John gives practical, experiential guidance on how growth *really* can happen — for you.

JOHN ORTBERG, author and pastor,
Menlo Park Presbyterian Church

Here's a phenomenal book for anyone looking to get closer to God — from a guy who knows what it takes. John's one of the few people I know who's engaging with regular people who have ever-increasing relationships with God, as opposed to just theory that doesn't get played out in the real world.

BRIAN TOME, senior pastor of Crossroads,
author of *Welcome to the Revolution*

John Burke stands out from so many other Christian leaders as he truly does understand the hearts and minds of those who may not connect with "Christianity" but are seeking a true and living connection with God. *Soul Revolution* moves us into a vibrant, very real way of following Jesus and growing in our love for God and others.

DAN KIMBALL, author of
They Like Jesus but Not the Church

Also by John Burke

No Perfect People Allowed

Resources

To download a small group guide to use with this book
or to find other helpful resources visit:

www.Soulrevolution.net

JOHN BURKE

How

Imperfect

People

Become

All God

Intended

 **ZONDERVAN®**

WILLOW
Willow Creek Resources

ZONDERVAN.com/
AUTHORTRACKER
follow your favorite authors

ZONDERVAN®

Soul Revolution
Copyright © 2008 by John Burke

Requests for information should be addressed to:
Zondervan, *Grand Rapids, Michigan* 49530

Library of Congress Cataloging-in-Publication Data

Burke, John, 1963–
    Soul revolution : how imperfect people become all God intended / John Burke.
      p. cm.
    ISBN 978-0-310-27646-3 (softcover)
    1. Self-actualization (Psychology)—Religious aspects—Christianity. 2. Spiritual
formation. 3. Spirituality. 4. Spiritual life—Christianity. I. Title.
BV4598.2.B86   2008
248.4—dc22   2008010806

All Scripture quotations, unless otherwise indicated, are taken from the *Holy Bible, Today's New International Version*™. TNIV®. Copyright © 2001, 2005 by International Bible Society. Used by permission of Zondervan. All rights reserved.

Other Scripture versions used: NLT—from the *Holy Bible, New Living Translation*. Copyright © 1996. Used by permission of Tyndale House Publishers, Inc., Wheaton, IL 60189 USA. All rights reserved. NIV—from the *Holy Bible, New International Version*®. NIV®. Copyright © 1973, 1978, 1984 by International Bible Society. Used by permission of Zondervan. All rights reserved. MSG—from *The Message*. Copyright © by Eugene Peterson 1993, 1994, 1995, 1996, 2000, 2001, 2002. Used by permission of NavPress Publishing Group. CEV—from the *Contemporary English Version*. Copyright © 1991, 1992, 1995 by the American Bible Society. Used by permission. AMP—*The Amplified Bible*, New Testament. Copyright © 1954, 1958, 1987 by The Lockman Foundation. Used by permission.

Interior design by Melissa Elenbaas

Printed in the United States of America

12 13 · 25 24 23 22 21 20 19 18 17 16 15 14 13 12 11 10 9

Contents

TO MY CHILDREN,

Ashley and Justin.

God has met so many

of my deepest longings

through the two of you;

I could not imagine a greater blessing.

I pray you will follow Christ

moment by moment

throughout your life

as there is no greater way to live.

Foreword

I remember when the publisher sent me a copy of John Burke's first book, *No Perfect People Allowed*. I have to confess, I had a thought that I often have when a new book comes out on spiritual growth. I feared that it was going to have the same three-point outline that many Christian books seem to have:

1. God's good.
2. You're bad.
3. Try harder.

But when I began to read it, I sensed something much different. I was reading someone who understood that the "try harder" gospel was not the true gospel at all and that Jesus has something better than that for all people. It was refreshing.

Then, as I continued to read, I began to see why. John Burke was not writing about some idea, doctrine, or theory. He was writing from a wealth of experiences where he had seen the very real power of God change people's entire existence. He was talking about what happens to people when we do not require them to get good enough to pass some Christian exam in order to be part of the club — or judge them if they don't. He was describing what happens when a community of faith does what Jesus said he came to do — "to seek and save that which has been lost." I resonated with his message so much that I arranged a get together with John Burke to talk more about how to reach those who have little interest, or even *negative* interest, in God or the church. When we met, I found a genuine person who was engaged in more of an adventure than a method.

In this book he takes it to the next level. He outlines the method and says that the method *is* to have an adventure. It is the adventure of ongoing connection with God, with his people, and with his ways. It is an adventure of seeing what God does when we step out in a mustard seed of faith — just once an hour, every sixty minutes, for sixty days. What happens is exactly what Jesus said would happen. We grow and "do not even know how" (Mark 4:27), as if we were asleep at the wheel. It is the essence of what Jesus said in a thousand different ways, that if we *abide in him*, we will see him and we will thrive.

What I love about John's message is the absence of religion. If we are to grow, and if we are to successfully invite other people to grow as well, then we cannot practice or preach religion. It neither works nor is attractive to those outside its walls. In fact, whenever Jesus did get mad, it was at the religious people, never the strugglers. To the struggler, he did not offer religion. He offered himself. He offered a relationship. A moment-by-moment adventure of asking him where he is, what he is doing, what he wants us to do, and then responding as he reveals himself. It's not about obeying a bunch of religious rules. it's about responding to him and his love every hour, every day. John reminds us of that reality and shares with us the stories of others who have experienced its truth.

The best books, I believe, have nothing new in them. Instead, they cut through the clutter of all the new noise that keeps us from seeing what has always been. John does that well, as he takes us back to the old message of the Gospel, the one of Jesus who just walked into people's lives and said a simple "follow me." And when they did, those people began an adventure that became the method itself— the adventure of abiding in relationship with God and each other. But the paradox is that this "non-method" turns out to get the results that all the other religious methods do not. The moment-by-moment power of relationship turns us into the kind of people that we were intended to be. That is a message that is both fresh, and old.

But isn't that like Jesus? He's the eternally old One, who surprised humanity with such a fresh appearance that no one even recognized it as the God who had always been, and his same method that had always been as well: "Just trust me, Abraham."

So jump into this book and try it. Invite others to do the same. What you will find is what Jesus said would happen if we held to his teaching: "You will know the truth, and the truth will set you free" (John 8:32).

God bless,
Henry Cloud, Ph.D.
Los Angeles, 2008

Deep Longings—
MY JOURNEY OF FAITH

All [people] seek happiness. There are no exceptions....
Yet all [people] complain.... A test which has gone on so long,
without pause or change, really ought to convince us
that we are incapable of attaining the good by our own efforts.
BLAISE PASCAL

Two dates and a dash.

One hot summer day a few years ago, I stood under the huge oaks shading my father's grave and recalled his last words. He had spoken them after a life that most people would have considered quite successful: "I'd give it all back if I could just have my health and family."

I pondered his last thoughts and looked at the dates on his headstone: 1933 – 1980. The first was the year he was born, with hope for a life of meaning, love, and purpose ahead of him. The second was the year he died. It's strange how life gets summed up with two dates and a dash in between. We get a birthday, we get a death day, and we have little control over either. But we can choose whether the dash in between will mean everything — or nothing.

My childhood memories of Dad came to mind. Once we built a model train set together. It was one of those lifelike electric trains, around which we decided to create an entire elaborate world. We got a 4 x 8 board for the base; we used wire, wood, and papier-mâché for the mountains and rivers, towns and houses; and we bought miniature people and cars. The track made a large oval around the board, through the mountains, over the bridge that crossed the river. We framed it, sculpted it, wired it, and painted it for about a year — it was incredible. Finally the day came to plug it in and watch it go. I couldn't wait.

We celebrated as the train went around the loop, through the town, back

9

out to the loop. Dad and I high-fived — it looked amazing. But as the weeks went by, I started to lose interest. It didn't take me too long to figure out it was just going around in circles. I could pretend it had some purpose by making up some GI Joe adventure, or I could pretend the little green army man stranded on the tracks needed to be rescued. Eventually it developed into experiments with train wrecks. The problem was — it was just going in circles.

"It wasn't the elaborate train set I loved," I thought that day by the graveside. "It was building it together, doing it alongside my dad. Without that relationship — the train got old pretty fast."

Life is like that. We chase something we think will bring us life. In our fast-paced society we talk fast, drive fast, think fast, eat fast, but have you ever thought about *why* you speed through life — going around in circles on this giant ball of dirt? Most of us spend our lives trying to get what we *think* we want, but often when we get it, we ask, "Now what?" Most of us never slow down long enough to consider what that dash on our headstones will some day represent.

What drives us to strive so hard? What are we really after? What do we long for?

Or let me make it more personal: What do *you* long for? What does *your* heart *really* desire?

All of us have deep longings that are from God. Some of us feel these longings intensely, while others sort of hydroplane across the surface of life. Perhaps deep hurts have even caused some of us to lose touch with our deepest desires.

But you have them. From early in your life you devised a strategy to get those deepest needs met, and even now those deep longings drive your behavior, choices, and goals (or lack of goals).

I've come to believe that our deepest longings only find fulfillment through relationships — with God and with other people. Without those relationships, our pursuits and goals and dreams and achievements are like that train going around in circles — what's the point?

But how do we *do life* in relationship with God?

It starts with a seemingly simple yet powerful virtue: willingness.

WILLINGNESS

I first experienced the power of willingness when I was a new Christ-follower. Only half emerged from my old life, a life of partying and all that entailed, I lived on a spiritual roller coaster. I'd go from a spiritual high (after each small group where we studied Scripture and discussed life with God) to a spiritual low (each weekend, doing things I knew were not what God intended). But that was my shallow strategy for attaining what I thought was the good life.

Late one Saturday, after a night of overindulgence, I lay down in bed and began to say my nightly prayers. The room spun around my head as I pretended nothing was wrong. Suddenly, it dawned on me — "I'm not fooling you with my inauthentic prayers, am I God?" So, realizing I couldn't put one over on God, I decided to be brutally honest: "I don't *want* to talk to you about my partying because I already know that I want to do it again! I'm afraid if I follow your will, I'll never have fun again. So if you want me to stop, you've got to help me see a better way. I'm willing for you to help me."

Little did I know then about the power of willingness, but when God met me in that willingness, new attitudes began to replace the old. The change seemed almost effortless. Within months, I was living more in God's will and actually enjoying life more! In time I began to see that God wanted to take my "life's a party" strategy and fulfill me in a more soul-satisfying way: with uninhibited fun and laughter, excitement, spontaneity, and transparency with close friends — and without a crutch. That year I began to see that life with God brings a greater thrill, deeper relationships, and a more heightened experience of life than my shallow strategy of instant gratification ever could.

As I continued to grow spiritually, God showed me other strategies I'd been using to meet my deepest longings, not that they were "wrong" or "sinful," but just misaligned. For instance, I'd always wanted to be successful. I'd even mapped out my strategy: I'd start my own company, be my own boss, and become financially independent. Then, I assumed, I'd be fulfilled, happy, secure, and living up to what my peers and parents expected.

But right in the middle of my sophomore year in college I got sick. I was bedridden for a week. With nothing to do but lie there, I thought, "Why am I working so hard, killing myself to 'succeed'?"

It was the first time in my life that I'd asked myself "Why?" I didn't know the answer. I'm now convinced the "why" came from a belief that "success," as I defined it, would meet my deepest longings to be highly valued, loved, fulfilled, happy! But the "why" was so buried in my psyche, I couldn't see it.

Then another question popped into my head: "God, how do *you* define success?" My father defined it as starting his own company, attaining financial security, never depending on anyone — and he achieved incredible success by those standards. Now I was following in his footsteps.

Again, my father's last words dug deep into my conscience, "I'd give it all back …" "If I achieve success like my dad's," I wondered, "will it be enough? What's life really about if all our worldly achievements get stripped away in a moment? God … what is success to you?"

Reading the Bible that week, I happened across Hebrews 11, a chapter that celebrates people who were successful in God's eyes. I read it and reread it. They all had one thing in common — great faith! This verse stuck in my mind: "Without faith it is impossible to please God" (Hebrews 11:6).

So I had my answer: God defines success in terms of faith, not just professed belief in him, but active, daily, risk-taking trust like that of the great people of Hebrews 11. Trust and faithfulness form the foundation of every relationship.

That week I began to question my success strategy, and I prayed a second honest prayer of willingness: "God, I'm scared to trust you with my success. I'm afraid you'll make me unsuccessful if I follow your will — that's the honest truth. But I also know my fear is unfounded — if that's what you want, you don't really need my permission to take away my success, do you? So I'm willing to seek success on your terms — help me be a man of faith. Help me succeed in your eyes."

I began to keep a journal that year. Even though I wasn't really the journaling type, I started writing as a way to track this journey of faith. I wanted to see if God would really guide an imperfect, struggling person like me, if only I remained willing to trust, to take faith risks. I chronicled my prayers, decisions, and risks. Looking back after a couple of years, I was blown away to see God's many answers, as well as his direct, tangible involvement in my life. The more willing and radically responsive I became, the more I realized the immeasurable personal benefit that comes from following God daily.

I've chronicled this journey of faith for more than twenty years now. Whenever I reread my journals, I'm astounded! While working in the business world during those first few years, I experienced that God was truly interested in me and every little aspect of my life. I adopted the mantra "If you're too scared to trust, you'll never know." I experienced guidance in my job decisions, relational decisions, and daily work decisions, and looking back, I can see so many God-coincidences, literally hundreds of tangible examples of God interacting with me as I trusted.

Journaling this adventure has helped me see patterns not only of how God leads, but also of how he is relational and creative and can't be put in a box. Over the years, I've learned that to benefit from God's plan, I have to be willing to let go of my own. This is scary at times.

For instance, I worried that no woman I'd want to marry would want to marry me if I were really to follow God's leading. Ironically, it was *because* of his leading that I met and married the most beautiful person I've ever known! God takes our willingness and leads us mysteriously down the path where our deepest longings will finally be met in relationship with him and others.

Relationship is what it's all about.

Over the years, I've heard many stories from imperfect people like myself. Some of these people weren't even sure God exists, but at least they were showing the first signs of willingness. Others were new to faith. Still others had been grasping at faith for years. One thing I've seen, however, is that God could care less about how messed up you are, how far you've fallen, or how "good" you've been. What he wants to know is, "How willing are you right now — in this moment?"

In the stories that follow you'll see how God takes imperfect but willing people and leads them into life's greatest adventure — the relational journey toward their hearts' greatest desire.

CAN YOU HEAR ME NOW?

Unfortunately, many who profess to follow Christ have never really experienced this adventure. Jesus often said, "Whoever has ears to hear, let them hear" and "Whoever has eyes to see, let them see."[1] I'm pretty sure most all the people Jesus addressed had two ears and two eyes. What was he talking about? He was referring to a realm of spiritual listening, seeing, and understanding. He said, "This people's heart has become calloused; they hardly hear with their ears, and they have closed their eyes. Otherwise they might see with their eyes, hear with their ears, understand with their hearts and turn, and I would heal them" (Matthew 13:15). Who was Jesus talking about? By and large, he was speaking of the devoutly religious people as the ones who couldn't hear or see or understand.

Pollster George Barna has reported, "Of more than 70 moral behaviors we study, when we compare Christians to non-Christians we rarely find substantial differences."[2] And if you ask non-Christians for one word that comes to mind when they hear the word *Christian*, the most common answer is "judgmental," even though Jesus said he came into the world not to judge it, but to save it.

Something's terribly wrong. What is it? I'm convinced we've lost the ability to see and hear and understand how to truly follow the way of Christ moment by moment.

In this book, I hope to take you on a journey to discover how we learn to listen and see and experience this journey of faith that begins to meet the deepest longings of your soul.

Imagine yourself two years from now. How would you like to be free from the maladies that plague so many in our generation — loneliness, fear, anxiety, anger, bitterness, insecurity, lust, and the keeping-up-with-the-Joneses syndrome? What if you could be free of the need for praise or approval from others? Imagine that worry and stress no longer overpower and push you down under their weight, and in their place you feel calmness every night when you lay your head on your pillow. Who wouldn't want a life in which joy erupted from your spirit at surprising times? Who wouldn't want a life in which you can enjoy each moment, thankful and content and relishing the gift of life with the people around you? Imagine feeling so well off that you don't need more money or more stuff to feel content. You might even find yourself becoming increasingly generous. Who wouldn't want to be a more loving person year after year, the kind of person that others are grateful to have around because you're making a lasting difference in their lives? Imagine being able to act lovingly toward even the unlovable people in your life. That would be a soul revolution — wouldn't it?

Is this really possible? Only if Jesus was telling the truth! He insisted that God intends for you to live a life that fulfills your deepest desires and transforms you into a life-giving person. God says he will produce a life-giving reservoir inside you — but only if you let him. How? That's what this book is about.

Chapter by chapter, I plan to challenge you with a simple Sixty-Day Experiment in Faith, an experiment to see what happens if you stay connected to God at least every sixty minutes for sixty days. We called it the 60-60 Experiment at our church, and thousands of people have done it with amazing results. Whether you've followed Christ for years or aren't even sure who he is, commit as much of yourself as you understand to as much of God as you understand for sixty days and see what happens. I think you'll be amazed. Like many people in this book, if you go all out in seeking a radically responsive relationship with God, I believe you'll discover a way of life you'll want to continue. Because this experiment is about loving God and people, I would encourage you to find a small group or at least one or two trusted friends (I call Spiritual Running Partners) to do this 60-60 Experiment with you.

But first you must decide, "What do I really want? Am I willing to go all out for sixty days to see if God's revolutionary ways lead to the life I desire?"

If you'll take that risk, I believe you'll see that God takes imperfect people, and as we are willing, he helps us become more and more of what he intended us to be — and in the process we find our deepest longings finally being met in relationship with God and others. That's what I've personally experienced, and what I've heard in story after story of willing people, many whom you'll meet in this book.

Are you willing?

PREPARING FOR THE 60-60 EXPERIMENT

1. Take a sheet of paper and make a list of all the things you long for in life. Don't edit out anything; whether you think it's a good desire or not, just write.

2. Now look at your list and circle the three to five most important things on your list (what you don't want to live without). Why are those things most important to you? What do you hope they will bring you? Is there a deeper spiritual quality you're hoping that desire will bring? Is that spiritual quality a top priority on your list?

3. If it's true that our deepest longings are good and from God, how might God want to meet the deepest longings that your top priorities reveal? Discuss that question with your small group or someone you trust.

4. Do you trust that God wants to meet your deepest longings? What fears do you have in all-out trusting him? What might you gain from fully trusting God for the next sixty days? What might you lose?

PART 1

PREPARING FOR A SOUL REVOLUTION

CHAPTER ONE

Shallow Strategies

It had been a perfect night out for John and Dalia. Dennis Quaid's annual benefit party had been a blast. A few drinks, great entertainment, lots of laughs. The kids were asleep, and John was in the mood as they undressed for bed.

"John, can I ask you something?" The tone in Dalia's voice revealed a deep hidden fear.

"Sure, honey, ... what is it?" John took Dalia in his arms and pulled her close so as not to lose the moment.

"Have you been unfaithful to me?"

Dalia's words penetrated John's soul like a dagger. She had asked him this two or three times before, but this time, somehow, the words struck more deeply.

Time seemed to stand still as John's mind raced back across the years. Once, while he was engaged to Dalia, he had gone to a work party one night without her. It had been a hard week; he deserved to unwind and have some fun, he'd told himself. The drinks flowed, and when the cocaine came out, he was up for some heightened pleasure. The woman doing coke with him got flirty. John rationalized: soon he'd be married, no more chances for a thrill like this. Before the night ended, he had cheated on his fiancée.

John recalled another occasion early in their marriage when he'd spent a weekend away with some work associates, most of them single. John knew where a night out with them might lead, but he'd told himself he could "read the menu without buying." Besides, he had thought, what's wrong with having a little fun if it's not hurting anybody? The booze, the drugs, and a willing woman took him on the same dead-end ride he'd traveled so many times since his junior year in high school when he started "having a little fun." Only this time — he felt something. It was his conscience.

The next morning, guilt and shame had covered him like a wet, smelly blanket. *What have I done? . . . Dalia!* John's friends assured him that if he never told her, the feeling would go away.

"Oh, if only I hadn't lied when she first asked," John thought now. The remorse over his hidden life and the strained intimacy with the woman he loved tickertaped red across his mind. He always swore he'd change — he'd stop drinking and never have another affair. He told himself he wasn't "that bad." He was a Christian, after all. He believed Jesus died for his sins. And he confessed each adulterous affair to God — but then had another and another.

Each time, John would tell himself, "I'm a good person — a successful lawyer, a volunteer at church. I'm not really hurting anyone by having fun." But "fun" always led to too much drinking, drugs if they were available, flirting, and wherever things led from there.

"Have you been unfaithful to me?" The question reverberated in John's head.

God had been working in John's heart since they'd started going to Gateway Church. He knew that authenticity was important for those who followed Christ. He'd heard stories of others who had failed and fallen, yet had truly decided to follow God all out. There was something appealing, even life-inspiring about breaking out of this self-induced prison. But fear always kept him locked up: fear of losing his marriage; fear of facing past failures; fear of feeling like a failure; and, if he was honest, fear of not having any more "fun." Ultimately, it was the fear of losing the only life he'd ever known.

Some life this has turned out to be! The thought struck deep and twisted in his soul. The realization of all the pain he had caused welled up in a reservoir of emotion behind the dam of his past lies.

"John, have you?" Dalia persisted.

"Yes."

It happened in a moment. All of the memories, all the truth, all the lies — all collided into one horribly painful moment.

"Yes." John dropped his head as Dalia's tears streamed down her face. All her long-held suspicions were confirmed. John never intended this — to hurt the one he loved. All the "fun" that life had promised only brought death — the death of everything he really wanted, of everything he cherished. It was the most terrifying, honest, freeing word he'd ever spoken.

"Yes."

For the next six months, John faced the reality of losing everything he loved most — Dalia, his children, the friends he'd lied to, the church friends he'd deceived. The proverb said it well: "There is a way that appears to be right, but in the end it leads to death" (Proverbs 16:25).

Almost three years later, Dalia recalled, "If John hadn't changed, I would have left him. But God really has changed his heart. He's a free man, and through rebuilding our marriage, I've come to realize how much I love him. It'll take years, perhaps a lifetime to regain all we lost, but we have a strength in our marriage that wasn't there before."

John said, "I had this work-hard-play-hard philosophy that drove me, going way back to high school. Even though I was a straight A student, a good athlete, and in student government, I wanted friends. When I changed schools, the group that reached out to me partied hard, so I partied hard to fit in. That began a life of drinking, drugs, and sex.

"I can't even imagine all the people I've hurt. I've prayed for forgiveness. I was just blind. All I desired was to belong and be loved, yet you get so turned in on yourself, so self-centered, that you can't see that the path you're on will destroy you and those you love. I had Jesus way up in the clouds, removed from my real life. I felt I could tap into God when I needed him, but there was no daily, regular connection — I didn't know how to relate to God. Honestly, I knew very little about him. I hadn't taken time to study the Scriptures to know his character. I hadn't honestly surrendered my will to follow Christ. I wanted to have my cake and eat it too — but that never works.

"Since then, I've developed the art of staying connected to God throughout the day, and God is producing something in me I always wanted — peace, faithfulness, love, self-control. Since I confessed, God has been gently pulling me out of this deep hole I've dug, but I find there's still something in me that wants to keep my foot in the hole, because deep down I feel I may want to crawl back in it. It's that 'sin nature' in me wanting to go back to the only life I've known. Yet I'm tasting something I've always wanted growing within — something full of life — peaceful, yet exciting at the same time."

FINGER POINTING

God wants to meet our deepest needs, but early in life we get wired to meet our needs without God. It never works. We think our fulfillment strategies will bring life, but they usually destroy the life we desire. Our deepest longings are good. But just as thirst points us toward water, our deepest longings point us toward Someone who can actually satisfy our thirsty souls.

A Zen master once said, "A finger is excellent for pointing at the moon, but woe to him who mistakes the finger for the moon." I believe we must follow our deepest desires with spiritual eyesight so that we can see exactly where they are pointing.

This book is your guide for this journey. In preparation, let's explore the life your heart and soul craves, which you may just find is the life God intended for you all along. Begin with these questions:

- What do I really desire?
- How will I really get it?

WHAT'S YOUR STRATEGY?

All of us have strategies — mostly shallow ones — for quenching our deepest thirsts. What's yours? Identifying your main strategy can be tricky, like trying to see your nose without a mirror. Often our plan to "find life" gets so woven into our psyche that it becomes invisible. Even when we do identify that strategy, it's terrifying to imagine life without it.

Are you willing to reconsider your strategy? It may not be bad, but it may also be far less than God intends for you. Ask yourself, are you open to growth — to *change*?

One way to begin to uncover your current strategy is to fill in these blanks:

"If only _____,

or if I just _____,

then I will have the life I've always wanted."

Write down some phrases in those blanks. Be honest. Don't edit your thoughts because you feel your desires are wrong — just be rigorously truthful. What are you hoping for? What are you counting on?

Let's probe some common strategies with spiritual eyes for a minute.

Some people bank on the strategy of finding Mr. or Miss Right, getting married, and having a loving family. That's all good, but a marriage license doesn't guarantee love, faithfulness, or security. Let's say you've found "the one," got married, have had the statistical average of 2.3 kids, but you don't have love, contentment, and security — would you be happy? I doubt it since your basic spiritual needs are still unmet. So how do you get spiritual qualities like love, contentment and security?

Maybe your strategy is: "If I can just reach a certain financial level, reach my career and lifestyle goals, then I'll have life!" Material success — not a bad thing in itself, but is it really enough? Is it *all* you want? (Maybe you're thinking, "All I want is a chance to *prove* that lots of money and success is not enough!")

Consider this: imagine you have all the money, status, and toys you ever dreamed of, but you aren't content, don't experience joy, and don't feel your life matters — is it enough? Or do you want real contentment, personal confidence, lasting purpose, and maybe even a generous heart too? Do these spiritual qualities really come from attaining more stuff? What are your heart's deepest desires?

Maybe you've been deeply wounded in the past. As a result, your strategy may center on becoming self-sufficient and independently strong. You don't need anyone. But can inner strength or lasting security be found in isolation? Where do you find the spiritual strength and security to displace all your fear despite living in a dangerous world?

For many in our generation, the strategy of choice is to live for the next extreme rush — instant-gratification purchases, quick-dry thrills to fill the cracks in your soul, endorphin-rushed romances and sexual highs, chemically dependent and uninhibited fun — all because it's the closest you come to feeling alive. But ultimately these strategies destroy the life you seek. Thrills get boring, highs leave you low, romance wilts as fast as it blooms, sex becomes a series of morning-afters. So where do you go to find lasting spiritual qualities, like excitement with peace, adventure with security, and lasting intimacy with sexual contentment?

As C. S. Lewis realized, the problem is usually not that we want too much; it's that we *settle* for too little. Deep down we deceive ourselves. We believe two things: "My strategy will work," and "God will get in the way of what I really want." But both are lies! Ultimately, God wants to meet our *deepest* desires.

SPRINGS OF LIVING WATER

As you read the Bible, it doesn't take long to encounter imperfect people. From Adam and Eve to the heroes of faith in Hebrews 11, God's faithful made huge moral blunders. So there's hope for you and me! How can God possibly work with imperfect people? Because they are *willing*. In one of my favorite stories, Jesus encounters a very imperfect woman, and through their interaction, he shows us the way God will gently uncover our broken strategies in order to quench our deepest thirst.

While traveling with his disciples through Samaria, Jesus came to a well called Jacob's Well. After he sent his disciples into the city to buy food, a woman came to draw water from the well. Usually, the women of the town would draw their daily supply of water in the cool of the morning. Conversation around the well would be the equivalent of our office water-cooler conversations.

Significantly, when this woman came to the well alone, it was around noon, the hottest part of the day, no doubt because she was avoiding the water-cooler group. Her past had been anything but perfect. She'd been married and divorced five times — a track record that would earn her several laps around the gossip circle — but the fact that she was now unmarried and shacking up with a sixth man was scandalous.

> Jesus said to her, "Please give me a drink." ...
>
> The woman was surprised, for Jews refuse to have anything to do with Samaritans. She said to Jesus, "You are a Jew, and I am a Samaritan woman. Why are you asking me for a drink?"
>
> Jesus replied, "If you only knew the gift God has for you and who you are speaking to, you would ask me, and I would give you living water." (John 4:7 – 10 NLT)

Jesus said, "If you knew *the gift* God has for you ... If you knew *who I am* ... you would ask me for the water I can give you." What was he talking about? Jesus was parabolic and chose the parable over the pragmatic.

Like a mystery novelist, he longs to draw our whole being into his plot. Like a master songwriter, he's not just interested in getting his point across; he engages heart, mind, and soul with his song. And I find he does the same with you and me as he did with this woman. Patiently and in mysterious ways, he engages us at the level of our desires, prodding us to reconsider what our hearts really long for and how we will really get it.

This woman knew that the prophets had foretold of a Messiah who would come "and explain everything to us" about God. Jesus later revealed that he himself was the long-awaited Messiah of God. But because she didn't really know who God is, she didn't ask for what he had to give.

Jesus said, "Everyone who drinks this water will be thirsty again, but those who drink the water I give them will never thirst. Indeed, the water I give them will become in them a spring of water welling up to eternal life" (John 4:13 – 14).

She didn't get it at first, and neither do we, most of the time. That's our main problem — we don't really know *who God is*, not just in name, but in character, so we don't make it a top priority to seek the living water he wants to give us to satisfy our thirsty souls. We keep trying to get our deep spiritual thirst quenched in shallow ways, which end up leaving us even thirstier.

IMAGES OF GOD

Many of us have an inadequate image of God. Our parents, other authority figures, our religious upbringing (or lack of it) can often paint an unappealing picture of God in our imaginations.

When Paula came to our church, she believed in a Higher Power, but to imagine God as "Father" was repugnant to her. She struggled with authority figures — a struggle rooted in deep pain, which drove her to drink excessively. After her drinking destroyed her marriage and contributed to her losing custody of her children, she found herself in recovery. While there, she came to terms with the abuse she had experienced as a child. Her father, a distinguished physics professor who traveled the world giving lectures, was an atheist and an alcoholic. Starting at age thirteen, Paula found favor with her dad by becoming his drinking buddy, but once he got her drunk, he would sometimes fondle her sexually. That became the primary image she had of a father's intimacy. No wonder "God as Father" made her gag.

Though Paula was initially freaked out by the Bible and any mention of Jesus, I showed her how the Higher Power she had come to trust experientially through recovery *is* the God Jesus revealed — a God who forgives wrongs and helps those who are willing to surrender their lives to follow his will. Paula recalls, "When I realized that Jesus revealed the Higher Power who had helped me, I gave my life to him and got baptized. Learning that Jesus said, 'Whoever has seen me has seen the Father,' opened up for me a way to redefine what 'father' was supposed to be. As I've studied the way Jesus treated people, I found healing from the distorted view of the Father my earthly father gave me."

As a result of our distorted images of God, his character seems less than appealing, and the gift we think he wants to give us pales in comparison to the life we imagine for ourselves. But that's because we have not fully used our imaginations.

IMAGINE

Imagine what God is really like. Unless we believe God is, above all, loving and good and *for* us, we won't be willing to seek him. The Bible says, "God is love. This is how God showed his love among us: He sent his one and only Son into the world that we might live through him. This is love: not that we loved God, but that he loved us and sent his Son as an atoning sacrifice for our sins" (1 John 4:8 – 10).

Do you see what this says? God *is* love. Is God a just judge? Yes — God will one day make right all the wrongs — but is he primarily a judge? No! Jesus came to show us that first and foremost, God is Love, and God loves us so much that there is nothing he won't do to deliver us from our broken ways and bring us into a shared life with him. Jesus even gave his own life so that "we might live through him" — starting now and forever more.

What if our deepest longing, sewn into the fabric of our souls, is to express and experience the love of the greatest, most beautiful, knowledgeable, caring Being in the universe? What if all our desires are fingers pointing toward God — the One who loves you more than any other and wants to provide good things for you, just as a good father does? What if God, who is aware of all the things we *think* we want, knows this would actually distract us from himself — the *only One* who can meet our deepest desires? That would explain why a loving God does *not* give us everything we want.

If God is love, and if we love him because he first loved us, what does that mean about all the love you've ever experienced? Think of all the love you've given or received — where did it come from?

It's borrowed!

It's borrowed from God.

You've never experienced a love whose source did *not* originate in God's love for you. It's true, whether you realize it or not.

BORROWED LOVE

This concept of borrowed love hit me years ago when my kids were little. I would lie in bed with them at night, praying for them as they fell asleep. As I lay there, thanking God for them, I felt an overflowing sense of love that was so great, it felt like my soul would burst!

I had never been a touchy-feely kind of guy. I'd grown up somewhat emotionally closed, but God had been changing me. One night, as I thanked God for this overwhelming love I felt for my children, I had a strange thought: "I love you more," God seemed to be saying to me.

It took me off guard. I'd never considered it before. All the love I experienced *was* from God — because God *is* love. My love for my wife and children was only a borrowed measure of God's love for me and them!* "We love because he first loved us" (1 John 4:19).

The apostle Paul prays for his friends to grasp this truth experientially:

> *I pray that from his glorious, unlimited resources he will empower you with inner strength through his Spirit. Then Christ will make his home in your hearts as you trust in him. Your roots will grow down into God's love and keep you strong. And may you have the power to understand, as all God's people should, how wide, how long, how high, and how deep his love is. May you experience the love of Christ, though it is too great to understand fully. Then you will be made complete with all the fullness of life and power that comes from God. (Ephesians 3:16 – 19 NLT, emphasis added)*

Most people don't seek God as the source of their deepest fulfillment because they don't understand who he is or what he wants to give them. We must first try to understand and *experience* the love of Christ that Paul talks about with spiritual eyes and ears and understanding.

Try this exercise to experience this for yourself. Think about a time when you felt the most loved as a child, the most validated, the most believed in. Who has loved you most in this world? Now picture being with that person, and recall that feeling you had in their presence.

Now listen with spiritual ears ... can you hear the truth? God's voice ... "That love came from me ... and I love you even more!"

Stop reading at this point, and close your eyes to ponder this.

Now picture the person or people you love more than any other. Think

---

* Technically God's love is freely given, as opposed to being "borrowed" in the sense of owing it back (though rejection of God leads to an eternity devoid of his love, so some do "give it back" I suppose). But the powerful concept that hit me is not merely that God's love has been given freely, but that I'm expressing and experiencing *his* love. I have it to experience because God gave it to me to use, so I experience a measure of his great love for me in my love for others.

about how you feel toward them — the good things you want for them. Now, connect this love to its Source — follow where the finger points with new eyes. Where does your love come from?

You see, it's all borrowed love. Listen with new ears for God's truth … "This love you feel … comes from me … through you … to them. I love you even more than you love them. I want good things for you, even more than you want good things for them."

This, Scripture declares, is the truth about your Creator. What if you experienced God as the one who loves you more than any other and wants to give you good things? Paul said, "Everything God created is good" (1 Timothy 4:4). There are no evil things, only evil uses of the good things God has given. And even our evil uses are often misdirected attempts to attain the good God wants to give. Jesus said, "If you, then, though you are evil, know how to give good gifts to your children, how much more will your Father in heaven give good gifts to those who ask him!" (Matthew 7:11). Jesus says, "If you knew who I am, and the gift God wants to give … you'd ask!"

GOD VERSUS GOD

This is the message God conveyed through Moses, the prophets, and finally through Jesus: No human being or material thing can satisfy our deepest longings because God has hardwired us for himself first. Just as birds are hardwired to fly south for winter, we were hardwired to seek God. We will never find the life we long for apart from him because he is the Source of all we love.

If we put other things, no matter how good, in the center of our lives, they become rival gods that lead us to destruction — the loss of the life our thirsty souls crave. But when a new vision of God's goodness motivates us to seek him with all we have, everything else comes alive. All our pursuits for relationship, success, security, and purpose get rightly ordered and become life-giving in new ways.

Jesus tries to help the woman at the well see this:

> Jesus answered, "Everyone who drinks this water will be thirsty again, but those who drink the water I give them will never thirst. Indeed, the water I give them will become in them a spring of water welling up to eternal life."
>
> The woman said to him, "Sir, give me this water so that I won't get thirsty and have to keep coming here to draw water."

He told her, "Go, call your husband and come back."

"I have no husband," she replied.

Jesus said to her, "You are right when you say you have no husband. The fact is, you have had five husbands, and the man you now have is not your husband. What you have just said is quite true." (John 4:13 – 18)

If we want our deepest desires satisfied, we must face the truth about ourselves. This is not easy, so Jesus finds creative, parabolic ways to get us to "see and hear." Though this woman's past was littered with broken ways of relating, Jesus didn't condemn her. He simply led her to face her broken strategy of filling her deepest longings in shallow ways. He asked her to face this truth about herself: that she continued to try to meet a thirst for love and security apart from God, and it wasn't working.

We must be willing to take a hard look at the shallow strategies that become rival gods in our lives, good things or destructive patterns that we count on to give us life. This is the first step toward drinking from the wellspring that truly satisfies. If you knew what God wants to give you ... you'd ask ... you'd seek ... you'd find. And you'll see, God still meets imperfect people today when they're willing.

Consider Brian's story.

LOOKING UP FROM THE BOTTOM

"The night was a blur as I sped home. Flashes of drinks, flirting, more drinks. The drinks made it easier to be funny in front of her. I love this part — speeding up the big hill." In the back of his mind, Brian knew he shouldn't be driving, much less speeding, but ego ruled this night.

"I'm gonna ask her out," Brian boldly decided as he flew past the other cars. "Wimps — can't keep up." He crested the top of the hill and looked back to see the headlights vanishing behind him. Then he saw it — flashing lights. Now the sound of sirens. Brian's third DWI. "Number three's a felony." The thought hit Brian so hard that it almost sobered him.

After a night in jail, an alcohol assessment, and a meeting with lawyers, Brian heard the news: "It's not good, Brian," the assessment counselor began. "Three DWIs, a public intox, drinking five or more drinks on an average night out, a high blood-alcohol level, and family history of alcoholism. This is serious. You seem like an intelligent guy, you have a degree, you own an architecture firm — but you really abuse this stuff."

As the counselor rattled off all the hoops Brian would have to jump through — alcohol awareness classes, MADD forums, and community service — one little abbreviation reverberated in Brian's head: AA. Sure enough, the counselor concluded with, "During all this you'll be required to attend twenty-eight AA meetings."

"What? Twenty-eight AA meetings? I'm not an alcoholic," Brian told himself. "What'll they make me do — explore these events more? Will it become obvious I have a problem, because I don't! ... Do I? I mean, I can't have a problem. I'm Brian, the good kid from Iowa, the nice guy, the successful guy.... I'm not an alcoholic."

At his first meeting, Brian admitted to himself he was afraid — afraid to find out what was behind all those shame-ridden feelings. "Why do I feel so guilty? Why do I feel so ... alone?" Brian sat in a cold metal chair, waiting awkwardly as the room filled up. He read the first few items on the poster on the wall to pass the time.

THE 12 STEPS:
We:

1. Admitted we were powerless over alcohol — that our lives had become unmanageable.
2. Came to believe that a Power greater than ourselves could restore us to sanity.
3. Made a decision to turn our will and our lives over to the care of God ...

"Hold on," Brian thought as he read that third step, "I'm here to get through this stuff. I don't have a problem, and I'm certainly *not* going to turn my life over to God. Spiritual awakening — ha! Are these people for real? My counselor didn't tell me she was committing me to church!"

Since age sixteen, Brian had given himself over to the pursuit of pleasure. As far as he was concerned, religion was just a means to control the masses. He often joked that he had sold his soul for eternal youth, holding an atheistic view of life in which his only purpose was his own amusement. By his own admission, it had led him to become a workaholic, an abuser of alcohol, sexually obsessed, and ultimately a lonely, bored, empty person.

Brian survived his first meeting without having to share in the group. Once home, he plopped down on the couch and opened up AA's *Big Book*. A participant had handed it to him after the meeting and said, "You only hit rock bottom when bad things happen faster than you can lower your standards." Brian had laughed when the guy said it, but now it started to haunt him.

"How many times did I justify my behavior, feeling it was okay — only based on a new lower standard." He cracked open the *Big Book* and began to read the story of Bill W., AA's founder. One particular statement in Bill's story caught Brian's attention: "I was to know happiness, peace, and usefulness in a way of life that is incredibly more wonderful as time passes."

"Happiness and peace are foreign to me," Brian admitted to himself. "My days are monotonous, boring, and aggravating. I always feel like I need something crazy or exciting just to get a temporary happy buzz. I can't just be happy." With that thought, Brian resolved to try to keep an open mind. He read on ...

Selfishness — self centeredness. That we think is the root of our troubles ... we could not reduce our self-centeredness on our own power. We had to have God's help. This is the how and why of it. First of all, we had to quit playing God. It didn't work. Next, we decided that hereafter in the drama of life, God was going to be our Director. He is the Principle, we are his agents. He is the Father, we are his children.... When we sincerely took such a position, all sorts of remarkable things followed. We had a new Employer. Being all powerful, He provided what we need, if we kept close to Him and performed His work well. Established on such a footing, we became less and less interested in ourselves, our little plans and designs. More and more we became interested in seeing what we could contribute to life. As we felt new power flow in, as we enjoyed peace of mind, as we discovered we could face life successfully, as we became conscious of His presence, we began to lose our fear of today, tomorrow, and the hereafter. We were reborn.[1]

One night several weeks later, Brian lay in bed reviewing the day's events: a lot of work, lunch, more work, a drive to the gym. That made him mad. Technically his work permit was for home, office, grocery store, and church — but it didn't cover his trip to the gym. "How come I can go to church to maintain my 'spiritual health' if I want, but not the gym to maintain my physical health? It's not fair." But he realized he couldn't let himself spiral down. He had to learn to appreciate the little things. He had to be grateful; that's what he was learning. And as he lay there alone, something happened.

"God, I don't know if you're there. I don't even know if you exist ... but thank you. Thank you for letting me drive to the gym tonight and not get caught." It was simple and felt dumb, but it was honest.

For the next few months, every night Brian would lay in bed, thanking God for the positive things he experienced in his life that day. "I felt like I started to receive little gifts from God every day," Brian recalls. "In my state at that time, little things like a smile and a good conversation at the coffee shop made my list of thanks. Every night I continued to thank a God I wasn't sure was there. But something was happening inside me."

Then came the trial. Brian recalls, "I was found guilty. I was facing jail time of up to a year, fines that amounted to more money than I had, a year of probation, which also costs money, and hours and hours of community service." For reasons that still shock Brian, after a miraculous plea bargain, he was given no jail time, and no fines. No explanation was given.

"It was amazing, and I gave God my biggest 'thank you' yet." Brian explained, "Only this time, I believed he was there. I truly believe this was given to me to reward the changes I'd made and to inspire me to continue seeking God. A few months later, a woman I knew invited me to Gateway after I shared my God story with her. I found the church inspiring on many levels. After a few months, Gateway held a sixty-day 'experiment' to connect every hour with God. I never made it every hour, but my once-a-day nightly connection turned into multiple connections every day. This transformed my new faith into a deeper pursuit of God and a Christian way of life. I began to see God at work in my life throughout the day."

A few months ago, Brian and I were talking about what God has done over the past two years since the DWI. I watched tears of gratitude well up in his eyes as he told me about his renewed outlook and energy, his new friends, and his renewed sense of purpose. He shared stories of the many ways God has tangibly worked in his life since staying willing and connected daily. He told me, "The little things that used to be problematic for me have just disappeared without any effort or sacrifice on my part. It's not that my life is perfect or trouble-free, but for the first time I know happiness and peace as a way of life, and I never feel alone anymore."

LIFE WITH GOD

As Brian discovered, God leads us to a soul-quenching experience of life better than any buzz, conquest, or thrill. Jesus said, "The thief comes only to steal and kill and destroy; I have come that they may have life, and have it to the full. I am the good shepherd. The good shepherd lays down his life for the sheep" (John 10:10 – 11). Jesus explained that someone out there wants to destroy your life and rob you of joy — but that someone is not God. The whole reason Jesus came was to lead us into life in all its fullness. That's what motivated him to lay down his life for you — so that you would trust him and follow him into a more fulfilling, life-giving experience than you can even imagine. When you truly start to believe this, it changes your experience of everything. Every moment can go from black and white into a high-definition, Technicolor experience of life with God.

Like the woman at the well, we keep thinking that someone or something here on earth can quench our deepest thirst, but earth has nothing that will truly satisfy it apart from God. God desires to give you a life that flows from within like living water. You can't grasp it, gain it, or attain it from anything "out there." It comes from God's Spirit within. But to experience the life we desire, we must be willing to lose the life we think we want, and that fear of losing life is what keeps most of us from ever finding it.

MORE PREPARATION FOR THE 60-60 EXPERIMENT

1. Write your answers to the questions: "What do I desire?" "How am I trying to get it?" Can you think of a time that you got something you really desired, that you really thought would be fulfilling, but it fell short of your expectations? Why was that?

2. When you imagine God, what characteristics come to mind? Write them down.

3. Now write down the characteristics of your father and mother. How many overlap with your image of God? What's distorted about your image of God? What's missing?

4. If you did not do so, do the exercise on page 27 – 28 connecting the love you've experienced and the good things you've been given to the Source of all love and goodness.

5. Where do you struggle to trust God's love or goodness? Why is this? Discuss this with a trusted friend or others in your small group.

CHAPTER TWO

RESTORE —
WHAT DOES GOD WANT?

"You what? You can't do that — we have a contract!"

"I'm sorry, but the manager who executed this contract had no right to do anything that might interfere with us showing movies." The General Cinema executive from Los Angeles remained resolute despite my pleas and arguments into the phone.

"Look, we've spent all our money preparing to hold church services here starting in two weeks — only because you signed a contract," I reminded him. "What are we supposed to do?"

"I don't know, that's not my problem," was his curt reply.

After twenty minutes of arguing, I hung up the phone and lay on the floor in shock. We had no other option; we'd searched the city. Our mailers announcing Gateway Church's opening service at the General Cinema were in the mail, and all our money was spent. Now we had no place to meet. "Why, Lord?" I asked, staring at the ceiling. "God, we planned and prayed and thought we were doing everything you wanted — how could you let this happen? What do we do now?"

Ted Beasley (who helped start Gateway) and I decided to call a special gathering of our core group of thirty-eight people and pray. I felt an aching in the pit of my stomach the next night as I prepared for the meeting. As I prayed, the phone rang. It was Brian Tome, a friend who had started a church in Cincinnati.

"Hey, I was sitting here at my desk," Brian began, "reading an email from a woman who came to faith in our church; she's moving to Austin. I want to get her connected with you guys."

I told Brian the uncertain future we faced. There was a long pause.

"You know, I think there's a young guy in our church who has some connection to the movie theater industry — you want me to talk to him? I don't know if he can help, but it can't hurt," Brian suggested.

"Sure — I've tried every angle, and I'm at a dead end," I replied. We hung up, and I left for our prayer gathering.

I told our young church the disappointing news. Our core group was made up of very messy, imperfect people, many who were just finding faith or returning to God. What would this do to their fledgling trust in God?

I told them it would take a miracle. I had talked to the highest level executives in the Los Angeles office that oversee the Austin theaters. I talked to a lawyer, and legal action wouldn't get us anywhere fast. We spent that night praying for God to show us his power.

After the gathering, I walked alone under a black, starry sky — confused and discouraged. "What are you doing, God? Surely you know what's up — this isn't taking *you* by surprise. Please, do something miraculous. If you don't, I don't know what to do — we're done. I guess I'll have to postpone Gateway until we . . . try again? I just don't get it; what are you doing? I left everything because I thought this is what you wanted."

For hours I poured out my disappointment. But when I looked up into the billions of stars, entire galaxies spanning billions of miles, I remembered: "None of this is beyond your ability. You created everything. So you must have your reasons. We're in your hands. I'll trust you. Show me how to move forward in trust."

I'd been here many times before — at this fork in the road of trust. It always begins the same way — severe disappointment, letting it all out, then remembering God's greatness and faithfulness. And finally, trust. I spent the next hour remembering the many ways God had been faithful to lead and guide me, even when I had faced disappointment in the past. I went to bed that night filled up with gratitude and even joy — a joy I can't explain.

I couldn't give up. Three days later, I went to meet the general manager who had signed the contract to try to get him to at least give us one month at the theater. His first words confused me.

"Well, I don't know what kind of connections you guys have," the manager began, "but they worked. The president of General Cinema in New York called the Los Angeles office and told them to 'work it out with the church in Austin.' So, you're good to go."

I walked out dumbfounded. I hadn't called anyone except my lawyer friend ...
How in the world? I realized later that Brian's little prompting to call me out of the
blue that day was a God-inspired leading. His friend *did* know someone, who knew
someone, who knew ... the president of General Cinema. We personally didn't
have that connection, but our whole church learned about God's connections, and
how to trust him through the disappointments.

DISAPPOINTMENT WITH GOD

Ever wonder why God allows disappointment? What's his purpose? Even our
General Cinema story took a disappointing turn later because within nine
months, we got the boot. So began our frustrating two years of moving between
two and three hundred people from one location to another, all across town,
sometimes with only five days' notice. During one period, we had to meet at a
different location or time every week for six weeks!

"What am I doing wrong?" I would cry out to God as I ran along the top of
the Mansfield Dam, overlooking the diamonds of sunlight dancing across the
waters of Lake Travis. "I just want to make a difference for you, Lord! Why are
you are fighting against me?"

I was confused. Kathy and I had stepped out in faith to start a church for
our unchurched generation because we had absolutely no doubt it was God's
will, God's calling — and yet, nothing was going according to God's will (as I
knew it should be)!

After two years of wrestling with God, I felt broken — like never before. I'd
take my mountain bike out into the hills and spend hours crying out, "What
am I doing wrong?" And when I received nothing but silence for a year, I finally
grew silent. Then, in the quiet, I began to hear in my soul not an answer to my
pleading, but a question in return.

"Am I enough? ... Am I enough?"

"Of course you're enough, Lord," I'd answer intellectually. "Haven't I given
my life to serve you? Didn't I prove I'd leave it all to follow you?" But when the
deep struggle for peace and joy wouldn't let up, I had to admit the heartfelt
truth: "No, Lord, right now you're not enough. I'm not at peace being faithful
to simply love you and my family and enjoy using my gifts to serve you. I need
things to go my way ... according to my plans ... that's the truth."

That's why I was struggling. My hurt and frustration with God, my lack of
joy and peace betrayed the truth. God was not enough. Faithfulness was not

enough. I needed God *plus* — God plus things going as I planned. I wasn't okay with God being God in my life if he didn't do what I thought he should. I wasn't okay with simply being faithful to live in his will each day.

I spent the summer wrestling to surrender, letting go of playing God and learning to follow … again. The sad thing is, I thought I'd already learned this lesson, but now I see that life with Christ is not so much a one-time decision to trust (though there is a first decision of faith*), but more like a series of daily decisions to trust.

At times this feels painfully discouraging, but more and more I see hopeful progress. Slowly but surely God's peeling back each layer to reveal who he really created me to be at the core. And the result is something inexplicable — a joy that bubbles up from within at the most surprising, unwarranted times. It's this experience of a far better life than just getting things to go my way — it's this spiritually fulfilling life I taste more and more that motivates me to write. But it doesn't come from the strategy of trying to control things, or to get God or others to do my will. It doesn't come from trying to "be good for God" so God will "be good to me." It doesn't come when circumstances change to finally go my way. That strategy doesn't work. This "my will my way" tendency we all struggle with is the reason God allows disappointments.

MOTIVATED BY LOVE

In the first chapter, we considered what we desire. But now we're asking, "What does *God want*?" I believe the only way to understand why God allows hurt and disappointment is to listen to his heart — to hear with spiritual ears what he desires most, and to understand with spiritual wisdom why this fulfills our deepest longings as well.

Paul gives us a hint when he links trials with joy and hope:

> *We can rejoice, too, when we run into problems and trials, for we know that they help us develop endurance. And endurance develops strength of character,*

---

* The first decision is to trust in God's grace and forgiveness offered through Christ. When we simply express to God in faith that we want what Jesus did to count for us, that willingness (faith) is all God needs. It's like the "I do" of a marriage relationship. God says he not only forgives all our past, present, and future wrongs, he draws us into the closest imaginable relationship (his adopted children). That secure relationship will never change, but like any relationship, it requires daily decisions of trust to grow closer. This is the lifelong journey we're experimenting with. (See Ephesians 2:8 – 10.)

and character strengthens our confident hope of salvation. And this hope will not lead to disappointment. For we know how dearly God loves us, because he has given us the Holy Spirit to fill our hearts with his love. (Romans 5:3 – 5 NLT)

For Paul, it all goes back to love — love is the reason God allows disappointment. Sound twisted? Hang with me, and I think you'll see.

God is love. Jesus revealed greater insight into the mystery of God who *is* relationship — perfect, loving relationship between Father, Son, and Spirit existing eternally. How else could God be love, since love requires an object — *other* persons to love? There's only one God, not three, but God at the center of his Being exists in loving relationship.*

As a husband and wife in a healthy, loving relationship discover, love creates children to invite into relationship, and in so doing love expands. God created us out of love and for love, inviting us into his Divine Community of ever-expanding love. All the prophets who wrote thousands of years before Jesus made it clear that loving relationship is God's motive for creating us. Listen to the heart of God conveyed to you through Moses:

The Lord will again delight in being good to you as he was to your ancestors. The Lord your God will delight in you if you obey his voice and keep the commands and decrees written in this Book of Instruction, and if you turn to the Lord your God with all your heart and soul.... Today I have given you the choice between life and death, between blessings and curses. Now I call on heaven and earth to witness the choice you make. Oh, that you would choose life, so that you and your descendants might live! You can make this choice by loving the Lord your God, obeying him, and committing yourself firmly to him. This is the key to your life. (Deuteronomy 30:9 – 10, 19 – 20 NLT, emphasis added)

---

*This paradox of God's nature was revealed down through the ages, hinted at through the prophets, revealed in Jesus (John 14:6 – 9). Though we cannot picture one God in three persons due to our limited four dimensions of space and time, this paradox resolves in higher dimensional space. The paradox comes from my limitations. If I created a two dimensional "flat" creature and penetrated his world, I would appear in his world as a two-dimensional flat circular slice (say a cross-section of my finger). If I said, "I'm actually a plurality of 'circular slices' but only one being" — that would be paradoxical in two dimensions. You can't have multiple flat circles that make "one" because you can't "stack" them on top of each other in two dimensions — it requires a higher dimension — namely "up" and "down." Yet that's what I am, many circular "slices" stacked on top of each other in a 3rd dimension. Jesus penetrated our four dimensional existence as God revealed in a "slice" of humanity (Hugh Ross delves into God's higher dimensionality in *Beyond the Cosmos*).

God tells Moses he delights in people who love him by following him. He desires to be good to you and see you prosper. You were created for God — for loving relationship with him. Understanding this is *the key to your life*!

God gives us free will, the ability to choose because love requires choice. You can't force someone to love you (even if you're God). People choosing their ways over loving God by following his ways causes the vast majority of hurt, suffering, and evil (and affects even innocent victims). God allows the consequences of our choices for a time, so that we will choose him and learn to love and follow him, even through the trials. In love, God allows the willful evils of a world gone astray to affect all people, in hopes that we will see that something *is* wrong. We were meant for more than this life can ever offer. God's desire is for us to commit ourselves fully to loving God — the solution to the problem of evil and the key to the life we deeply desire!

Down through the ages, when people turned to other ways to find life and fulfillment by putting other gods first (whether idols made of wood or paper money or the praise of people), God expressed his heart to them in graphic ways. Theologians call them "anthropomorphisms," meaning God is described in human terms. But we can't miss what these humanlike emotions convey. Remember, God is no *less* loving, feeling, or expressive than the creatures he created in his image. And so, through the prophets, God uses every human relationship as a metaphor to describe an even greater relational intimacy he desires with you. Jeremiah says,

> The Lord gave me another message. He said, "Go and shout this message to Jerusalem. This is what the Lord says: I remember how eager you were to please me as a young bride long

---

FROM LEGALISM TO LIFE

After decades of involvement in a legalistic church, I burned out and was unchurched for eight years. I came to Gateway this past April (that was good), I joined a small group in July (that was very good), and now I'm doing this 60-60 Experiment (this is great). Perhaps it's just the right time in my life, but regular contact with God is having very definite positive results for me: peace where there was turmoil, confidence where there was doubt, feelings of closeness where there was distance, and there are more. Suffice it to say, I'm extremely grateful for this experiment. —Wade

ago, how you loved me and followed me even through the barren wilderness. In those days Israel was holy to the Lord, the first of his children.... What did your ancestors find wrong with me that led them to stray so far from me? They worshiped worthless idols, only to become worthless themselves.... For my people have done two evil things: They have abandoned me — the fountain of living water. *And they have dug for themselves cracked cisterns that can hold no water at all!" (Jeremiah 2:1 – 3, 5, 13 NLT, emphasis added)*

Like a husband's first love for his young bride, that's how God feels about you. Like a loving parent desires his children to trust his guidance, God longs to lead you into life. But when we put things that are worth less first in our lives, before God, we end up feeling worthless ourselves. We can never feel secure enough, we can never get enough, because we've abandoned the fountain of living water to dig wells for ourselves that are full of cracks and can never satisfy our deepest thirst. God pleads with people through the prophets to return to putting him first:

"My faithless people, come home to me again, for I am merciful. I will not be angry with you forever. Only acknowledge your guilt. Admit that you rebelled against the LORD your God and committed adultery against him by worshiping idols under every green tree. Confess that you refused to listen to my voice. I, the Lord, have spoken! Return home, you wayward children," says the Lord ...

"I wanted nothing more than to give you this beautiful land — the finest possession in the world. I looked forward to your calling me 'Father,' and I wanted you never to turn from me. But you have been unfaithful to me....You have been like a faithless wife who leaves her husband....

"My wayward children," says the Lord, "come back to me, and I will heal your wayward hearts." (Jeremiah 3:12 – 14, 19 – 22 NLT)

God longs for one thing — faithfulness! Loving relationship motivates all God does. He longs for children who call him "Father," and who never turn away from him. He longs for us to be intimate with him (more intimate than our closest relations) by listening with spiritual ears to his voice and doing all of life with him as he leads us to good places. And he reveals his heartbreak over people who reject or ignore or just forget about him most of the hours of most of their days, putting other things first in search of life, but never finding what they're searching for. And that's also why sin, from God's perspective, feels like adultery.

SIN IS ADULTERY

The word *sin* has lost its meaning in our culture. Wonderful tasting foods are marketed as "sinfully delicious." Sin is sexy, exciting, fun, and thrilling, and greatly misperceived as "something fun and enjoyable that God doesn't want me to do." We rarely think of sin as the source of all we hate in life ... of all that steals, kills, and destroys.

Sin at the core is choosing my will and ways, despite what God declares about

LETTING GOD IN

I had a very "normal" family growing up. My sister and most girls were extremely mean to me because, I came to find out, I was a "pretty girl." I became interested in alcohol, marijuana, and sex at age thirteen. I was grounded ninety percent of my high school life. When I was seventeen, my parents thought I was into cocaine and sent me to rehab. I had only used coke once, but after rehab, I started using it regularly. I dated a guy I knew I wanted to spend the rest of my life with, got pregnant, but had a miscarriage. A year later, in a drunken rage, this man I loved more than anything turned into a monster. He took my keys, my phone, pushed me around and threatened my life. I fought him off me, but he choked me, spit on me, tried to rape me, and then held a loaded gun to my neck all night long. The next day, I called 911 and had him arrested. The next year I got a DWI, dropped out of school, and got pregnant by who knows whom. I had an abortion, though I knew it was wrong. At the lowest point in my life, I went to see a counselor. One counseling session, I told her that I knew what I needed in my life to be happy and succeed. I knew something was missing, and I knew it was God, but for whatever reason I could not let him in. She had me write down how I see myself and how I think God sees me. It was a huge step in the healing process. Shortly after, a friend invited me to Gateway. You all introduced me to God and to a life that I did not know existed. I know my life will never be perfect, and I have a lot left to learn; I'm only twenty-two. But my heart is filled with peace and love, with forgiveness and a happiness that I never had before. I have a longing to know Christ. I have forgiven myself for a lifetime filled with self-destructive patterns. I've let go of my fears and anxieties, and I have given myself completely to God. I truly believe God has a special plan for me, and loves me more than I could ever imagine. —Cindy

his will and ways that lead to love and life. Basically, when I don't trust that his ways will get me the life that satisfies, I choose my will and ways — that's sin. To most, it feels like no big deal because it's the way of the world.

To God ... it feels like adultery.

"Your children have forsaken me and sworn by gods that are not gods. I supplied all their needs, yet they committed adultery" (Jeremiah 5:7). "When the Lord began to speak through Hosea, the Lord said to him, 'Go, marry a promiscuous woman and have children with her, for like an adulterous wife this land is guilty of unfaithfulness to the Lord'" (Hosea 1:2).

Through prophet after prophet, God unveils his heart — when we put other things before God, who loves us and desires to lead us into satisfying paths, it feels like adultery to him. That's why God's first concern is not our behavior, but our hearts. The Pharisees had "near perfect" external behavior, "but their hearts are far from me," Jesus said, quoting the prophet Isaiah. Our behavior simply indicates how willing we are to love and trust and follow God. Relationship is what God desires; faithfulness pleases him most.

Jesus was asked: "Teacher, which is the most important commandment in the law of Moses?" Jesus replied, " 'You must love the Lord your God with all your heart, all your soul, and all your mind.' This is the first and greatest commandment. A second is equally important: 'Love your neighbor as yourself.' The entire law and all the demands of the prophets are based on these two commandments" (Matthew 22:36 – 40 NLT).

The point of life is relationship. Loving God and loving people sums up what God created us for; everything else written in the Scriptures is commentary on what that means. So spiritual growth is relational — the goal is relational, the means is relational, the measure should be relational. When we get clear about this, and actually begin to live life with God at the center, it's amazing how everything else gets rightly ordered because we were made to love God. But how do we actually love God? By staying connected and willing to do his will.

THE 60-60 EXPERIMENT

One day while mowing the yard, I began thanking God for the many ways I was experiencing more and more of this fulfilling way of living — staying moment by moment connected to him. I pastor a church comprised mostly of young adults, many who have tried most everything under the sun for finding the good life, yet still didn't find what they were looking for (as U2 memorialized in a song). As I prayed, "God, I wish I could get them to go for it long enough to see how good life is with you," a thought popped in my head: Do an experiment — challenge them to an experiment to stay in continuous connection and radical responsiveness before God. Have them set a watch to beep every sixty minutes as a reminder. If they'll do it long enough, they'll see how awesome life is connected to God!

Nearly two thousand people agreed to do this 60-60 Experiment, and the results for those who *went all out* were astounding. You'll hear some of their stories in the pages ahead. My prayer is that they motivate you, whether a seasoned follower of Christ or a skeptic with just an ounce of willingness, to devote sixty days to see for yourself.

So I want to challenge you starting today to do a 60-60 Experiment. For the next sixty days, try to stay in a continuous, honest conversation with God, willing to do his will moment by moment. Warning: This does not come naturally. Although this is exactly what it means to follow Christ, most Christians have never even tried to stay continuously responsive to God. We need something to interrupt our habit of not giving God a second thought most of our day, so we can turn and allow God to break in and lead and guide us.

> ### 60-60 IMPACT
>
> Hey, John, I'm Ted's MBA professor from UT. I got a God-prompt to encourage you. This 60-60 Experiment we're on is incredible. It has had such an impact on me, I am stunned. I've been a Christian for thirty years, but in just three weeks I see the basic character of my walk with God in a hugely different way—and I am acting on it! There are many little (huge for me) personal items as evidence of this ... and I won't take your time recounting them. But I hope you will take the bottom line for encouragement—this is transformational! —Linda

I suggest you get a watch with a beeper or some kind of alarm that can go with you that will beep every sixty minutes as a reminder to stay connected.* Also, put sticky notes on your mirrors, computer screen, and in your car to remind you — "Re: 60-60." The goal is to stay consciously aware all through your day that God is with you and desires loving, trusting relationship. Try to turn your

---

* Any discount store or sporting goods store will carry an inexpensive watch with a countdown timer, but you can use anything that beeps or catches your attention at least every hour as a reminder. (For more suggestions visit *www.Soulrevolution.net*)

thoughts back to God throughout the day as often as you can — as you work, talk it over with God. At every interaction ask, "What do you want me to say?" At every decision consider, "What's your will here?" As you stay increasingly in conscious contact with God, willing to follow, he will lead you into the life you deep down desire. You'll see, this simple conscious contact with God is not easy to do, but it's *all you have to do* — everything else will begin to fall into place over time.

Even if you're not yet convinced this is true — try it! At least every sixty minutes for sixty days, stop and recall, "God is with me right now. He loves me and desires to give me good things — better than I can imagine," and let that propel you to ask God, "Show me your will this next moment. I want to be willing to do your will as an act of love toward you."

We'll add texture to this 60-60 Experiment along the way. God cares about everyone. As we live in right relationship with God, he will guide us to live in increasingly life-giving ways with each other. So I want to encourage you to find a small support group, or at least one or two other people to do this experiment with you (small groups or classes can download a free curriculum at *www.Soulrevolution.net*).

God wants to use us together to do his work in the world. As you follow God's revolutionary will and ways moment by moment, God will begin restoring his kingdom ways to the broken places in your soul and then in your world through you and your friends. You can't even imagine what God might do in and through you as you're willing moment by moment.

After we did the first version of this experiment, I learned of a man who did a similar experiment earlier this century who had remarkable results that changed the world. Listen to what Frank Laubach discovered when he reoriented his minutes to stay connected to the God who wants to do life with us.

HOW TO DO THE 60-60 EXPERIMENT

1. Get a watch with a count-down timer, or some other means of reminder that will beep or interrupt you every sixty minutes. You can also make "Re: 60-60" stickers to put on your watch, computer, or rearview mirror as reminders. The more reminders the better.

2. The goal is an ongoing, minute-by-minute conversation of willingness with God. You will fail more than you succeed, and that's why you need the reminders. So every hour or every time you're reminded, remember God is with you, and re-engage in conversation with him.

3. As you begin this experiment, reflect every hour on the character of God—the one who loves you most and is "on your side." Thank him for his character throughout the day. Thank him that he promises to give you good gifts as you follow his will. If you're not sure of God's character, write down what God says about his love and goodness toward you, and then read them each hour your watch beeps. (See Jeremiah 29:11 – 13; 31:3; Matthew 6:26 – 33; Romans 8:31 – 32; 38 – 39)

4. Journal or blog your discoveries each day as you're doing this experiment. Share your insights with others and learn from their experience on our blogspot: *www.Soulrevolution.net*

 **PART 2**  **LOVING GOD**

CHAPTER THREE

Reorient—
DOING LIFE WITH GOD 60-60

For the first forty-five years of his life, Frank Laubach lived a pretty average life. He was an American-born Christian living in a remote part of the Philippines, yet on his forty-sixth birthday he wrote in his journal,

> I no longer have the sense that life is all before me, as I had a few years ago. Some of it is behind — and a miserable poor part it is, so far below what I had dreamed that I dare not even think of it. Nor dare I think much of the future. This present [moment], if it is full of God, is the only refuge I have from poisonous disappointment and even almost rebellion against God.[1]

Yet that year, 1930, despite the disappointment of life so far, something changed. By 1970, when Laubach passed away, his influence had spread worldwide. The *Encyclopaedia Britannica* notes he was perhaps the single greatest educator of modern times, voted "Man of the Year" in America.

In the last forty years of his life, Laubach developed the Each One Teach One literacy campaign, used to teach sixty million people to read in their own language, all across the globe. He wrote over fifty books and became an international presence in literacy, religious, and governmental circles — having an influence on poverty, injustice, and illiteracy worldwide. His influence spread to presidents as well as across the underdeveloped areas of the world.

What changed in that year of 1930 for Frank Laubach? Many who have written about him say little about his spiritual life because they don't understand it, but in his own words, 1930 was the year he began to experiment with a reorienting, revolutionary kind of prayer that changed everything.

In Laubach's journal, published under the title *Practicing His Presence*, in January 1930 he wrote,

> Two years ago a profound dissatisfaction led me to begin trying to line up my actions with the will of God about every fifteen minutes or every half hour.... [People] said it was impossible. I judge from what I heard that few people are really trying even that. But this year I have started out to live all my waking moments in conscious listening to the inner voice, asking without ceasing ... "What, Father, do you desire this minute?" It is clear that this is exactly what Jesus was doing all day every day.[2]

Laubach began an experiment — much like the 60-60 Experiment — in moment-by-moment continuous conversation with God. Laubach said, "It is exactly that 'moment by moment' surrender, responsiveness, obedience, sensitiveness, pliability, 'lost in His love,' that I [desire] to explore with all my might."[3] After thirty days, Laubach already felt a joy he had never experienced in sixteen years as a Christian.

> This sense of cooperation with God in little things is what so astonishes me.... I need something, and turn round to find it waiting for me. I must work, to be sure, but there is God working along with me. God takes care of all the rest. My part is to live this hour in continuous inner conversation with God and in perfect responsiveness to his will, to make this hour gloriously rich. This seems to be all I need think about.[4]

After sixty days, Laubach wrote,

> The experiment is interesting, although I'm not very successful thus far. The thought of God slips out of my sight for I suppose two-thirds of every day, ... [yet] this thing of keeping in constant touch with God ... is the most amazing thing I ever ran across. It is working.... As I analyze myself I find several things happening to me as a result of these two months ... this concentration upon God is strenuous, *but everything else has ceased to be so.* I think more clearly, I forget less frequently. Things which I did with a strain before, I now do easily and with no effort whatever. I worry about nothing, and lose no sleep.... If He is there, the universe is with me. My task is simple and clear.[5]

Nearly a year later, Laubach wrote,

It is difficult to convey to another the joy of having broken into the new sea of realizing God's "hereness." . . . How I wish, wish, wish that a dozen or more persons [would try this] . . . and write their experiences so that each would know what the other was finding as a result! The results, I think, would astound the world. At least the results of my own effort are astounding to me.[6]

Can you hear it in Frank Laubach's journals — this eternal quality of living that comes flowing up from within as we do life in relationship with God?

LIFE WITH GOD

"Jesus stood and said in a loud voice, 'Let anyone who is thirsty come to me and drink. Whoever believes in me, as Scripture has said, rivers of living water will flow from within them.' By this he meant the Spirit, whom those who believed in him were later to receive" (John 7:37 – 39).

Jesus' message was: The life your parched soul craves is now available to all who learn to do life moment by moment with God. As we become comfortable doing life with God, we begin to experience the power of his life flowing up into our often lifeless world — a power that brings peace even in the storms, a power that gives self-control even when we're angry, a power to live a life of freedom from the chains that enslave us, a power to develop deep, authentic relationships, a power to love even the most difficult people, and the power to experience a joy in the moments of each day as every moment of life becomes alive with new possibilities.

What if Laubach's vision could happen in our generation? What if hundreds or even thousands of people did this simple experiment and learned from each other's results? It might change our world. Imagine what God might do in and through you if you simply learned to reorient the moments of your day to do life with God.

That's why I'm challenging you to do this 60-60 Experiment for the next sixty days. As you go through your days, seek a continuous conversation with God, using every sixty minute beep of the watch as a reminder to reorient yourself into a continuous conversation of willingness. Keep a journal of what you discover — the ups and downs, highs and lows — and let's learn from each other like Laubach suggested. Post your discoveries on our blog at *www.Soul revolution.net* and find out what others are discovering. Let's see if the results don't astound the world! So what do you say? Will you seek to completely reorient for sixty days? What do you have to lose?

I'm convinced this revolutionary way of doing life with God is at the center of what it means to follow Christ — to develop the habit of staying in a continuous conversation with God, willing to do his will. If we would simply learn to do this, we would become more and more of who God intended us to be — radically alive, life-giving people. But that's a BIG "if."

I also believe one of the reasons the name "Christian" has such a negative connotation in America today is that most Christians do not, in fact, follow Jesus in this way. As the apostle Paul warned the religious people of his day, "As it is written: 'God's name is blasphemed among the Gentiles because of you'" (Romans 2:24). Maybe the reason many people today have a negative view of Christians is because we have not followed Christ moment by moment like this.

Clearly Jesus modeled living in constant contact with God the Father. Jesus said, "The Son can do nothing by himself; he can do only what he sees his Father doing, because whatever the Father does the Son also does. For the Father loves the Son and shows him all he does" (John 5:19 – 20). "My food," said Jesus, "is to do the will of him who sent me and to finish his work" (John 4:34). Paul explains that prayer should be an ongoing conversation with God — not a formal ritual to observe: "Rejoice always, *pray continually*, give thanks in all circumstances; for this is God's will for you in Christ Jesus" (1 Thessalonians 5:16 – 18, italics mine). "Pray in the Spirit *on all occasions* with all kinds of prayers and requests" (Ephesians 6:18, italics mine). This is reorienting prayer at the center of this soul revolution — forming a new habit of continuous, honest conversation with God, willing to do his will.

WHAT'S CENTRAL?

As I alluded to earlier, my father died of cancer when I was a teenager, and his final words reoriented my understanding of life, because they conveyed what mattered to him most.

Jesus' last words convey what mattered most to Jesus. What was central to him?

John 13 – 17 record Jesus' last words (great chapters to meditate on during this experiment). You'll notice that he keeps saying the same thing over and over again in different ways: basically, love God by staying obediently connected so you can love one another as I have loved you. As Jesus eats his last supper with his closest friends, he reminds them of the goal of life: "A new command I give you: Love one another. As I have loved you, so you must love one another. By this everyone will know that you are my disciples [followers], if you love one another.... Trust in God; trust also in me" (John 13:34 – 35, 14:1).

The goal is relational — loving God by trusting him and his Messiah, so he can lead us to love one another in a new way that reorients our little self-consumed worlds. Jesus invites us into this deep mystery about God. At the center of the universe is a relationship of self-surrendering love between Father, Son, and Spirit who want to continue working through those who are willing. Jesus explains:

> *I am the way and the truth and the life. No one comes to the Father except through me. If you really know me, you will know my Father as well. From now on, you do know him and have seen him.... It is the Father, living in me, who is doing his work.... Very truly I tell you, all who have faith in me will do the works I have been doing. (John 14:6 – 7, 10, 12)*

This Divine community exists in love eternally and invites us to share in this love. Jesus is the door through which we enter. When Jesus says, "No one comes to the Father but through me," that must be so if Jesus is telling the truth. It's like me saying, "No one can marry John Burke unless they marry me." Of course, because John Burke and I are one in the same. Jesus is the most relatable representation of God we can know. Reject him and you reject the one claiming the clearest expression of God's personhood.*

Jesus goes on to explain that we demonstrate love for him by trusting (having faith) in what he says, and God's Spirit comes to live in us forever. As we trust, our faith is reciprocated by God allowing us to see and know more of him as his Spirit does his restorative work in the world through us:

> *If you love me, you will obey what I command. And I will ask the Father, and he will give you another Counselor to be with you forever — the Spirit of*

---

* God foretold his coming as Messiah through the prophets. For over 1000 years before Jesus' birth, God put signposts along the roadway of history pointing to the time and place and activity surrounding God's coming, so all who have eyes to see can "see." For more on this, read Psalm 22 (David forecasting Messiah's crucifixion 1000 years prior), Isaiah 9:1 – 7 (written about 680 BC, forecasting Messiah as a descendent of David, living in Galilee), Isaiah 53 (reason for his crucifixion and resurrection), Daniel 9:20 – 27 (the time of Messiah's coming is given — right before the destruction of Jerusalem and the temple — which happened in 70 AD).

truth. The world cannot accept him, because it neither sees him nor knows him. But you know him, for he lives with you and will be in you.... Whoever has my commands and obeys them, he is the one who loves me. He who loves me will be loved by my Father, and I too will love him and show myself to him.... But the Counselor, the Holy Spirit, whom the Father will send in my name, will teach you all things and will remind you of everything I have said to you. (John 14:15 – 17, 21, 26 NIV)

Spiritual life is incredibly simple — love God by responding in trust to God's Spirit as he reminds you of Jesus' teachings. Let him lead you moment by moment into a life of authentically loving people in a new way, and you will begin to see God "show himself to you" as you experience a life of love in Divine community.

Doing life with God *is* central. This 60-60 Experiment is a path to actually living out the *one thing* most important to God. Get this right, and you fulfill all the other commands (Matthew 22:37 – 40). But let's be honest; it's simple, but not easy. It's against our independent nature that turns self-ward more than God-ward throughout the day, so it takes time and intentionality to establish a new habit of doing life with God.

AROUND THE TRACK

I remember when I first came to faith. Intellectually, I was convinced that Jesus is the Messiah, foretold by the prophets. I came to believe that God exists and wants a relationship with me, and so I prayed a prayer of faith. My friends and spiritual mentors told me this would begin my relationship with God through Jesus — kind of like the first step on the journey.

But six months later I started to feel funny. I'd been praying daily, but it felt like talking to myself. I got no response, heard nothing, felt nothing, never saw sparks or fireworks, had no tingly feelings — nothing. I was reading the Bible, but honestly, at times it was just downright confusing as to how to relate it to my daily life.

As I was out running on a track one day, I remember thinking, "Maybe this is just a joke. Maybe it's all wishful thinking — how can I tell? If God is really here and wants a relationship with me, he seems extremely shy. Maybe I've been duped. Am I just an idiot?" I considered throwing in the towel and going back to life without God.

But another thought came to mind, "Maybe it takes time! Maybe God wants to see how willing I am to really seek him. Maybe it's like every other relationship — it takes time logged together learning to trust each other. I guess I'll never know unless I really go for it." And that thought turned me around.

Decades later, I'm glad I listened to that quiet thought. Little did I realize then but that was the first time I responded to the whisperings of God's Spirit. It was the beginning of learning how to do life with God by listening with spiritual ears. As in any relationship, you have to stick with it long enough to learn the other person's relating patterns and develop trust.

STAY CONNECTED — FRUIT HAPPENS

His last night on earth Jesus said, "Come, let's leave," and he and his disciples left the upper room and walked across Jerusalem toward the garden of Gethsemane. When I visited Jerusalem, I walked the path they would have traversed — from up on Mount Zion, down through the Kidron Valley, which is a very deep valley between Jerusalem and the Mount of Olives, where Gethsemane is located. A natural spring flows into the Kidron Valley, so no doubt that's where vineyards and olive groves would have been located.

Jesus knew how easily this central idea of doing life with God can get lost in religious activity, busyness, and the worries of life! So I imagine Jesus and the disciples walking through the vineyard, Jerusalem-side of the Kidron Valley. He sees the vines and wants to illustrate what matters most. So he paints a picture of how life works:

> Remain in me, as I also remain in you. No branch can bear fruit by itself; it must remain in the vine. Neither can you bear fruit unless you remain in me. I am the vine; you are the branches. If you remain in me and I in you, you will bear much fruit; apart from me you can do nothing. (John 15:4–5)

See it? Stay connected to God's Spirit, as a branch connects to a tree — and fruit grows naturally. The branch doesn't have to strive to produce grapes — if the soil is right and it stays connected — fruit happens! (Sounds like a bumper sticker, doesn't it?)

But when you're disconnected — nothing grows. Disconnected from the trunk, the source of nutrients and life, a branch dies and is worthless. Now, maybe you're thinking, "Wait a second. What do you mean I can't do anything apart from God? I can do lots of things ... I can build a successful business, I can have a loving family, I can be a good moral person, I can build an empire!"

That's true! What Jesus is saying, though, is that apart from God you cannot grow into the person God intended you to be. You can't accomplish or become who he created you to be without him — because *you were created to do life with God*! Without staying connected to him, you can gain the whole world but lose your soul — and lose everything of lasting value and worth in the process! That's the point. This is central to life — stay connected.

Spiritual growth is simple: Stay connected to God's Spirit moment by moment, and he does the rest: "So I say, let the Holy Spirit guide your lives. Then you won't be doing what your sinful nature craves.... The Holy Spirit produces this kind of fruit in our lives: love, joy, peace, patience, kindness, goodness, faithfulness, gentleness, and self-control" (Galatians 5:16, 22 NLT). You don't have to try hard to change or grow; just focus on one thing: Stay connected — fruit happens.

Three weeks after we started our first 60-60 Experiment at church, a guy walked past my car in a grocery store parking lot and asked, "What does 'Fruit Happens' mean?" I walked around to the back of my car to find that some practical joker in our church had made me a "Fruit Happens" bumper sticker because I said it sounds like one. I'd been sporting it around town for three weeks! Personally, I'm not into bumper stickers, but if there's one thing we need to be reminded of at every turn it's this: Stay connected, fruit happens.

Brian, the former atheist with the DWI from chapter one, explains how this reality happened for him:

> I broke up with the woman who introduced me to Gateway, and not in a very healthy or mature way—old wounds still not healed. But I continued to go to church, which was a huge deal because relational isolation was usually the path I took. As I kept doing the 60-60, staying connected to God several times a day, my habits of looking lustfully at women and Internet porn started to decline. I didn't really try; it just didn't appeal in the same way. In fact, it rarely crossed my mind. That's the beauty of God's hand in our lives. I didn't have to struggle with the decision because there was no decision. God was taking the impulse away. The 60-60

led to a major growth period. I have an excitement and thriving interest in all the things God has for me—it's been filling the void I could never fill. I've read the entire New Testament, all kinds of Christian books—soaking everything up. After reading the New Testament, I came to a conviction about sex before marriage, mainly because God had changed my heart to want more of a connection with others. Jesus' definition of lust is adultery, and I found Jesus changing my whole mindset toward women. Instead of seeing women as sex objects, I find I look at them in a totally different way. I think about what I want in a relationship rather than fantasizing. When I got into a new relationship, for the first time we talked about God and his will early on. Amazingly, I find this new way of relating much more fulfilling.

God created you to do life with him, right *now*, moment by moment. Think of it this way, you can't control the future, you can't change the past, but if you can have a good moment *right now* by living faithfully with God, followed by another and another, you'll have a good day — a faith-filled, fruitful day. And if you have a fruitful tomorrow, and the next day, and the next, you'll end up becoming all God intended! It's that simple. But it's difficult to stay connected and willing moment by moment. So how can we do this better as we use these 60-60 reminders to reorient us?

CONTINUAL AWARENESS

When my daughter was young, we used to lie in bed each night and read *Where's Waldo?* Ever seen those books? Page after page of noisy, busy, overcrowded scenes (kind of like our lives). Somewhere in the jungle of people, Waldo, this guy with a funny hat, is lurking and you have to spot him. Ashley and I would have nightly "Where's Waldo" races. At first, it's really hard and annoying, because you can't see him, but Waldo's there. The more you practice, the easier it gets to spot him. Soon you're able to retrain your eyes to look at the page in a new way, and spot Waldo faster and faster.

It's the same with awareness of God's presence. Your Creator is with you, always has been! Have you noticed? We must learn how to become aware in a new way. As you practice, over time, it gets easier and easier. Paul explains to the Athenians, "God [created all people] so that they would seek him and perhaps reach out for him and find him, though he is not far from any one of us. 'For in him we live and move and have our being'" (Acts 17:27 – 28). God is with us, sustaining our very being, but we live mostly unaware.

The truth is, many of us live everywhere except in the moment. Some of us are so busy living in the future, consumed with worry about what might or might not happen tomorrow, that we miss the only moment guaranteed — this one moment with God. Some of us are stuck in the past. We feel so bad or so guilty about our wrongs or so resentful or bitter about the wrongs of others, we miss what God has for us *this moment*. God paid the price through Christ's death to forgive us fully and set us free from the past, and to ease our future worries with his relational security, so we would stay connected to him today.

Pause for a second, take a deep breath, and consider: "Am I even aware of this moment? What thoughts are scrolling through my mind? Am I aware that God is here with me and is capable and willing to interact with me, right now, even as I read this?" Take a minute to pray and reorient your spiritual eyes to "see" the God who is with you — this moment!

HOW GREAT IS YOUR GOD?

In the movie *Gandhi*, a clergyman and Gandhi are walking together on a boardwalk in South Africa. They are accosted by some brutish-looking young white men who seem ready to hurt them. Just then, the ringleader's mother yells from an upstairs window and commands him to leave Gandhi alone. As they walk on, the clergyman exclaims, "That was some good luck."

Gandhi comments, "I thought you were a man of God."

The clergyman replies, "I am, but I don't believe he plans his day around me!"

It's a common but mistaken view of God — that our lives and ordinary days are too small and insignificant to get his attention. After all, he's got a universe to run, lots to do, supernovas to explode, the laws of nature to keep in line, and, of course, an occasional interaction with certain "special humans" — like Moses or Abraham, Mother Teresa or Billy Graham, and, of course, professional athletes. He's too big to care about the moments of my life.

Some think this view honors God's greatness, but it does just the opposite. Lack of belief creates lack of awareness. You see, God is *SO* great that he alone can indeed plan his day around me, and you, and every one of his creatures, and attend to our requests and be intimately involved with us — all at the same time. That's just *how great* God truly is. He's not limited by time and space — he is here with you, right now, everywhere, always!*

You don't have to be perfect for God to enter into life with you — that's the message of Jesus. You can let him into the messes in your life, and he will begin to reorient you and direct you, and do things for you that you couldn't do for yourself. But it starts with a continual awareness: Where's God? Right here! "God, you are here, right now ... in this moment. Thank you for wanting to do life with me, to guide me, comfort me, teach me, love me."

How often are you aware of this truth? Do you believe it? As the day begins — are you aware of God's presence? As you drive in traffic — in that ungodly mess, are you aware? As you crank out your work or struggle to get motivated — are you aware? As your kids are whining and cranky and driving you up the wall — are you aware? He's there!

What might God do in you as you start to train yourself to be more and more aware of his presence in each moment? Use each beep of the watch, every sticky note reminder, to reorient and acknowledge God's presence. How might it change your life to realize you're never alone — the only one who fully knows you, completely understands you, sees your potential, and is on your side, is always there with you. It starts with awareness that leads to communication — the more you communicate, the better you relate.

CONTINUOUS CONVERSATION

Let's say you know a couple who comes to you complaining about not feeling very close or loving toward one another. They're beginning to not trust each other anymore. Knowing that good communication is ninety percent of the secret of any close relationship, you begin to ask questions. "How often do you take time to share what's on your heart and mind?"

"Oh, we don't need to do that," the guy replies. "We already know everything about each other."

"Do you ever spend time together or do anything fun or memory making?" you inquire.

"I don't have the luxury of that kind of time," she says. "I'm a very busy lawyer."

---

* Joshua 1:9 and Matthew 28:20 speak of God's presence with us always. Astrophysicist Hugh Ross explains how one extra dimension of time would allow God to be present in each moment with billions of people simultaneously (*Beyond the Cosmos*).

You can't believe they don't understand why they don't feel close or trusting or loving. It seems so obvious — you can't relate if you don't communicate. But they don't get it.

I hear people complain all the time about not feeling close to God, not sure they can trust him, not sure God cares. But they never committed to staying connected to God in their daily life, and when they do take time to communicate, the communication is all one-sided. Rather than doing life with God, it's all a religious, formal, ritualistic meeting for them. I'm convinced God desires an unrehearsed, gut-level, rigorously honest conversation throughout the moments of the day. Darin explains how this kind of continuous, authentic struggle led to a breakthrough for him:

> I've been terrible in my every-hour consistency during this 60-60 Experiment. For awhile, I was in a state of total apathy toward God. I didn't want to do his will. I didn't even want to want his will. I just didn't care. So my prayer each hour was, "God, kill my apathy." The crust of apathy eventually was scraped off, only to reveal the stench of sinful desires festering beneath. The Adversary switched from apathy to misdirected desires going full throttle. I wanted these other things; I did not want to do God's will. I did not want to relinquish control. So, I just began speaking frankly to him, "Lord, I don't want to give this up. Please help me to want to." The struggle of the flesh did not abate, but my prayer gradually evolved: "Lord, I want to give this up to you, give me the strength." The battle proved bloody. There were times I would have an all-out brawl with God for almost an hour. I would rationalize a way for the flesh to win ... but then that blasted watch beeper would go off, and it would start all over again! I felt liberty to not have to be "spiritual" before God, but instead raw and visceral, telling him exactly what I felt and why I didn't want to do his will. Shame and guilt from my sin usually shuts me down, causing me to hide in the shadows away from God's presence. Instead, I stared carelessly into the Sun and had my words with it. In a strange, beautiful way, wrestling with God like this allowed me to remain in him even when that was the last thing I wanted to do. As I kept talking to God about everything, he slowly formed me. A lifetime of 60-60 won't make me perfect, but I'm astounded at his grace: patiently molding my desires into his desires, breaking me from my bondage, healing me,

*and reigniting a passion in my soul to follow his will as I stayed
connected through the struggle.*

Staying connected in a brutally honest, continuous conversation allows
God to do for us what we can't do for ourselves. See, you're having a continuous
conversation with yourself all the time anyway. Ever notice that? Even while
reading, you may be talking to yourself about your own struggles and about
whether this 60-60 Experiment will really help.

But the goal is to stop just talking to yourself in your head and enter into
conversation with the God who created you for himself. Get honest with God,
process what's most on your mind throughout the day, and keep your mind
open to his thoughts. That's how you begin to develop an authentic relationship
with God. He will honor that effort.

So you're getting cranked up at work, your stress level starts to red-line, and
the beeper goes off — or you see the sticker on your computer, "Re: 60-60." Are
you aware? God's here! Open the conversation even as you're rushing to meet a
deadline. "Lord, I'm getting wound up here. I'm feeling burdened. Jesus said,
the life you want for me isn't burdensome* — so I'm doing it wrong here. Help
me. Show me how to do this your way."

Or maybe you're right in the middle of some thought or action you know
is wrong. The temptation is to hide from God, but do you really think that's
possible? *No* — it's just detrimental. So instead, you open up communication
and ask, "God, what am I doing? I know this is not your will. Thank you that
because of Christ, you forgive me for this too, so I don't have to hide from you.
Come help me. Help me do the next right thing."

As we learn to reorient our moments to stay connected, God leads us. But
can we really talk to God like this? Is this really okay with God? Let's look at
how Jesus taught us to pray, and I think you'll start to understand how much
God cares about every aspect of our lives.

THE 60-60 EXPERIMENT

God wants to do life with you moment by moment. As you
are willing, he will guide you into an amazing experience of
life. Not where everything goes as you wish on the outside,

---

* See Matthew 11:28 – 29. For a topical list of promises about God's will in our struggles, check
out *www.Soulrevolution.net.*

but where God produces what you've longed for on the in-side. This 60-60 Experiment can start you down that path as you learn to connect with God in a continuous conversation, using reminders every sixty minutes to reorient. The goal is a moment-by-moment connection, but this takes practice. Don't worry if you get sidetracked or off course along the way; just begin again. Focus on two things:

1. **Be aware of God's presence.** With every beep of the watch or every reminder you see, stop and simply acknowledge God's presence with you, and thank him that he cares about you and wants to help you through your day. You may want to memo-rize 1 Peter 5:7 to remind yourself that he cares: "Cast all your anxiety on him because he cares for you."

2. **Converse with God about everything.** The goal is to be mind-ful all the time. Open your mind to talk over with God all your thoughts, worries, work challenges, decisions, temptations, and failures throughout your day. Instead of just talking to yourself about them, talk it over with God. He will honor this as you stay diligent.

CHAPTER FOUR

Reconnect—
PRAYER AS A WAY OF LIFE

Jesus taught us how to pray. Basically he said don't pray like religious babblers who chant rote prayers they memorize. God is a person! Instead, pray like this ... and he taught us the Lord's Prayer: "Our father who art in heaven, hallowed be thy name. Thy kingdom come, thy will be done, on earth as in heaven. Give us this day our daily bread and forgive us our trespasses (if you're Presbyterian) debts (if you're Baptist) ... lead us not into temptation ... blah blah blah." (Matthew 6:5 – 15 has the real version).

We memorized it! We think we know it, but we babble it meaninglessly just like Jesus said *not* to! How would you like to have kids who only talked to you in memorized, canned phrases? "I love you, Mommy Dearest; you're a kind, benevolent being." No, you want to connect with your kids. You want honest, authentic, heartfelt connection. Jesus' model prayer is actually about a heartfelt, honest, continuous conversation with God, willing to do his will. Let's look beyond the words to the meaning of this way-of-life prayer.

YOU'RE GOD I'M NOT
"OUR FATHER IN HEAVEN, HOLY IS YOUR NAME"

The first thing we need to remember, Jesus says, is God's character! Jesus says that God is like a perfect loving Parent — your Father, who, unlike your earthly parents, is always good, always seeks your best, and is always with you. Jesus instructs us to talk to God throughout the day as a loving Parent who is there to guide us.

But Jesus also reminded us that God is holy. *Holy* just means "set apart," *very* different from what's common. In other words, Jesus says as you talk with God, remember: "God, you're God, and I'm not." What does it mean to love God *as God*? It means to put God first and not let anything else be your guiding factor. That is the first of the Ten Commandments.

You see, there's really only one Sin with a capital *S* (this is important to understand). That Sin is breaking the first commandment — putting something before God. We've all broken this one. As Keith Miller likes to say, we have fired the rightful CEO of Life — the Founder and rightful Owner — and taken control of the operation ourselves. All the other little sins come from this big one. And that's the root of the problem: Self-centeredness rather than God-centeredness.

Amy had come to faith in Christ at Gateway and had been growing several years when the leader of her small group quit. She approached our director of small groups about leading. Amy explains what resulted from that conversation:

> During the leadership process, Gary asked me if anything kept me from growing closer to God. I told him, "I smoke." He said, "Why don't you quit." I said, "Because I like it." Gary asked, "Why don't you pray for God to help you?" I forthrightly explained, "Because I like it, and I feel like a hypocrite asking God to take this away when I don't want him to!" Gary suggested, "Pray for willingness; maybe that's all you need." That Sunday, I heard a message on Jacob wrestling with the Lord, and that night I wrestled all night with God—tossing and turning, pleading and crying, trying to hang onto my habit saying, "Why is it wrong? It's not hurting anyone." I kept sensing God saying, "Because you put it above me, you love it more than me, and it's a harmful crutch you don't need." The next morning, I was worn out from wrestling all night. I stepped out on my patio, lit up as I did every morning, drew smoke deep into my lungs . . . and I hear . . . "Amy! You wrestle with me all night long and you do this? You can't call on me with the first craving of the day? What was all night about?" I sheepishly put my cigarette out and said, out loud, "You're right. I'm sorry. I'm done with this." That was the last puff of smoke I had. That was four years ago.

As you do life in honest conversation with God's Spirit, and you find yourself stressed or anxious or angry or deceitful or worried or just plain out of control — remember, "Father, you're God, and I'm not. Help me put you first this moment, willing to do your sovereign will rather than getting bent out of shape that my will is not sovereign. Help me do the next right thing that I can do to follow your will in this situation." Watch what happens as you willingly put him first.

HEARING GOD'S VOICE
"YOUR KINGDOM COME, YOUR WILL BE DONE . . ."

That leads to the next part of Jesus' prayer, and the next problem: How do we know God's will? How do we hear God's voice? Jesus said to pray, "Your kingdom come, your will be done." How do we learn to listen willingly? Our side of this conversation means that as we remain aware throughout the day, we acknowledge his presence and converse silently in our spirit about what's on our minds. But how does God talk to us?

I'm writing down my thoughts in this book so that you can have them as a permanent record of what I'm thinking. That's what Scripture claims to be — God's written communication — the recording of God's interaction and will and revelation of what he's like, chronicled throughout the history of civilization. Scripture reveals God's loving character, just nature, and perfect will. Jesus claimed to be the fulfillment of all that the prophets recorded in the thirty-nine books of the Old Testament (called the Law and the Prophets in Jesus' day) which were written down over about a 1,000-year period. He explained:

> Do not think that I have come to abolish the Law or the Prophets; I have not come to abolish them but to fulfill them. Truly I tell you, until heaven and earth disappear, not the smallest letter, not the least stroke of a pen, will by any means disappear from the Law until everything is accomplished. Anyone who sets aside one of the least of these commands and teaches others accordingly will be called least in the kingdom of heaven, but whoever practices and teaches these commands will be called great in the kingdom of heaven. (Matthew 5:17 – 19)[1]

That's why we need to read the Scriptures, so that we might know what God has revealed of his character and will. The Bible doesn't communicate specifically, but generally. It tells us it's not God's will to lie, steal, or commit adultery, but it doesn't tell us specifically what to do when you're in an argument with a spouse or seeking career guidance. But Jesus said his Spirit lives in us if we've invited him in, and his Spirit will lead us into truth and life specifically — if we're listening.

Through the prophet Jeremiah, God says, "*I spoke* to them, but they did *not listen*; I called to them, but they did not answer" (Jeremiah 35:17, italics mine). God communicates with us, but we must learn to listen with spiritual ears. And unlike us, God's not limited.

Every week, as a pastor, I speak my thoughts in sermons. My goal is to get my thoughts into the minds of the listeners. The problem is I'm limited. I need English words and stories that paint mental pictures; I need my vocal chords, sound waves, a listener's ears, and most importantly their willingness and co-operation. If they're not willing to listen carefully and consider my thoughts that are reaching their brain through the airwaves, I can't influence them.

Now what would be really cool is if I could just directly place my thoughts into the minds of the people to whom I'm speaking. I'd love it! It would make communication much more direct and much less limiting. Of course, my thoughts would appear to them as another one of their thoughts, and they could still choose to "hear it" or just ignore it, but it sure would be a much more direct form of communication.

Fortunately for others, I can't do that. But God can! God can place his thoughts *directly* into yours. Like those nudgings you've probably felt before in your conscience, God does communicate to you, but you must learn to "have ears to hear."*

I remember as a college student first discovering this listening kind of prayer. I was praying one morning very specifically for some of my friends, when I had this thought: "I need to call Alison." Alison is my little sister. She was in high school at the time. Since it was a Monday, I knew she was in school, so I brushed off the thought.

As I continued praying for my friends, the same thought came again: "Call Alison." But again, I ignored it. I had never considered that God-thoughts could be commingled with my own. When the thought to call my sister kept recurring, I stopped and asked, "God, do you want me to call Alison? Is that why I keep thinking about her? She's not home — you know that, don't you?"

And I thought, "This is crazy, but I'm just gonna do it. What can it hurt?" So I called home — and Alison answered! She had stayed home from school, depressed about the way kids were treating her. As we talked, I was able to encour-

---

* Direct thoughts is one way God communicates with us; of course there are others. He can communicate through other people's words to us (Numbers 23:5), through dreams (Numbers 12:6), through signs or circumstances at times (Acts 16), and through the Scriptures (which should serve as a check against deception sneaking into the more subjective ways of communication — which is always possible).

age her. I hung up the phone blown away. "Wow! Was that just a coincidence?" But I now have about twenty years' worth of journals full of "coincidences" like that! I've discovered that the more I position myself to hear promptings and respond, the more "coincidences" occur.

We expect God to show up and communicate in big, dramatic ways, but God doesn't often speak through the obtrusive, commanding ways we expect. Rather, he speaks in unobtrusive ways — in a gentle whisper that's barely discernible — so quiet it can be mistaken for our own thoughts unless we listen closely.

Why does he do this? Because he knows that people who don't seek his guidance won't listen anyway. What we need most is not more booming commands — we've got those (you can read them in the Bible!). We need humble, willing hearts, quiet and ready to listen and respond. "The eyes of the LORD search the whole earth in order to strengthen those whose hearts are fully committed to him" (2 Chronicles 16:9 NLT). When our hearts are in the right place, it's amazing how much clarity comes to mind.

WHAT'S ON YOUR MIND MOST?
"GIVE US THIS DAY OUR DAILY BREAD . . ."

Jesus continues his model prayer with "Give us this day our daily bread." What does that mean? It means God cares about the things *you* care about. Basic needs probably occupied the minds of most people in Jesus' time. Having food each day is one of our most basic needs. It's okay to ask God for the things we feel we need. As Peter reminds us: "Give all your worries and cares to God, for he cares about you" (1 Peter 5:7 NLT).

We often think we have to talk to God about lofty things like world peace or ending poverty, but God's will comes one life at a time. As you seek to stay in continuous conversation with him, tell him about the things that are *really* on your mind — what your real needs are and what kind of help you really need. See prayer as talking with God about *everything* that most occupies your mind — because that's where you really live, and that's where God wants to do life with you. As you do this, you'll find that God cares for you personally, even about the little things.

After college, I took a job as a reservoir engineer in Ventura, California. It was the first big decision I had prayed about, and it demanded that I step out in faith to trust — telling God I wanted to be his representative in the business world. It was a dream job with lots of responsibility and a good salary. Best of all, I could live by the beach and surf real waves! Having grown up on the Gulf Coast, the California surf seemed like Nirvana. But being from Austin, I knew no one in California, so I prayed that I'd meet people who would be a positive spiritual influence on me.

Before starting work that summer, however, I had planned to travel through the Soviet Union, smuggling Bibles behind the Iron Curtain. It all sounded like a high-stakes faith adventure. But a month before I was scheduled to leave, my company announced the largest layoff ever. I called my boss. He said, "You still have a job, but get out here right away."

I hung up the phone and felt sick. I had committed to going to Russia, yet my boss was saying, "You can't go if you want your job!" As I prayed, I felt it was a test. I told God I wanted to be fully devoted to his will in my career. On one side, I thought this job was his will, yet I could lose it. On the other side, I had a team depending on me, and I knew this would be my only shot at a two-month ministry project like this. So what could I do? Either choice would be an act of trust.

After two days of praying for direction, I decided, "Okay God, I knew it would stretch my faith to do this ministry project, and I think it's what you want me to do, so I will trust you with my job. If you want me to have it, I'll trust that it will be here when I get back. If not, you'll provide something better."

Nervous, I called my boss. "I really want the job, but I've committed to this team of people and to God that I'd do this project, and I feel like I can't break my commitment." It was out — I'm a Christian, and my faith could cost me an awesome career opportunity.

"Well, I can't promise you anything then," was all he said. "Call me when you get back, and we'll see." That's all I had to go on for the next three months.

While in Russia, I met a guy named Dave. He was involved in starting a new campus ministry at the University of California at Santa Barbara — which meant I now knew one Christian in California. Still, that was more than an hour from Ventura, and what's more, I still didn't know if I had a job.

When I returned, I couldn't believe it — my boss told me I still had my job, so I packed up and moved to Ventura. I kept praying, "Lord, just help me meet other Christ-followers here in town." But it just didn't happen. After months of isolation both at the office and at home, I felt like throwing in the towel and going out to bars just to meet people. But I knew that would take me back down a path I didn't want to travel. I was desperate. I kept crying out to God, "Help me find some friends who are good for me — I'm miserable."

Not long after that, I got a call from Dave in Santa Barbara. His roommate had moved out, and he wanted to know if I'd room with him. As I hung up the phone, I said, "Lord, is *this* your answer? Tell me it's not true! Dave lives over an hour away, and I can't make that commute every day!" Still, thinking this might in fact be God's response to my prayer, I called Dave back and said, "Let's try it out this weekend."

So I drove to Santa Barbara — one of the most beautiful places in America — and at Dave's church, I met a group of people who invited me to go rock climbing. I had a blast. It was a college town with loads of people my age, and Dave needed more help getting the new campus ministry started. They needed both a music leader and a PA system, and for some reason, I'd kept my college band's PA, which was now serving as my dinner table. Santa Barbara seemed like the answer to all I'd prayed for — except the commute.

On that Monday, I got up at 5:30 a.m. to try out the hour-long commute down Highway 1. As I drove, I talked to God about my dilemma: "It's perfect — but why Santa Barbara? I was hoping for friends in Ventura. I can't make this commute every day; it'll cost more in gas than I can afford. God, why is it that I've met no Christian friends in Ventura, but here, in one weekend, I meet tons of new friends in Santa Barbara? If only there were a carpool so I wouldn't burn so much gas. Then again, I guess I could use the commute as a prayer time — and it's not the worst commute, driving along the Pacific Ocean."

I rambled on, talking over these little concerns, not sure what to do. When I got into the office, I went to the lab.

"Hey, I'm Pete — you the new reservoir engineer?" the guy on the computer next to me asked with a smile.

"Yeah, I'm the new guy," I volleyed back. We made small talk for awhile until Pete asked, "Was this fog here all weekend?"

"Don't know," I replied, "I was in Santa Barbara all weekend. It was beautiful up there. You live in Ventura?"

"No, I live in Santa Barbara and carpool with three coworkers. It's a great place to live," Pete enthusiastically replied.

Pete couldn't see it, but my jaw hit the table and bounced back up. Did he just say he carpools from Santa Barbara?

"I'm thinking about moving to Santa Barbara," I said. "You have any room in your car if I do?"

"Actually," Pete said, "we don't right now, but one of the guys is moving this fall, so we'll have room in a couple of months."

So I carpooled with them for the next two years.

Looking back, these small decisions of faith were responsible for so many blessings in my life. I learned that when you trust God, he begins to do all these little things that you might be tempted to write off as coincidences — but *don't do it*! Thank him instead! Acknowledge his caring presence, because in these "coincidences" he shows you that even the little details of your life matter deeply to him.

FORGIVE US OUR WRONGS
"FORGIVE US OUR SINS, AS WE HAVE FORGIVEN
THOSE WHO SIN AGAINST US . . ."

Of course, you realize that even when you sincerely try to stay connected to God, you'll fail more often than not. In fact, you'll become more aware of how often you wander from God's path and do things contrary to his will. Paul said, "Christ Jesus came into the world to save sinners — of whom I am the worst" (1 Timothy 1:15).

Once during our church's 60-60 Experiment, a guy emailed me: "Over the past twenty-four hours, I've practiced awareness every sixty minutes to see if I thought I could keep a commitment like that. It's SOOOO HARD!! Man, I'm hardly ever where I want to be when that stinkin' beeper goes off!"

Many people even give up because they don't know what to do with their guilt. They have become more aware of God's will, and they realize their tendency to do the opposite, so they feel condemned and give up. They mistakenly think the goal is to *change themselves* to do the right thing every sixty minutes — big mistake!

Paul goes on to say, "But for that very reason I was shown mercy so that in me, the worst of sinners, Christ Jesus might display his *immense patience* as an example for those who would believe in him and receive eternal life" (1 Timothy 1:16, italics mine). This is why we need God's grace to grow. We can't change ourselves into what he intends. He has to do it. He has patience, and so must you. Whenever you are tempted to wallow in guilt or pretend you can hide from wrongs, remember that "there is no condemnation for those who are in Christ Jesus" (Romans 8:1). Let God help you do the next right thing.

> *For we do not have a high priest [Jesus] who is unable to empathize with*
> *our weaknesses, but we have one who has been tempted in every way, just as*

we are — yet he did not sin. Let us then approach God's throne of grace with confidence, so that we may receive mercy and find grace to help us in our time of need. (Hebrews 4:15 – 16)

Like toddlers learning to walk, at first we fall as much as we stand. But if we learn to stay connected more and more, we *will* walk. So how do you deal with spiritual failure? That's what Jesus taught us in the Lord's Prayer: "Forgive us our sins, as we have forgiven those who sin against us."

FAILING FORWARD

If you are trying the 60-60 Experiment, you've probably realized by now how many times you *will* fail. Jesus says, you *will* need forgiveness — it's a given. And I bet you figured that out, didn't you! You've become aware of how often you don't let God's thoughts penetrate your thoughts and how often that realization catches you in the "oops" position. Sometimes you might know God's will but resist it because it's not easy or doesn't fit your plans. Imperfect people wrong God and each other. We need forgiveness, and we must forgive one another. Here's how to deal with it and move on:

If we confess our sins to him, he is faithful and just to forgive us and to cleanse us from every wrong. If we claim we have not sinned, we are calling God a liar.... I am writing this to you so that you will not sin. But if you do sin, there is someone to plead for you before the Father. He is Jesus Christ... the sacrifice for our sins. He takes away not only our sins but the sins of all the world." (1 John 1:9 – 2:2)

Moment by moment, as you become aware that you've gone against God's will, stop, confess (admit it to him), and reconnect. Then move forward. Jesus taught us to forgive others not just seven times, but seventy times seven. That's 490 times! That's once every two minutes if it all happens on one day! That's how often we are to forgive, and that's how often God forgives us.

Confession and forgiveness work like this. If my kids go against my will and do something wrong, I still love them. I don't disown them. Our relationship is secure. But their unwillingness to admit their wrong and respond to my guidance keeps us from experiencing closeness. And as long as they stubbornly hold out, unwilling to respond or obey, they'll feel distance between us. But as soon as they admit they're wrong, ask for forgiveness, and become willing again, I quickly forgive and can continue to guide them. We can enjoy life together once more.

Like a loving parent, God shows us patience through our messy spiritual stages from toddler to child to adolescent — he's there to pick us up, brush us off, and keep us walking. You may have to confess and turn back seven times or seventy times a day — but that's okay. Just stay willing to learn and respond next time. That's how we grow. But if we keep resisting and ignoring God when we know what his will is, eventually our hearts will become hardened and our spiritual ears will shut. We won't hear a thing.

TEMPTATIONS

"LEAD US NOT INTO TEMPTATION,
BUT DELIVER US FROM EVIL . . ."

In the early days of Gateway, Ted was interviewing a woman for a leadership position. In the middle of the interview, out of nowhere, Ted had this thought: "She's sleeping with her boss." That was a pretty strange thought when he didn't even know if she had a boss — so Ted wondered: "God, is this from you? What do I do with this?"

(*A word of warning*: when prompting thoughts like this involve others, you've got to be extremely careful. We can be deceived just like Peter when he thought he clearly knew God's will for Jesus — and was dead wrong.)

So Ted asked a question (which is always the way to go when these sorts of promptings involve others): "This may sound strange, and forgive me if I'm wrong — but there's not anything going on between you and your boss, is there?"

She looked shocked and with indignation said, "No!"

Ted quickly apologized. "Sorry for asking. I just had a weird thought and wanted to check it out."

Two days later, she called Ted and admitted to an affair with her still-married boss. Now what's more disturbing to me than her admission was that she *kept having* the affair! Even though Ted showed her why this was against God's will, and even though God obviously tried to lead her out of temptation and wrongdoing, she couldn't hear. Her spiritual ears were closed, and she destroyed a family in the process.

This is a warning for many of us. If you know what God is telling you but you keep on shutting your ears, eventually you won't hear at all. The Scripture says we grieve God's Spirit when we do this — it's relational unfaithfulness toward God. "Do not bring sorrow to God's Holy Spirit by the way you live.

Remember, he identified you as his own, guaranteeing that you will be saved on the day of redemption" (Ephesians 4:30 NLT). Don't just assume, "I can always choose to follow God later." That may not be true if your heart becomes too callous. Jesus says, "For the hearts of these people are hardened, and their ears cannot hear, and they have closed their eyes — so their eyes cannot see" (Matthew 13:15 NLT).

Earlier, I told you that I almost gave up praying during my first year of faith. I was partying hard with my friends at the time and doing things I knew were not God's will. Honestly, I didn't want to respond to that gentle nudging in my conscience; I wanted to keep doing those things because they were part of my life. I had selective hearing. I wanted to hear God answering all my requests, but I didn't want to hear God's will if it was contrary to what I wanted.

Some people are more comfortable with specific direction from God than they are with general direction. They want to know God's will about a career path or a potential spouse, but they don't want to stop getting high or filling their minds with porn or being unloving toward their family. Bad news: it doesn't work that way. If we stubbornly plug our ears to God's will in one area, we won't hear in any area.

Maybe you've tuned God out for years in one area of life. If so, all it takes is confession, reconnection, and most importantly, willingness to respond. God is always there, patient, merciful, and willing, but *you* must be willing to turn back and follow.

That's why Jesus taught us to pray: "Lead us not into temptation, but deliver us from evil." This means praying, "God, as I stay connected to you, lead me away from tempting situations where I might fall prey to evil — give me the inner strength to not turn from you, but to do your will." This doesn't mean we won't be tempted. This way of praying proactively prepares us to stand strong and respond to truth in times of temptation. And the better we understand how temptation works, the easier it is to not be led into it.

MIND GAMES

Evil emanates from lies. I'm convinced the only power evil has over us comes from the lies we believe. As a result of evils done to us as children or bad choices we've made, we often internalize lies about ourselves. Those lies get reinforced by other painful triggers, and we live with a void in the soul.

I knew a man who was adopted as a child and suffered from chronic asthma. He had a perfectionistic, emotionally cold, workaholic father whom he could never please. Because the asthma almost took his life, he felt weak and interpreted his father's emotional distance as rejection due to his weakness. As a result, he believed several lies: "I'm not lovable. I'm weak. If I want love and approval, then I must prove that I'm not weak."

As he grew up, I watched him live out of these lies for years, always trying to prove that he was strong and capable, that he was a fighter. Whenever some situation in his life triggered his painful memory of rejection, he would react by dredging up all those associated lies. When someone in college called him a wimp, triggering all his pain of feeling rejected and unloved, he nearly killed the guy — and got kicked out of college as a result.

Eventually he met the love of his life. They married — but divorced six years later. He had drifted into alcoholism as a way to escape the pain. When his wife suggested that he find help, it triggered those lies all over again: "If I'm in need, I'm weak. If I'm weak, I'm unlovable." It was all subconscious, but the power of those lies caused such uncontrolled rage that his wife eventually couldn't stand it anymore.

Not until he discovered God's truth and started making a deliberate effort to follow God's will moment by moment did he find freedom from this cycle.

As we internalize lies like these, we become prone to the lies of others. Sometimes their attitudes suggest that we have to prove our worth before we can have our deep needs met, be safe and secure, or be loved and accepted. It starts out innocently enough, but step by step, as we follow one deceptive thought after another, we can become more and more deluded by lies. We believe all kinds of rationalizations and justifications, hurting ourselves and others along the way, but never really seeing the dangers until they nearly destroy us or we destroy them.

Just consider the power of lies. Imagine what I could do to you with a persistent lie. If I slowly convince you that Jews are not really human beings, then who knows what you might be willing to participate in — perhaps the slaughter of six million Jewish people.

If I could persuade you that black people are inferior to whites, I might be able to get a society of otherwise good "Christian" people to enslave blacks — all because of a lie.

If I could convince you that you're fat, even though your weight is normal for your height, and kept telling you "thinner is better," I might actually get you to starve yourself to death.

If I could lead you to believe your spouse was the source of your problems, I could create deep bitterness, resentment, and hopelessness in your marriage. If I could do the same with your spouse, I could destroy your marriage — just with my lies.

If I could entice you to believe that just one cigarette, one drink, one hit, one look won't hurt, then, one seemingly unimportant decision at a time, I could keep you enslaved to habits that could destroy you.

If I could get you to believe the future is hopeless, and bombarded you with thoughts that death is the only way out, then I could get you to destroy yourself.

Wow! Just imagine the power I would have if you would believe my lies!

So think about it: what evil lies have power over you?

THE TRUTH WILL SET YOU FREE

Jesus explained that the antidote to such lies comes from opening your mind to God's truth, then radically responding moment by moment throughout your day: "If you hold to my teaching, you are really my disciples. Then you will know the truth, and the truth will set you free" (John 8:31 – 32). Jesus' last words reiterated this, "When the Spirit of truth comes, he will guide you into all truth" (John 16:13 NLT).

You overcome temptation by catching the first subtle lie as it tries to detour you from the path that leads to life. If we stay connected, bringing every thought to God's Spirit, who lives inside every believer, he will guide us into truth. The secret is in catching the first thought. "We take captive every thought to make it obedient to Christ" (2 Corinthians 10:5). We overcome temptation one thought at a time, paying attention to the truthfulness or deceptiveness of every thought, because our thoughts lead our lives.

As he first tried to recover from an addiction to alcohol and crack cocaine, Trey recalls the importance of catching deceptive thoughts:

> I remember one specific lie that would come to my mind. Like so many lies, it seems so obvious looking back. I used to buy crack near a particular gas station. This particular gas station was close to my job and had some of the cheapest gas in town. This is where the subtle lie began. "You need to be wise with your time and money," the voice would tell me. Rather than take that thought captive and ask God to show me the truth, I would simply respond to that lie

and drive in and buy gas. It worked just fine on several occasions, even though I could see my crack dealer's house as I pumped the gas. "No problem," the lie would tell me. "I'm strong enough now. I don't have to worry about being near this old temptation. Besides, I'm being responsible with my time and money."

Then one day—boom! About the fourth time I went there, I found myself driving up to my old dealer, and before I knew it, I was talking to him about purchasing crack. Fortunately, I had enough connection with God, and just in time I came to my senses and sped away. Had I purchased crack that day, I truly believe I would have gone on a possibly life-threatening binge.

That situation really opened my eyes to my ability to rationalize an obvious lie. From that point forward I immersed myself into God's truths in Scripture. When we did the 60-60 Experiment, it helped me not get sucked into gas-station-style lies because each time my watch beeped, I would automatically ask: "God, is this where you want me to be? Is this what you want me to be saying? Is this who I should be hanging out with? Am I trusting and obeying you right now?" I've been sober for six years now, but more importantly, I'm connected to God moment by moment and feeling free at last!

Fighting temptation is that simple — you catch the first thought.

But the first thought can be deceptive. It's usually something innocent, designed to coax you into proximity to your greatest temptation. So by staying connected to God's Spirit moment by moment, submitting your thoughts to him, you let him show you the truth.

Paul reminds us to stay humble, because when we think we're most bulletproof and don't need God's help, trouble is right around the corner. "If you think you are standing strong, be careful not to fall. The temptations in your life are no different from what others experience. And God is faithful. He will not allow the temptation to be more than you can stand. When you are tempted, he will show you a way out so that you can endure" (1 Corinthians 10:12 – 13 NLT).

There's always a way out, and you can always resist because God is with you. He will show you the way and give you the power to pursue it — but only if you are willing to radically respond. The way out probably won't be the path of least resistance; it won't be easy. But the path will always be there, along with the power to overcome every temptation. As we respond to God's Spirit to lead us out of temptation, we find more freedom — freedom to enjoy life without the treadmill of always needing another hit or look or fling or possession.

When we view prayer as a way of life, communicating continuously, God leads us moment by moment to become more of the people he intends us to be. And the result is the life we were longing for.

There's just one condition: when God speaks, you must respond.

THE 60-60 EXPERIMENT

1. **What's on your mind?** Continue to use the sixty-minute beep on the watch and take advantage of every reminder to stay connected moment by moment to your Father who guides you. Talk with him about what's most on your mind. Ask for what you need, and trust that he will provide what you truly need for that moment. If you don't have an accurate view of the Father, read through one of the eyewitness accounts of the life of Jesus (Matthew or John — one chapter a night for sixty days will get you through both). As you read, open your mind to consider: If Jesus reveals God the Father, what new things do I learn about how to relate to this Parent who wants to guide me through life?

2. **Practice "taking every thought captive."** Talk with God about thoughts that lead you into temptation. Ask God to show you those seemingly insignificant thoughts that lead you into proximity to your greatest temptations. As you "catch them" get raw and honest with God about those thoughts. He will honor this.

3. **Fail forward.** As soon as you become aware of thoughts or actions against God's will (sin), just admit it. Confess it to him, thank him for already forgiving all your sins (Jesus paid the price of God's justice — nailing it to the cross). Since Jesus paid, you don't have to pay by staying separated from God — reconnect and move forward. Memorize 1 John 1:8 – 9 as a reminder of how to fail forward:

   "If we claim to be without sin, we deceive ourselves and the truth is not in us. If we confess our sins, he is faithful and just and will forgive us our sins and purify us from all unrighteousness."

Respond—
ENGAGING IN RISKY BEHAVIOR

One winter in college, I went skiing with three friends in Crested Butte, Colorado. Midway through the week, we spotted four attractive female skiers who looked like they could ski circles around us. Having no sense of humility, we tried to keep up with them. Somehow we managed to strategically cram into their gondola and strike up a conversation. Being locals, and seeing that we were easy Texas bait, they asked us if we wanted to do some *real* wide-open skiing with them.

Being arrogant Texan college boys who thought we had skied it all, we couldn't resist a challenge like that. So we went to the top of the mountain and started following them onto an unmarked trail. I began to feel a little nervous when they instructed us to take off our skis and hike, through powder up to our knees, over a ridge known as "the Outer Bounds."

When we crested the ridge, I got a sick feeling in my stomach. I looked out across a huge bowl of nearly virgin powder and down a slope that looked like it was nearly a straight drop to the bottom. I'd never even considered skiing something so steep! At that moment, two fears overwhelmed me: first, the humiliation of imagining myself rolling into a snowball; second, the fear of death.

One of the women could see the cockiness draining from our faces like bad engine oil. With some compassion she asked me, "Ever skied anything like this?"

My survival instincts got the best of me. With my voice in an upper octave I hadn't used since middle school, I said — "No."

She helpfully explained, "You can't be afraid of the mountain. You can't hold back. If you do, you'll lean back too far and wipe out. You have to go wide open like you're falling down the mountain — then you can get in a rhythm like *this*." With that, she plunged down the drop-off, carving back and forth with freedom and grace — it was amazing.

With a surge of confidence, I plunged forward, made one turn, then accelerated so fast that my fear took over. I leaned back to avoid death, and before I knew it I was snowballing head over heels right past her. I finally stopped another fifty feet down the mountain.

She retrieved my lost ski and reminded me again, "You can't let fear get the best of you. Throw yourself down the mountain; go wide open and let your turns slow you." Finally after a few more falls, I conquered my fear enough to do what she said. Though it felt counterintuitive to throw myself down the mountain, I did it. I found a rhythm in the powder, and soon I was experiencing a rush like never before. It was the most fun and freedom I'd ever had skiing.

At the bottom, I looked back up at this mammoth mountain and felt a huge sense of accomplishment. I had conquered my fear. The rest of our stay, that's all I wanted to do — wide-open skiing.

So I need to caution you right here: this 60-60 Experiment, however simple, won't work unless you do it wide open. You have to take the plunge off the mountain, not worrying about what others will think or what the future might hold or whether God's sometimes counterintuitive ways can be trusted. You have to go for it! You must get into a daily rhythm of *radical response* in obedience to God's Spirit.

Because one thing I've noticed — it's only when you respond in obedience to those God-thoughts that you *see* and *understand* God's presence and guidance in your life — and that's a rush like no other — it's Life "Wide Open." But the key is getting into the rhythm.

BELIEVING IS SEEING

Hopefully, you've been trying this experiment in moment-by-moment conscious contact with God. As your watch beeps every sixty minutes, you're turning your thoughts to God, talking over what's on your mind, willing to do his will. Of course, our goal is continuous conversation, moment by moment, breaking our old habit of ignoring God in order to grow in our ability to stay connected.

You may be asking, "But how do I know if these prompting thoughts are from God? What if they're just my random thoughts?"

The answer is: you only learn by responding. Act in faith; then, when you look back, it will be clear whether the thought was a God-prompting. I'm almost never sure if my thought is God-inspired until I respond. Then, looking back, I can see. Sometimes you'll get it wrong. You'll follow a prompting and in hindsight realize that it wasn't God at all. But as you're learning, you must give yourself permission to miss.

One Friday morning I was working hard to meet a deadline. As I searched through hardcopies of my old emails, my eyes locked on one in particular.

"I wonder what ever happened to Jerry," I thought. I recalled meeting with him and his girlfriend, Christy, a year before. I'd never heard such a "Job" story before. Jerry had lost his entire family in a matter of years. When he came to talk, he was struggling for a reason to live.

Christy had convinced Jerry, who had been agnostic most of his life, to come to Gateway because she heard about our "come as you are" attitude. She didn't feel as though they belonged in church, but she knew they desperately needed help. She didn't know where else to turn.

"Lord," I prayed, "I don't know what happened to Jerry." I glanced back over his email. "I don't feel like I helped him much, and I haven't seen him and Christy in a year. I know he doesn't believe in you, but please help him come to know your love, and have mercy on him."

After praying, I went back to my work, but for some reason, I still couldn't get Jerry off my mind. It bugged me that I'd failed in helping him see God's love for him. "Lord, bring someone into his life who can show him," I prayed as I worked.

"Maybe I should email him," I thought. "Man, I'm so behind — stay focused, John!" I went back to work. Five minutes later, my mind wandered back to Jerry. "Yeah, I should email him. I wonder if that address is still good. Will he remember me? I'll email him . . . later."

Back to work I went, but the thought nagged at me. Finally, unable to get Jerry off my mind, I asked, "Lord, do you want me to email Jerry right now?" (I'm a little slow). I didn't get any clarity as I prayed, so I said, "Okay, Lord, I don't have time for this, but I'm gonna step out in faith and shoot him an email, just in case this is your prompting."

The following Tuesday morning, Christy drove Jerry home from the hospital in silence. Christy wondered how much more of this she could take. After a weekend in intensive care, Jerry had survived a near-fatal suicide attempt the Friday before (the day I emailed him), but he didn't seem any better. She loved Jerry, but he wasn't her husband, and he was destroying both their lives. She felt so unworthy of God's help, but for a season, going to Gateway, she had started to believe that maybe God was *for* her and not *against* her. She cried out, "God, please help Jerry, and help me know what to do."

That morning, as Christy checked their email, she noticed the one from me. As she read it, she couldn't help but feel as though God had answered her prayer. She printed it out and handed it to Jerry, who sat comatose on the couch.

That same afternoon, Jerry walked into my office looking like the living dead. I'd assumed it was the deaths of his family members that had driven him to want to end his life, but I was wrong.

"I just can't get rid of this guilt," he confided. "I miss my family terribly, but what haunts me is what I did to my brother. I loved my twin brother and looked up to him my whole life. But he resented me after I started dating a girl he really loved. He felt betrayed by me and told me, 'You're no longer my brother.' For years we didn't talk because he refused to see me. I wanted to resolve it, but before I could, he died. I feel so horrible for what I did to him; I just don't want to live."

I read passage after passage to Jerry about God's grace offered in Christ to remove our guilt.[1] As I read the Scriptures, I noticed tears of relief pooling in Jerry's eyes. He accepted God's forgiveness and grace. I suggested he go home and write a letter to God about all the things he'd like to tell his brother, and then read it out loud to God. Later, in an email to me, Jerry recalled what happened that night.

> As I read the letter out loud to God that night, it felt like a huge weight lifted off my shoulders. I wept tears of release as I felt the guilt finally leave. Not long after, I got involved in Gateway's Depression Support group, where I made some wonderful friends who taught me how to grieve and experience laughter and joy again. After years of therapy, pills, medical bills, and an attempted suicide — to think I could have found this relief by accepting the grace of God offered in Jesus Christ. It would have saved me years of guilt and wouldn't have cost me a dime.

I have no doubt that God prompted me that day, but I only got to see God's heart and share in his redemptive story when I responded to a simple thought: "Email Jerry."

GOD COINCIDENCE

During an early morning event, I had some time to kill and decided to take the opportunity to read a small-group assignment that had been bumped up by a week. Later that day, I was in a meeting at a location I've never been to before. The meeting ran over an hour longer than scheduled, and I had a lot to get done that day but sensed I needed to stay. I responded trusting God had some reason. Stopped at a red light on my way home, thinking of how to make up for lost time, my cell phone rang. "I'm in the car ahead of you," I looked up to see her waving through her rear view mirror. This was a friend I hadn't seen in many months. After talking for a couple blocks, I sensed something was wrong. I knew she was seeking God. Wondering if this was more than coincidence, I responded by inviting her to stop for coffee. Her worried feelings and unwarranted guilt she confessed to me related exactly to one of the chapters I had read earlier that morning called "Faith and the Feminine Soul." My meeting happened to come just after a church service explaining how God prompts us with thoughts in our minds. Eighteen months ago, I was a devout atheist who would have agreed with your article arguing against "faith" as a viable way to know anything. Today after my own leap of faith, I'm a devout Christian merely recounting one of many "coincidental" experiences in my last year and a half that display the amazingly unexplainable love of God. —submission to *Wired Magazine* from Brian (DWI story from Chapter 1) in response to the cover story "The New Atheism, the Probability of God is Disappearing."

ENGAGING IN RISKY BEHAVIOR

The main reason we don't see God at work is fear. We're afraid to take the risk and respond. He prompts us to say something encouraging to a friend, but we fear what they'll think. He prompts us to meet a need, but we're afraid our efforts will be misunderstood. He prompts us to get involved, but we fear we won't have time or know what to do. He prompts us to stand for what's right, but we fear the consequences. Only as faith conquers fear will we see with spiritual eyes.

I find it ironic that our generation is so scared to engage in God-induced risky behavior. Think of all the nutty risk-taking things that our generation finds perfectly acceptable — drinking ourselves into oblivion, drugging for the next high, engaging in risky sexual behavior, even base-jumping off cliffs for a thrill! Isn't it kind of odd that we'd be so scared to go all out in God-inspired risky behavior? Yet for some reason it feels like a greater risk to let go and follow God wide open than to let go and give ourselves over to high-risk activities that can enslave our wills. God will *never* enslave your will!

So how do you know if promptings are God-thoughts or just your thoughts? Take the risk to respond in trust. Only when you respond will you know! Jesus said, "Anyone who chooses to do the will of God will find out whether my teaching comes from God or whether I speak on my own" (John 7:17). You see, we get to know God by doing his will. Jesus' last words made it very clear that loving God comes from responding in obedience:

> *If anyone loves me, he will* obey *my teaching. My Father will love him, and we will come to him and make our home with him. He who does not love me will not* obey *my teaching. . . .*
>
> *If you* obey *my commands, you will remain in my love, just as I have obeyed my Father's commands and remain in his love. I have told you this so that my joy may be in you and that your joy may be complete. (John 14:23 – 24, 15:10 – 11 NIV, emphasis added)*

Scripture is clear. God isn't out to prove himself to you or me. He doesn't reveal himself to those who put themselves at the center of the universe and shake their little fists at God, demanding that he do what they want or else. God looks for hearts that are humble and seeking a relationship with him, willing to respond in obedience to his guidance.

Once you respond, you see little "coincidences" happening — not *all* the time, but *over* time. You begin to see God's wisdom lived out, bringing rest in the midst of chaos, peace in the middle of turmoil, forgiveness to the most unforgivable people — and you start to see God working through *you* to care for others. Over time, you build a history in relationship with God; you experience his love. You get a backstage pass to see what he's doing behind the scenes — sometimes in life-altering ways.

BIKER GOD

Renee jumped in her van and started the engine. Something was nagging at her — almost like a nervous feeling in her gut mixed with the thought to take her bike instead. "I don't want to take the Harley today," she reasoned, "I'm going to visit Autumn at school."

As Renee pulled the van out of the garage and down the driveway, the prompting persisted, "Take the motorcycle." Reluctantly, she put the van in park at the bottom of the driveway. Over the past two years, she'd been learning to respond to God's Spirit. She had learned that when God prompts, you obey. But she still had a rebellious streak that made her argue.

Renee had never been the churchgoing type. As a motorcycle stunt rider for Hollywood movies, she never felt she fit in a church. Plus, there was still that acrid, bitter taste in her mouth from her early years. "Every Sunday we sat in the front row of our very traditional church," Renee recalls, "with our little white gloves and our patent leather shoes, and my mom would talk about the heathen in the back row. Then we'd go home and all hell would break loose. I had a raging alcoholic father who beat the hell out of us and sexually abused me from as young as I can remember. My mom's response to everything was to run into the bedroom and shut the door and pretend it wasn't happening."

Renee ran away at age eleven and was picked up off the streets by a biker gang that raised her. Introduced to amphetamines by her biological father, she kept using them — stealing to get dope, sleeping with people to get dope, walking all over people to get dope, just to quiet the painful noise in her soul. She finally cleaned up at age sixteen when her biker "family" took her to treatment.

Decades later, Renee's daughters started nagging her to go to church. "My kids dragged me to church. They wanted to go to an Easter service three years ago. 'I don't do church,' I told them, 'but if you want to discuss Easter on Sunday, great ... but no church.' I was having panic attacks just thinking about it."

But Renee attended our church that Easter, dressed head to toe in black leather, just to prove she'd be rejected. She was surprised. As Renee and her daughters kept coming, Renee renewed her faith in Christ. "It was during the 60-60 that I made peace with the fact that God wants good things for me. I'd never accepted that because I always felt 'less than.' The voices kept telling me, 'you'll never amount to anything.' As I learned to trust and respond, I experienced that I'm okay as I am.

"I'm so stubborn, but I've learned to stop and listen," Renee admits. "I talk to God all the time. I had a sense he was prompting me that day, so I put the van in park, and I argued, 'I don't want to take my Harley; I want to take the van.' When I couldn't get peace about taking the van, I figured maybe the van was gonna break down and make me late, so I gave in and took the motorcycle."

At lunch, Renee started heading toward her daughter's school. She had to cross an intersection under construction that narrowed into two lanes with concrete barricades on either side. Renee approached the intersection at thirty-five miles per hour. Then she saw it.

"It all happened in a split second," Renee recalls. "I saw the eighteen-wheeler coming fast — thirty miles an hour over the speed limit, I later found out. It hit a bump in the road and started to jackknife through the construction zone. I was committed. It felt like time slowed down as I watched this metal dinosaur slide sideways into my lane, directly on a collision course with me."

Renee's stunt-rider training took over as she went on autopilot. She tucked in and swerved to the right, her right knee barely missing the concrete construction barricade, as the eighteen-wheeler slid past on her left side.

"I heard a voice say 'Not today' as I somehow squeezed between the concrete on my right and metal on my left. The truck came so close I could have licked it with my tongue. I felt something hit my left foot, and again I heard the voice say, 'Not today.'"

Renee came out of the accident with a broken left foot, but otherwise not a scratch. "If I'd taken the van, I'd be dead," Renee insists. "There wouldn't have been anything to dig out of the wreckage."

Renee came to talk to me that week. It shook her up because she had a sense that God had an even bigger purpose for her life. Such knowledge felt overwhelming to her. I assured her that all she needed to do was to keep on listening and responding obediently moment by moment. God would take care of the rest.

THE FIRST DIMLY LIT STEP

Every time I sense a God-prompting, it requires wisdom and discernment. God never lights the whole path ahead and says, "Go *there*." Instead, I take one step, dimly lit, until I respond in faith, then another step, lit just enough for the next step of faith. This is what I see in Paul's journey in Acts: "Paul and his companions traveled throughout the region of Phrygia and Galatia, having been kept by the Holy Spirit from preaching the word in the province of Asia" (Acts 16:6).

The apostle Paul undoubtedly followed the leading of God's Spirit, but it was more interactive than just receiving a clear map. Paul apparently felt compelled to go to Asia to proclaim the message about Jesus, but the book of Acts says that the Spirit redirected him.

As God guides us, he still wants us to use our minds, pray, and think things through. But we must trust he will guide us as we step out in faith and act. In the Psalms God says, "I will instruct you and teach you in the way you should go; I will counsel you with my loving eye on you. *Do not be like the horse or the mule*, which have no understanding but must be controlled by bit and bridle or they will not come to you" (Psalm 32:8 – 9, italics mine). God does not want to guide us as though he were steering a car. He guides us the way a parent guides children into maturity.

This means he will not override our wills. Rather, he works with our wills. He doesn't bypass our minds, but he interacts with us as we use our God-given capacities. Following the Spirit doesn't negate strategic thinking, planning, or seeking wise counsel — God uses all of these things along with his promptings.

Paul prayed, had a sense of what seemed right, and took a risk by moving forward. Only then did he get greater clarity. The only way to *know* is to *go*. Remember: "Without faith it is impossible to please God" (Hebrews 11:6 NIV). So nearly every time I try to follow God's lead, I pray and sort through my motives, asking if I'm fully willing to do God's will in this. I ask for guidance as I think and plan and seek wise counsel. Sometimes I do this for weeks or months if it involves a big decision. But in the end, I have to take one step forward, saying, "Well, God, it seems like this is the right step — so here goes. I trust that you're guiding. And if I've missed it, I trust you love me and you're big enough to redirect me." Then I step out.

WHEN GOD REDIRECTS

When Paul can't get to Asia, he doesn't stop. He prays and moves forward trusting that God can and will redirect him. "When they came to the border of Mysia, they tried to enter Bithynia, but the Spirit of Jesus would not allow them to. So they passed by Mysia and went down to Troas" (Acts 16:7 – 8).

Paul and company end up in the seaport of Troas, wondering why they got redirected there. "During the night Paul had a vision of a man of Macedonia standing and begging him, 'Come over to Macedonia and help us.' After Paul had seen the vision, we got ready at once to leave for Macedonia, concluding that God had called us to preach the gospel to them"(Acts 16:9 – 10).

Paul's Spirit-led journey concludes with God redirecting them and opening a door to go to Philippi in Macedonia to start a church (the book of Philippians is addressed to that church). Sometimes God may redirect, close a door, or even ask us to step through one door whose only purpose is to lead us through another door that we would not have seen without obediently moving forward. A couple of times I have had the chance to see God clearly redirect and lead through one door only to show me another.

When we moved to Austin from Chicago, we sold our little starter home, and in the less expensive Austin market, we could afford a lot more space. We were like kids in a candy store. The more we looked, the more we saw, and the more we saw, the more we wanted, until finally we decided — this is our chance — we'll just *build* the perfect house.

So we picked a floor plan, chose all the goodies we wanted to put in it, and pretty soon we realized that "creep" had set in. The house now cost a little more than we had budgeted, so we decided to trim the budget in other places.

When the time came to sign the final contract, Kathy and I prayed for God's guidance. We sat there all day, frozen, unable to sign. We had been praying all along for God's guidance and, if needed, redirection, and now we both had an uneasy feeling. Thinking it was just a case of pre-buyer's remorse, we agreed to keep praying, asking God to give at least one of us peace if this was his will. Peace never came!

After two days of discussing, fasting, and praying, neither of us had peace. It was weird. The homebuilder kept calling, nagging us to sign. We felt guilty about not signing and confused about God's will. But we agreed, if neither of us had peace after the third day of praying — the deal was off.

On day four, I called the builder and canceled the contract. Aside from losing our earnest money, we didn't have a place to live in Austin. We started praying for a month-to-month rental, but every place we contacted required a one-year lease as a minimum. Then, a month before moving, some friends found us a house we could rent for three months.

On the second day in our rental house, as I was jogging in the neighborhood, I ran past a "For Sale" sign in front of the house directly behind our rental. We looked at it the next day, and it was just what we had been wanting — and cost even *less* than we had budgeted! Our home has been great for our family.

Still, an even more awesome God-moment came two years later, when we could see how all the puzzle pieces fit together.

GOD OPENS DOORS

While we were still in our rental house, I talked with Joe, our next-door neighbor, one night on the driveway. He asked me what I did, and I told him we were starting a church in Austin.

"How do you start a church?" he asked, puzzled.

I told him the truth: "I'm not sure!" and then we had a long conversation.

I didn't see Joe much after we moved into our permanent house. Over the next two years our church met in six different locations, while we searched the city for a long-term facility we could afford. Finally, we found an old, abandoned movie theater owned by the school district. Although it was farther out than we liked, our desperation led us to believe this was God's answer.

We prayed, we bargained, we bartered with the school board, and they would be about to sign the lease when something would stall the deal. We'd work out one problem, and something else would keep them from signing. We prayed for confirmation, but for almost a year we couldn't get the lease signed! Finally, in frustration, I gave up. I told God, "I don't know why you can't get them to give us a yes or no, but I'm gonna let go of it. We'll stay put until we get forced to move again."

One Saturday a few weeks later, my kids came running from the backyard, yelling, "Fire!" I ran outside to find a fire blazing in the easement behind our fence. Joe and his son were already out there, and I helped douse the flames. Afterward, Joe and I got to talking, and he asked how the church was going. I told him great, except we couldn't find a place to meet.

Joe said, "You know, I'm the executive director now of a nonprofit retirement home in the city, and we just bought this synagogue we're going to tear down. But just this week, I started feeling really bad about destroying the place. We're just tearing it down to save taxes until we decide to build on the land."

"You should feel bad!" I poked. "Let me look at it!"

After looking at it the following night, I drove straight to Joe's house and told him, "It's perfect; let's make a deal."

"Honestly, I don't think our board of directors will go for it," was Joe's reply. "They're a bunch of no-nonsense business guys, and there's really nothing in it for us. You couldn't pay us enough to make it worth it."

Miraculously, and despite Joe's misgivings, the board decided to lease it to us for just what we could afford — one fifth of market rate!

Joe said, "Man, you guys have uncanny timing. A week earlier and I wouldn't have considered it. A month later, and it would've been demolished!"

Our church met for the next four years in that old synagogue and grew from 300 people to 2,000. We now refer to that event as our "Burning Bush" moment, but it all started with a prompting, redirecting my family from our "perfect" house into Joe's neighborhood. Sometimes God's goodness requires that we don't get what we want when we want it.

■

So as we radically respond to God throughout the moments of our days, we get to "see" more and more of God at work in our lives. But Jesus made it clear that what matters most to God, second only to staying in loving connection to him, is how we love people. Believe it or not, where we need to "see" God's power the most is not in miraculous provision, or even in breaking harmful addictions. We need his power most to break a much more harmful, powerful addiction — the addiction to self. Only with God's moment-by-moment help can we learn to be other-centered. That's what we'll explore next on this journey of relationship — how to love people in God-inspired ways.

THE 60·60 EXPERIMENT

This week, as you seek to stay continuously connected, get radically responsive. Go for it wide open and take risks as you sense God's Spirit prompting.

1. **Pay attention to promptings**. With every beep or reminder, take a minute to reflect on the past hour. Ask God to show you where he might have been prompting you to respond differently. Ask him to guide you and help you respond better to promptings in the next hour.

2. **Take risks to respond**. When you think God might want you to respond, don't let fear of people or fear of the future hold you back. Engage in some God-induced risky behavior and see what happens. Make notes about what you learn throughout the day.

3. **Know God's will**. It's impossible to respond to God's will if you're not really sure what his will is in the moment. Browse

www.Soulrevolution.net to access an interactive resource to help you understand what God says in Scripture about issues you may be facing.

4. **Connect to others**. Talk to a friend or small group to discuss what you're learning about yourself and God. Be sure to record in a journal and on our blogspot what you discover about responding to God's promptings. It's always helpful to learn from each other's discoveries.

PART 3 **LOVING PEOPLE**

Revolution—
KINGDOMS IN CONFLICT

Jerry Root, a Wheaton College professor and close friend, was speaking at Oxford University one time. Before his talk, he was invited to eat at High Table, a very pretentious faculty affair where the professors wear their academic gowns, and it's so stuffy you can barely breathe. Jerry sat next to a woman who taught history.

Knowing that Jerry was from Wheaton, she asked, "Why are you a Christian?" (Another faculty member later told him that this woman sounded as though she were preparing to devour him as the main course.)

Not wanting to provoke an argument, he answered, "Because I'm aware of failure and deficiency in my heart, and I follow Christ because God demonstrated through him that he loves me and forgives me and will lead and guide me, and I need his guidance. I believe in justice, but I'm not always just. I believe in love, but don't always act loving. There's something wrong with me, and I need his forgiveness and help. That's why."

"I can appreciate that, but it's just not my issue," was her response.

"I think I understand," Jerry said. "I became a Christian in my first year of college, and I didn't become perfect overnight — it took two or three weeks!"

She burst out laughing and the whole table, who had been watching the hunt, laughed as well.

Jerry said, "Your laughter betrays you. We just met, you don't know me, but you know that my statement is nonsense. You must understand, either by your study of history or by awareness of your own heart, that no one is perfect."

She said, "You got me."

So he asked, "How do you live with yourself each day, knowing what you do about yourself?"

"I have faith in humanity," she replied.

"I'm open to that," Jerry said. "I'm open to anything that will help guide us on a right path to love each other, but how does that work pragmatically? Have you ever been wounded by another human?"

"Of course," she said.

"Have you ever wounded another human?"

"I suppose so," she hesitantly admitted.

"So how does faith in humanity work when humans have this tendency to be both wounded and wounders?"

Another faculty member interjected, "How does it work pragmatically for Christianity?" Jerry talked about God's gift of grace and God's plan to enter into life with all those willing — to lead and guide the humble of heart moment by moment to willingly follow his will.[1]

We need God, because we're stuck in this catch-22. James explains it well:

> *Where do you think all these appalling wars and quarrels come from? Do you think they just happen? Think again. They come about because you want your own way, and fight for it deep inside yourselves. You lust for what you don't have and are willing to kill to get it. You want what isn't yours and will risk violence to get your hands on it.*
>
> *You wouldn't think of just asking God for it, would you? And why not? Because you know you'd be asking for what you have no right to. You're spoiled children, each wanting your own way.*
>
> *You're cheating on God. If all you want is your own way, flirting with the world every chance you get, you end up enemies of God and his way. And do you suppose God doesn't care? The proverb has it that "he's a fiercely jealous lover." And what he gives in love is far better than anything else you'll find. It's common knowledge that "God goes against the willful proud; God gives grace to the willing humble." (James 4:1 – 6 MSG)*

Our deepest longings are relational. God designed us to need each other, but we hurt each other by playing god (thinking our ways should rule). God is jealous for our love, not because he needs us, but because we were created for him. After so many years of the human experiment to find life and fulfillment and peace on our own terms, you'd think we'd be willing to wholeheartedly seek God's ways, but we're slow learners.

KINGDOMS IN CONFLICT

We were created for a loving relationship with God first, then with others. God's will is that we learn how to love him so that he can lead us to love others. But there's a problem. We live in a world of conflicting kingdoms with conflicting desires. We all have good God-given desires to be loved, to have purpose, to feel secure, to be at peace, yet all these desires are relational — we need each other!

I'll never feel loved if I'm disconnected from people. I may accomplish great things, but if no one values me or needs me, I will feel purposeless. Until I'm confident I'm loved by a few significant others, I'll never feel secure. Identity only comes through community. I cannot be at peace if I'm at war with others.

But here's our catch-22: our deepest desires are only met relationally — and yet we are always hurting each other. We're not so much "wounded healers" as we are "wounded wounders"!

This, of course, is why we desperately need God. His desire is to lead us into right-relatedness with himself and others, but history confirms that our world breeds conflict between the kingdoms. People choose their wills and ways over God's will and ways — and even with the best of intentions, we hurt others.

God allows all of this hurt, disappointment, and struggle for a time, in hopes that we will wake up and realize something's wrong and freely choose to seek the will of the King. Out of love for us, he allows the pain and suffering our choices cause so we will not cling to this life or the things of this world more than we cling to the Creator of life.

GOD'S KINGDOM OR YOUR KINGDOM

Jesus' central teaching was "The kingdom of God is near." The "kingdom of God," or the "kingdom of heaven" is explained about 150 times in the New Testament, but what does that mean? What is a kingdom?

Well, each of us has our own kingdom or queendom! Yours is the sphere of influence you have, where your will is done and where you decide what happens. That's your kingdom.

God created us this way. In Genesis 1 it says God gave us dominion — co-rulership — over his creation. Our job is to take care of it — at least the parts over which we have influence.

This is why even two- and three-year-olds want to show that they too have a kingdom. Some of the first words kids learn are "mine," "let me do it," and "watch me." That's God-given. They're discovering they have a will and a kingdom. They start exercising control over their own bodies to start with, but soon the little kings start pushing for more territory, throwing temper tantrums when their will is not done. They soon learn there are other kingdoms to respect as well. And so it goes. As you grow up, your kingdom extends to the sway you have over others at work or with your kids or maybe even over whole companies or cities.

God's goal in all this is that we should willingly align our kingdoms under the loving rule of his kingdom and exercise our wills under the direction of his loving will. Only that way will we stop acting like two-year-olds. Under God's rule, we don't use our power to dominate or abuse or use or force or manipulate or deceive for our own personal gain.

Just imagine the chaos of millions of little kingdoms not fully aligned under God's loving rule, and you start to understand what's wrong with this world today. It's a battle of wills in a very broken world. Everyone thinks, "If only everyone else would just do things my way, there would be no problem!" What we need is nothing short of a kingdom revolution.

REVOLUTION

Picture a husband and wife locked in a battle for whose ways should prevail. She wants him to help out more and stop spending so frivolously. He wants her to stop acting like his mother. She wants him to care more about her day. He wants her to be more physically engaged in the marriage. Back and forth they go, trying to manipulate and dominate. They need a kingdom revolution.

Or think of a mom who can't keep it together with her kids. She's aware of her own impatience and anger, but she can't help it. She knows she needs help. She knows she's damaging her kids, but pride gets in her way. She needs a kingdom revolution.

Imagine a father who gets so wrapped up in his work that he totally disconnects from his family. He takes out his anxieties on them and uses his power to exert his will at home because he feels out of control everywhere else. He doesn't know it, but his out-of-control kingdom is slowly killing his family. What he needs is a kingdom revolution.

Or consider the woman who was abused by her father — a man who thought having his way sexually wouldn't hurt his little girl. At the age of thirty-three, she still carries the pain. She's become isolated in her kingdom of self-protection — tough, aggressive, successful because she's a survivor. But she can't keep a relationship together because she can't trust anyone. She drinks too much because it's the only time she can loosen up and feel good. She needs a kingdom revolution. Her dad needs a kingdom revolution.

We all need a kingdom revolution!

This is a world of kingdoms run amok, where people think their own wills and ways are the right ones, or at least the most harmless ones, and yet we all damage ourselves, each other, and God's creation in the process. This is our world, and on a large scale it gets nastier than we often even realize.

Think about the kingdom of Enron that wreaked havoc financially on millions. Consider the kingdoms of oppression that create ghettos of poverty. Recall Hitler's kingdom and the kingdoms of Rwanda. Even religious kingdoms have used God's name to manipulate people against his will, to go on bloodthirsty crusades — and even to crucify his Messiah.

And the worst part about our little fiefdoms is the spiritual blindness that causes us to all subtly think, "I'm right, they're wrong; I don't need God's help — but they do!"

Jesus responds, "Whoever has eyes to see, let him see."

WILLINGNESS: THE KEY TO THE KINGDOM

Coaches, counselors, mentors, guides, and gurus will tell you: If you aren't willing to trust and follow, there's no point in guiding you. Willingness is the key! Maybe that's why God remains so hidden. Surely God could *make us* do his will if he wanted — right? But why doesn't he make us do his will? Because he's waiting for *our* willingness.

The kingdoms of this world are a mess, yet Jesus came into this mess with a message about a kingdom revolution — "the kingdom of God is near." There's a better way to live than the conflicted kingdoms of this world offer. "Jesus went into Galilee, proclaiming the good news of God. 'The time has come,' he said. 'The kingdom of God is near. Repent and believe the good news!'" (Mark 1:14 – 15 NIV)

HEALING OUR HURTING

I started drinking and smoking pot when I was fifteen, about the time I felt the weight of responsibility to take care of my depressed, suicidal father and my often-drunk mother. After finishing graduate school, I joined the Peace Corps. During that time, I realized I needed God in my life. I realized how sin patterns in my life were dishonoring to God, and for the first time, I wanted to change. When I returned to the States, I found Gateway Church. During the 60-60 Experiment, two messages really hit me: I realized life with God is meant to be an adventure, and I discovered all God needs is our full willingness. I decided to completely give myself to God and to ask him to take my life and do with it what he will. Since then, I feel like I have been in an incredible phase of growth, growing in my love for God and his creation, growing in my desire to be closer to him and become more of who he wants me to be, and growing in my relationships with others. God is teaching me to forgive, to love people in their brokenness, and even to see the good things in people who treated me in unloving ways. He's teaching me how to use words to help and to heal as opposed to using them to hurt, or oppress, or control others. —Marie

When my generation hears that message, however, many picture a guy like the one I saw coming home from an outdoor music festival. He had big placards and a bullhorn yelling, "Repent or burn in hell, the kingdom of God is near." That sounds like bad news to a lot of people, who must think, "So either I repent and become like one of these weird fanatics or I burn in hell. Hmm, is there a *third* option?"

Yes!

Jesus said, "The kingdom of God is near — and this is good news." Why is it good news for imperfect people like you and me? Because life in God's kingdom — the way God intended us to live, with him, with each other, and in relation to our world — is now available to ordinary, imperfect, messed-up people. That's the revolution! It's a completely revolutionary way to live right now, superior to our own kingdoms where we battle for power and worth and control.

This is good news for all willing humans because God has a plan to restore what has been lost and broken relationally, one willing life at a time. It's good news because it's an invitation into the life we're searching for in all our relationships.

GOOD NEWS FOR IMPERFECT PEOPLE

This is what the religious people of Jesus' day didn't understand:

> Jesus said to [the religious leaders], "I tell you the truth, the tax collectors and the prostitutes are entering the kingdom of God ahead of you. For John came to you to show you the way of righteousness, and you did not believe him, but the tax collectors and the prostitutes did. And even after you saw this, you did not repent and believe him." (Matthew 21:31 NIV)

Jesus says, it's not religious observance, but willing relationship that God's after. What you must do is repent and trust in this good news. The Greek word usually translated "repent" is the word *metanoeo* — which literally means "to change your mind" or "have a change of mind and actions." If you're only living life for the sake of your own little kingdom, you must change your mind, turn from your old ways, and begin to live within God's kingdom. And that's good news — you can do it! But you have to believe it's good news or you can't take advantage of it.

Dallas Willard, professor of philosophy at the University of Southern California, gives a good example that helps us understand what Jesus is saying. When he was growing up in rural Missouri, the only electricity around was in the form of lightning! When electrical lines were finally extended near his house, many rural farmers didn't understand that it was *good news* to have electricity so near. Many didn't understand the life-changing potential of living within the kingdom of electricity. So, in essence, the message had to be proclaimed:

> Repent, for the kingdom of electricity is near. Turn from your old kerosene lamps and lanterns, turn from your iceboxes and cellars, turn away from hand washing and rug beating and battery operated radios. The power of life within the kingdom of electricity is now available, and you can live a whole new way.[2]

Jesus explained, "The kingdom of God does not come with your careful observation, nor will people say, 'Here it is,' or 'There it is,' because the kingdom of God is within you" (Luke 17:20 – 21 NIV).

Do you realize how great the news is that Jesus brings to all humanity? Jesus paid the price to hook you up to a revolutionary way of life. Because of what Jesus did for us on the cross, you are now invited to "Come as you are";

God takes you "as is" so you can begin to live life restored into a right relationship with him. As you're willing, God leads you into a life that grows within and then gives life to others. This is *good news* because it's a better, more powerful, and more loving way to live!

It's not *religion* that God wants. *Relational revolution* is what he's after. It's not about jumping through spiritual hoops; it's about living in intimacy with God and others, so that God can begin to heal and restore what's broken in our world. Life in God's kingdom is relational. The means and the measure of maturity is relationship! That's why true spiritual maturity is not measured with how religious or outwardly righteous we behave. It's measured in how willing we are to trust God, do what he says, and let him lead us to become loving, life-giving people to one another. God lives his life of love in us and through us as we're willing. In the next two chapters, we'll explore God's ways of relating that finally bring peace to our kingdoms in conflict.

THE 60-60 EXPERIMENT

As you continue to practice staying connected and responsive to God, begin to pay attention to the way you deal with the people around you.

1. **Stay connected.** Keep trying to improve on how often you turn your mind back to conversation with God. Use each sixty-minute beep to stop and reflect on how you did the past sixty minutes. Be sure to celebrate the successes, not just feel bad about the failures. Are you failing forward? Getting better at staying connected? Improvement, not perfection, is the goal each day.

2. **How am I treating those around me?** This week, be aware of your relationships in relation to God's will. With every beep or reminder, ask God to show you where your kingdom comes in conflict with others. Ask God to show you his kingdom will for how you should deal with those you do life with daily. Respond!

3. **Journal and blog your discoveries each day.** Share your relational insights with others on our blogspot: *www.Soul revolution.net.*

CHAPTER SEVEN

Relate—
A NEW WAY TO LIVE TOGETHER

"What do you *want* me to say? My boss *saw* you kissing him, Stephanie, so don't lie to me. I know you're cheating on me."

Greg's red-hot anger overflowed like lava from the mouth of a volcano as he thought about his wife with another man.

"I'm not happy, Greg. I'm miserable. I can't live this way . . . I want out." Stephanie didn't see any hope after five years of marriage to the tin man. Greg felt like a hard, cold stone — lifeless, uncaring, an obstacle in the way of what she'd never really experienced — freedom, fun, excitement. Her neighbor on the block spurred on the affair, reminding Stephanie often of her brother-in-law's attraction to Stephanie. It happened one weekend while Greg was out of town on business. Now the adrenaline of romantic interest had taken over the decision-making process. Not even her two toddler boys could motivate a change of heart. She wanted "freedom."

"Fine — go to bed with whomever you want, but not in my house. Get out!"

Greg may have been accused of never feeling anything, but he knew how to feel anger. Growing up with a dad who would take off for six-month stints at sea, leaving him and his older sister with an emotionally unstable, suicidal mom had not exactly taught Greg good relating patterns, but he knew how to feel hurt, anger, and cynical distrust.

Greg's dad couldn't teach Greg healthy relating patterns either. His dad never had a father. Greg thought of his dad as a robot — a stoic army engineer who came home only to discipline him. He had no idea what it was like for Greg and his sister while he was away — to have their mom spend all their money, then, when she got depressed, lock herself in her room for days at a time while Greg and his sister fended for themselves. Greg lived out the only relational training he'd received — survival.

Stephanie's preparation for marriage rivaled Greg's. When she was five, her father committed suicide, and her mother remarried. From age eight to twelve, her stepfather molested her. She kept asking him to stop, threatening to tell her mother, but it was all so confusing. Finally at age twelve, she told a friend who told the school officials. Her stepfather's conviction and ten-year probation forced him to move out, but her mother stayed married to him. Soon it was all brushed under the rug, where all problems in Stephanie's family seemed to migrate.

Through her teen years, Stephanie dreamed of the man who would fulfill her deep longing for a trusting, secure relationship. Taught by her stepfather that her sexuality had no respectable boundaries, Stephanie frequently used sex as a means to an end. When she met her first love, she saw her dream coming true. A year later, she was pregnant. Her first love departed, leaving her as an angry teenage mom with deeply etched scars of distrust.

At nineteen she met Greg, fell in love, and they moved in together. She had her second son two months before they married. She could never trust, and he could never connect. Now the marriage was over.

"After a few years of trying to salvage our relationship," Greg recalls, "we filed for divorce. I hated Stephanie and wanted to get even with her for all the hurt she caused me during her affair. When Stephanie lost her job, we both agreed the boys would be better off living with me. Being a single dad smacked me in the face like a cold-water wakeup call. I didn't know how to be a good dad; I'd never had one. I knew how to be a stoic, intellectual engineer, but I knew that fell short.

"I'd considered myself an atheist for most of my life, but I met some Christians at work who lived out a faith that made their lives attractive. They weren't pushy, they didn't seem ashamed to talk honestly about real-life struggles and how God helped them. So when one invited me to Gateway and told me their slogan was 'No Perfect People Allowed,' I decided to give it a try."

"I was just cold-hearted at that point," Stephanie recalls. "I didn't care who I hurt. I was worried about myself and making myself happy, and I thought this affair would bring me life. I blamed Greg for my unhappiness, but I feared talking to him about it. I knew he'd just get mad. I just wanted to party and be 'free.' Greg and the boys held me back from what I thought I wanted — I was so deceived."

"Before coming to faith in Christ," Greg admits, "my life was just a maze. I felt lost, never knowing if the person I knew myself to be, or at least hoped to be, would ever come out. I wasn't a very good person growing up. The only thing I valued was being successful and 'right,' yet deep down I never felt I lived up to that either."

At Gateway Greg began to hear and understand about God's grace offered in Christ. He found a sense of hope in knowing there just might be a God willing to forgive him, care about his life, and even help in practical matters.

"Over a six-month period, I came to believe in God, without a doubt," Greg recalls. "As I began to talk to him about my problems, asking for help with my boys, I began to see little traces of evidence that he really cared. As I learned about Jesus' teachings, I realized my entire purpose centers in relationship — which had never occurred to me before! I'd always had the goal of being a successful engineer, and I defined myself by accomplishments. Relationship had nothing to do with it.

"When I started realizing that how I get along with my kids and the people I live with *is* my whole purpose in life, I admitted to God I had a problem. As I talked to God about my struggle to let others in, I found myself taking new risks and actually developing friendships. It changed the way I related.

"I always saw myself as one of those 'unreachable people,' but our church really emphasizes 'come-as-you-are' grace and 'no-perfect-people-allowed' acceptance, so I felt accepted and free to be me, to be in process. I started serving in the kids' ministry because I saw how much my kids loved it. This community helped me understand that I matter, like a piece of a puzzle ... I'm an essential part, a unique piece of God's great relational plan."

While Greg found authentic faith and started growing relationally, Stephanie sensed a dramatic shift. "As we interacted about the boys, Greg changed before my eyes over a six-month period. I saw a person who actually focused on caring about the people around him. My boys were happy — they had a real dad in their lives. I was jealous! That's what I wanted, and now I was missing out. The day before the divorce was final, I asked Greg if we could call it off. He said no."

Even though Greg had started dating someone else, Stephanie began attending Gateway at Easter 2003. Knowing little about Jesus or the Bible, she was intimidated at first. "I soon realized it's okay to not know anything yet," Stephanie recalls, "but as I learned more about Jesus' teachings and how to do life with God, I found a desire to follow Jesus. When I saw Greg connected and growing and helping teach kids, I felt I could belong too — even with my imperfect past. I got connected with our Comfort and Hope ministry to survivors of sexual or physical abuse."

Connected to a community and learning to follow God's Spirit, Greg and Stephanie grew relationally. "We became better friends than we'd ever been," Stephanie says. "With our newfound faith, we learned to relate in caring ways. We even helped each other with relational issues with people we were dating — it was crazy."

"With Christ in my life, I not only forgave Stephanie," Greg admits, "but I wanted her to find the faith and life I was discovering. As I experienced her growing and changing, I found myself falling in love with her again."

Three years after the divorce, Greg and Stephanie reunited in marriage — truly a work of God's Spirit.

ALL ABOUT RELATING

God is in the process of reclaiming, redeeming, and restoring what our broken little kingdoms have destroyed, and he's doing it by guiding us into new, Christ-like ways of relating. The way we relate to one another is important to God. When asked for the greatest commandment, Jesus gave two: First, love God. Then, he says, "A second is equally important: 'Love your neighbor as yourself.' The entire law and all the demands of the prophets are based on these two commandments" (Matthew 22:39 – 40 NLT).

Though only asked for one, Jesus could not disconnect the command to love people from the command to love God. Spiritual maturity is measured relationally: "This is love: not that we loved God, but that he loved us and sent his Son as an atoning sacrifice for our sins. Dear friends, since God so loved us, we also ought to love one another. No one has ever seen God; but if we love one another, God lives in us and his love is made complete in us" (1 John 4:10 – 12 NLT).

You can't love God or follow his Holy Spirit without following him into a new way of loving others. If you follow God's lead, listening and responding, you will learn how to truly love people, and you will fulfill the purpose of all the commandments of Scripture. Simple — right?

Simple, yes, but far from easy. It would have been far easier if Jesus had said, "Love God and love your dog — don't worry about the neighbor thing" But he didn't. Instead, he promised his Spirit, who will lead and guide us into his kingdom way of relating — a way that goes against everything that comes naturally to our own self-centered ways.

When our church did this 60-60 Experiment, as I mentioned, nearly 2,000 people started journaling to chronicle what they were learning. A young single guy, who came to faith two years before our 60-60, wrote this:

> Before starting this experiment, I was feeling like my relationships with friends and family lacked substance. I wasn't being open, and I was going back to old patterns of withdrawing from people whenever challenges or fears crept up in my life. In the past, I have felt like an egomaniac with an inferiority complex (I'd either feel superior or inferior to most everyone). I would think to myself that if people really knew me, they wouldn't accept me. I started this 60-60, having honest conversations with God — talking to him about my faults and confessing my shortcomings. Ironically, the feelings of inadequacy began to dissipate. Then I began to feel the need for others, without that tendency to either feel superior or inferior to other people. As I've stayed connected to God these past few weeks, I'm feeling a shift relationally. I am not as afraid to go deeper with people in conversations. I feel free to be more open about my faith. I'm feeling more free to just be me.
>
> — Steve

God wants to lead you into a freedom to fully be you — who he created you to be — free to respond to him and better love those closest to you. So as you respond to the Spirit's leading moment by moment during this 60-60 Experiment, his primary agenda will involve your key relationships — those people you do life with the most! So pay attention to how you treat those closest to you.

LOVE — NOT THE EASY THING

U2 sings, "Love is not the easy thing, the only baggage you can bring is all that you can't leave behind."[1] Why is it so difficult to love? Because we all have lots of relational baggage we've picked up from our world's broken ways of relating.

Pollster George Barna surveyed Americans: "What do you want out of life?" "Health" was number one; "a marriage that lasts" tied for second with "integrity;" and "close, personal friends" came in third.[2] Good relationships top our highest priorities; and yet, for some reason, we can't get what we want. Though "a marriage that lasts" was ranked so highly, our broken world trains us to divide and divorce — close to fifty percent crash and burn.

Even though "close, personal friends" ranked high, George Gallup, who studies American social behavior, now calls us "the loneliest people on the planet."[3] He says ours is a crowded loneliness. In other words, we have lots of people we call "friends," but we just don't know how to connect with them in life-giving ways.

God's Spirit wants to change that, if we will simply follow and respond. It will mean overcoming our fears — fears of trusting, fears of rejection, fears of being let down or hurt. That's why it starts with staying connected to God's perfect love: "If anyone acknowledges that Jesus is the Son of God, God lives in them and they in God. And so we know and rely on the love God has for us.... There is no fear in love. But perfect love drives out fear" (1 John 4:15 – 16, 18). So we must rely on the only Source of perfect love to displace our fears.

Still, fear is real!

We long to connect, but we are terrified of being hurt. We want deep relationships, but deep distrust keeps us relationally bankrupt. When we reach out to others, things always get in the way: jealousy, insecurities, fear of being rejected, indifference, busyness, annoying behaviors — a whole range of preoccupations that keep us from relating to others in powerful ways. As a result, our relationships never fulfill us or give us the life God intended.

But God's kingdom ways can break through our fearful isolation, if only we respond to his Spirit moment by moment. Let's look at four new ways of relating that God's Spirit will lead us into:

1. Grace-Giving Acceptance
2. Authentic Vulnerability
3. Healing Confession
4. Speaking the Last 10 Percent

For an expanded look at each of these, and how to create a relational soil in which God grows us best, see my first book, *No Perfect People Allowed: Creating a Come-as-You-Are Culture in the Church.*

1. GRACE-GIVING ACCEPTANCE
COME-AS-YOU-ARE GRACE

Deep down we all know something's wrong with this world. It's not hard for people to comprehend Paul's words in Romans 7: "I don't really understand myself, for I want to do what is right, but I don't do it. Instead, I do what I hate" (Romans 7:15 NLT). Ask anyone on the street if they can relate, and they'll say,

"That's in the Bible? Man, that's my life!" People naturally feel unacceptable when they don't perform up to standards.

What people don't naturally understand, however, is God's grace: "So now there is no condemnation for those who belong to Christ Jesus" (Romans 8:1 NLT). Because of Christ, God accepts us "as is." Rather than condemning us for our wrongs, he forgives and draws us out of hiding into the closest possible relationship.

> God saved you [made you rightly related to him] by his grace when you believed. And you can't take credit for this; it is a gift from God. Salvation is not a reward for the good things we have done, so none of us can boast about it. For we are God's masterpiece. He has created us anew in Christ Jesus, so that we can do the good things he planned for us long ago. (Ephesians 2:8 – 10 NLT)

We don't naturally *experience* this. We find it hard to believe that God looks past all the junk, all the wrongs, forgives us, draws us into relationship "as is," and now sees us as his masterpiece waiting to be revealed. But it's true. God wants a community of people who tangibly show his grace to one another — who demonstrate *his* acceptance and who draw near to each other without condemnation.

Imagine you found a Rembrandt painting covered in mud. You wouldn't focus on the mud or treat it like mud. Your primary concern wouldn't be the mud at all, even though it would need to be removed. You'd be ecstatic to have discovered something so valuable. If you tried to clean it up without the expertise, you might damage it. So you'd take the painting to an expert, who could show you how to restore it to its original condition. When people begin treating one another as God's masterpiece waiting to be revealed, God's grace grows in their lives and cleanses them.

GOD'S MODERN ART

When Brenda came to Gateway, she wasn't even sure what she was searching for. She didn't believe in God but was looking for something. She attended our Comfort and Hope class for recovery from sexual abuse. In that class she began to understand God's grace and love, and she learned how people who reject God's leadership often use, abuse, or neglect one another.

Because Brenda felt safe and accepted by this group, she took a risk. She told the group that growing up, her mother and stepfather had sold her and her little sister to a wealthy man who promised a better life for them in exchange for sex. She said it matter-of-factly, like that's just life, a mother pimping out her two daughters to a sex addict! At age fourteen, Brenda and her eleven-year-old sister moved from Missouri to New Mexico to live with this man. Brenda decided to not fight him in order to keep this pervert happy so he would not abuse her sister. After about five months, her adult stepbrother found out what was going on and rescued them. This resulted in living with a foster family that provided little improvement. Brenda ended up moving in with her teenage boyfriend and his mom who owned a methamphetamine lab.

Brenda started doing drugs just to numb the pain of all the anger she had bottled up inside. The next six years she went from one messed-up boyfriend to the next, using cocaine and pot to stay sane. When she came to Gateway, she was sexually promiscuous — basically living out the only life she knew, sex and drugs.

But as she learned about God's love for her and his hatred of the evils we do to one another, she found faith in Christ. In open, caring friendships with others at Gateway, she found the security to address all her anger, and God began doing a healing work in her life. She admitted to her group that she still smoked pot, but the group loved her anyway, encouraging her to see how God wants more for her than that. Since she is his masterpiece, the pot just keeps the painting muddied. They prayed for her as they continued to show her grace, but they also insisted she not come to the group high.

Months later, Brenda realized that the choices she had made were the same destructive choices her mom had made. So she quit the drugs, and she and her boyfriend decided to abstain from any more sex until marriage. As Brenda stayed in community and started counseling, God began to undo the cycle of use, abuse, and neglect. But it all started with grace-giving acceptance demonstrated by one small group.

The Scriptures tell us to "Accept each other just as Christ has accepted you" (Romans 15:7 NLT). It's not just in extreme situations where God's grace-giving acceptance is needed; it's in every marriage, every parent-child relationship, every dating relationship, every friendship. Our own little kingdom ways of relating can use, abuse, and neglect (all without our even being aware we're doing any harm). But as we follow God's Spirit to respond moment by moment with grace-giving acceptance, focusing first on the masterpiece rather than the mud, God begins to reveal something beautiful in us and in others.

Years ago, while practicing my 60-60, I hit traffic on the way to work one morning. Instead of letting it rile me, I decided to use the time to thank God for all the blessings in my life. I thanked him for my wife, who is my best friend. I thanked him for how enthralled I am by her beauty — more and more every year after 15 years! I thanked him for how much my own character has grown by being around her — she's so selfless and encouraging. As I thought about what an amazing mother she's been to our children and how much fun we all have together, I found myself overwhelmed with emotion. She is the biggest blessing in my life.

Then I had a prompting, "Tell her! Don't just think it, say it!" So I called her. As I told Kathy all these things about her I was thanking God for, my watch alarm beeped! I smiled as I sensed God's smile: "You're really growing in this."

As I've followed God's lead year by year, I've seen him change my once-critical spirit into one that can call out his work of art in others, and it has changed my relationships with my wife and kids in life-giving ways. But I'll be honest; I easily go back to old, critical ways that tear down and destroy the people I love when I'm disconnected from the Spirit.

How about you? Whom do you need to treat more like a masterpiece? As you try to stay connected, willing to respond radically, whom does God want you to show grace-giving acceptance toward this week?

Imagine all the marriages that could be saved, all the parent-adolescent relationships that could be salvaged, all the dysfunctional family dynamics that could be repaired if we would just respond to God in our moments of relating — calling out the masterpiece in each other.

2. AUTHENTIC VULNERABILITY
NO-PERFECT-PEOPLE-ALLOWED AUTHENTICITY

Once an environment of grace-giving acceptance is created, then people can be real. This is why grace forms the foundation for all spiritual growth. Grace allows people to come out of hiding, to be authentic, to stop concealing their wounds or pretending it's all good! If there weren't nasty, bad, ugly junk in my life — in your life — we'd all have the relationships we wanted, marriages would last, and the world would be a peaceful place — but that's not reality!

Without grace, we judge each other's faults, or withdraw and hide in fear, or attack in retaliation. But grace offers a new option, a new way to be together. As the apostle John writes, the way of Jesus is the way of authenticity. We can come out of the dark closet and walk in God's light of authenticity together. God heals us and grows us in community:

> This is the message we heard from Jesus and now declare to you: God is light, and there is no darkness in him at all. So we are lying if we say we have fellowship with God but go on living in spiritual darkness; we are not practicing the truth. But if we are living in the light, as God is in the light, then we have fellowship with each other, and the blood of Jesus, his Son, cleanses us from all sin. (1 John 1:5 – 7 NLT, emphasis added)

The word "fellowship," *koinonia* in the Greek, means "a common, shared life of intimacy." When the light is turned on, everything that's brought into the light can be seen clearly for what it is — nothing stays hidden. This passage implies several things about relating in a new way. First, if we claim we're connected to God's Spirit, walking in the light, but keep our sins and struggles hidden (from God and others), these "secret sins" actually blind us in spiritual darkness. And we're not fooling God; as the passage says, we're fooling ourselves.

Jesus butted heads with the religious leaders of his day, the Pharisees, for this very reason. They played a good church game, said all the right things, looked righteous, but they had secret sins — greed, lust, judgmentalism — that they were not willing to bring into the light. Their religion smacked of pretense rather than authenticity.

Jesus hates inauthenticity because it takes away our spiritual eyesight: "Woe to you, teachers of the law and Pharisees, you hypocrites! You clean the outside of the cup and dish, but inside they are full of greed and self-indulgence. Blind Pharisee! First clean the inside of the cup and dish, and then the outside also will be clean" (Matthew 23:25 – 26).

If we're honest with God and others, we'll walk in the light together. We'll share a common life of authenticity, and Jesus' sacrifice can then do its intended work. Notice that 1 John 1:7 says *we* will find cleansing from *our* sin-stained ways. See, it's not just an individual deal — the way of Jesus and his sacrificial work on the cross brings relational intimacy as we bring everything into the light of grace and authentic living.

At our church, we say "No Perfect People Allowed." We tell people, "If you want to pretend you have no struggles, no problems, no sins, no wounds, then go play that game somewhere else, because that's not real. But if we can agree to be authentic with our struggles, doubts, and temptations, then we can actually walk together, pray for each other, and help each other grow."

This is what everyone wants, and living out God's grace makes that possible. Only when I know you are for me, not against me, will I be vulnerable enough to let my weaknesses and struggles see light. And God does something mysteriously powerful and healing as we simply get honest together in the light of his community. As much as our families and the chaos of a broken, fallen world wound us, God's new family can restore and heal! As we stay connected and radically responsive, God intends to use us as healing agents in each other's lives.

3. HEALING CONFESSION

HEALING ONE ANOTHER THROUGH CONFESSION

It was the first night of our One Life Journey. Our church had to raise money to build a facility because we were getting kicked out of the old synagogue we'd been leasing. We called this journey "One Life" because that felt true to why we were doing it. One Life mattered enough to Christ to give his One Life, and we all have One Life to use to impact other lives. After an introduction video, we opened the floor to the hundred or so in the room. "Tell us what God has done in your life through our church family."

Jeff jumped up, unable to contain his excitement. "Ever since I was five, I've been confused about my gender. I was medically diagnosed as a male-to-female transsexual. I tried hormones a couple of times but life got worse and worse. I tried marriage, but that ended in tremendous pain. I tried the gay lifestyle but that didn't work for me either."

As Jeff opened up, I am ashamed to say my first thoughts were, "Oh no, this is going to freak people out!" But it was Jeff's uncompromising willingness to walk in the light that demonstrated the power of authenticity.

"Now that I've found my place with Jesus," Jeff continued, "I've noticed a remarkable change. In the past five months at this church, I've found a community of people who accept me and love me, who have helped me begin to explore my songwriting and musical gifts, who have helped me grow closer to the Lord than I ever imagined possible."

Jeff paused, fighting to control his emotions. "I used to blame God for this horrible burden and couldn't understand why God would do such a thing to a five-year-old boy. That part still confuses me. But for the first time in my life, I seldom feel the need to be a woman. God has used this church in a profound way. Now that Christ is in my life, I have a suspicion that he allowed this because he wants me to reach out to others who have the same problem. I can show them the love and forgiveness that he's beginning to show me through others, and I know that if I stay strong and do God's will, I'll be rewarded for all the pain and suffering I have been through my whole life."[4]

Instead of freaking out, applause erupted. People responded in awe to the power of God working through this authentic, grace-filled community. Others stood and shared powerful stories of healing and hope they too had found by bringing their junk into the light.

You possess a mysterious power! Other people possess it as well. We wield the power to either wound or heal one another. We've seen God's community heal broken marriages, substance abuse, anger issues, trust issues lingering from sexual abuse, pornography addictions — but healing almost always comes through community. It's God's plan. Spirituality is relational!

THE POWER OF CONFESSION

Carl Jung, one of the founders of modern psychology, observed that psychotherapy

---

THE POWER OF CONFESSION

Dear Sister,

I need to tell you honestly about the struggles I've had for a long time now. Since mom's death, I started drinking a bottle of wine a night, then a bottle of wine plus a six-pack, then I started taking painkillers. For more than two years, I faked being hurt to supply myself with painkillers. I also took them from others. Your bottles included. I'm so sorry for being selfish and deceitful. I hope you can forgive me and learn to trust me again. Ron's drug-related death was my awakening. I realized I've been living a lie. I am just as selfish, weak, deceitful, and unhealthy as he, and headed for the same fate. I checked myself into a rehab clinic several years ago. I've been honest about this with my husband, daughter, my church, and my work ... and now you. I truly am a new person in Christ, and I'm very thankful. I have times of real struggle and times that I've fallen off the path. They are most always little trips as I'm willing to come to God and those I love right away in order to prevent a spiral back into the hell I once lived in. I want to ask you to put your medications in a safe, private place so that when I visit, I won't be tempted. I created this and God has me taking responsibility regardless of the consequences. I hope you can understand. —Love, Christy

arose partly due to the void left in Christian community.[5] When we started treating confession as a private matter between an individual and God, or between a person and a "professional" who's paid to listen and keep quiet, society lost the God-given power of a grace-filled community.

There's a place for psychotherapy, but something powerfully healing happens when ordinary people simply confess their sins and struggles to God and to one another. Walking in the light, John goes on to say, involves confession: "If we claim to be without sin, we deceive ourselves and the truth is not in us. *If we confess our sins*, he is faithful and just and will forgive us our sins and purify us from all unrighteousness" (1 John 1:8 – 9, italics mine).

The healing power of confession comes not just in confessing to God but to one another as well: "Therefore confess your sins *to each other* and pray for each other so that you may be healed" (James 5:16, italics mine). Sin destroys the loving community God intended, and so God chooses to use his new community, who moment by moment follow the leadership of his Spirit, to heal and restore each other. We become wounded healers only as we rely on God's love, grace, and acceptance to enable us to walk in the light together without fear.

Psychologist Dr. Larry Crabb says,

> When two people connect … something is poured out of one and into the other that has the power to heal the soul of its deepest wounds and restore it to health. The one who receives experiences the joy of being healed. The one who gives knows the even greater joy of being used to heal. Something good is in the heart of each of God's children that is more powerful than everything bad. It's there, waiting to be released … but it rarely happens.[6]

Why does it rarely happen? Because we're scared. It's not natural for us to relate this way. We need God's help moment by moment. God wants to lead us to be a healing community as simple, ordinary people learn to accept, forgive, encourage, and walk with each other no matter how ugly or messy it gets. We have to courageously follow God's lead to bring our junk into the light of community, but when we do, it makes it safe for others to do the same. Suddenly we aren't alone in it, and God does something through us together that we can never do for ourselves.

As you do this 60-60 Experiment, can you hear God's Spirit whispering, "It's safe to come out of hiding, you can stop the game. My grace is sufficient. Walk in my light with others, and I will heal you and grow you together into powerfully loving people."

4. SPEAKING THE LAST 10 PERCENT
SAYING THE TRUTH IN LOVE

Sometimes love must be bold. Bold enough to say things to one another that we usually lack the courage to say. Bill Hybels calls it "saying the last 10 percent." We will usually say 90 percent of the encouraging words, or 90 percent of the hard-to-hear words of truth, but we usually hold back from that last 10 percent. But that last 10 percent is the part that often makes the most difference. As I'm willing to listen and respond to God's Spirit, I find he will push me to be bold, not worrying about what the person will think of me, and just say the last 10 percent — most often to encourage, but at times to confront.

Proverbs 27:6 says, "Wounds from a friend can be trusted, but an enemy multiplies kisses." It hurts to see the areas where you need to grow — we feel growing pains. It's hard to have blind spots pointed out or destructive patterns confronted. But if we know we're in it together — if I know these people are for me, not against me; if they know I'm for them — then we can work through difficulties, hurtful comments, annoying habits, and grow together. We need each other to grow.

As I stay connected to God's Spirit, he prompts me to live this way, but everything in me fights against it. This week, I woke up one morning and began a conversation with the Lord about the day ahead. As I got ready, talking to him about the things I needed his help with, a thought popped into my mind: "You lied yesterday." It actually came to me as a picture in my mind. I was standing in the hallway with Nate, a good friend, who asked me a personal question I didn't want to answer. But instead of questioning why he was asking, I told a half-truth — you know, a lie that you can justify to yourself as "almost true."

"You lied yesterday." Ouch! I wanted to push the thought away and hide it in the darkness. I'm a pastor; I don't lie; so my first inclination was to run and hide. "Let's think about something else!" But I knew God wanted me to confess.

Resistant, I admitted the truth to God first: "I didn't speak the truth, Lord. Why did I feel the need to lie?" As I prayed, I began to see fears of being misunderstood, fears of a lack of confidentiality, fears that drove me from the light.

Then, on my way to work, I called Nate and confessed to him. Like a trusted friend, he forgave me and lovingly asked, "Why did you feel the need to lie?" We had a great conversation about the last 10 percent, and it was healing for us both.

Paul explains that our Christian communities will grow up to be like Christ by speaking the last 10 percent: "Instead, speaking the truth in love, we will in all things grow up into him who is the Head, that is, Christ" (Ephesians 4:15). Jesus came full of truth and grace — he brought the two together: *truth*, which we sometimes need to shine its light into the dark recesses of our lives, but always in the hope of *grace*, which says we are more than the sum total of our past behaviors.

For most people, as soon as relationships get difficult, they bail out. They never let God lead them and grow them. But it is when things get difficult that God can teach us what love really does as we respond to him. The Scriptures command us to think creatively about motivating and encouraging one another: "Let us think of ways to motivate one another to acts of love and good works. And let us not neglect our meeting together, as some people do, but encourage one another" (Hebrews 10:24 – 25).

This is why you can't really grow as a Christ-follower and remain isolated from others. We need each other to become who God intended. Spirituality is relationship!

As you follow the Spirit's lead, you will grow to love others. But you can't really love others until you know them, and we don't really know each other if we haven't had to work through differences and difficulties. Until you understand why Jesus had to die for the sins of others, you don't really know them. And until you have to humble yourself and allow God to chip off your rough edges that wound others, you have yet to grow as God intends. The truth is you are not experiencing the kind of community God wants you to experience until the first fight breaks out! But have no fear — God is there to lead you into a new way of dealing with conflict too.

THE 60-60 EXPERIMENT

As you continue to listen and respond, you will see that God is concerned with how you treat your closest relationships. That's what we'll focus on here. Grace-giving acceptance, vulnerable authenticity, confession, speaking the last 10 percent —these aren't easy to do with lots of people. I suggest you start with just one or two people. If you were training to run a marathon, you'd need running partners to help keep you motivated, keep pace, and encourage you to keep going. In the same way, you need "Spiritual Running Partners" you trust who are going the way of Christ, willing to experiment in this new way of living.

1. **Respond relationally**. As you seek to get better and better at moment-by-moment connection and response to God, be aware of the people around you. With every sixty-minute beep or reminder, ask God to show you his will in the ways you relate to those around you. Take relational risks in response to God's prompting to accept, to encourage, to care, and to speak truth in love to those around you.

2. **Risk with spiritual Running Partners**. If you haven't already, find one or two people to regularly talk over this 60-60 Experiment with you (hopefully you are doing this experiment with others already, but if not, it's okay if they start a few weeks later than you). Agree to meet weekly for the rest of the experiment to talk about what you're learning and to take risks together. Use these questions to guide your conversation (be sure to discuss the successes as much as the failures—both are important to notice):

    a. What are you learning about God and yourself as you seek to stay continuously connected and radically responsive? (Loving God)

    b. How have you treated those you do life with? (Loving People)

    c. What recurring sin have you been conscious of this week? How have you dealt with it?

3. **Journal and blog**. Write down what God's showing you about yourself. What do you wish wasn't so, and how do you hide or compensate for that relationally? Write about how God leads you to show grace-giving acceptance, or how he prompts your authenticity or confession, or how speaking encouraging words to build someone up affects your relationships. Encourage others by posting your learnings on our blog, and be sure to read the blog to learn from the experience of others (*www.Soulrevolution.net*).

Reconcile 1—
IN THE RING

"I'm a bitch." The word shocked me as I sat across the table from this prim and proper woman who had spent her life in the church. "I've destroyed my marriage. My husband's having an affair with his work associate. All I wanted was to be in a secure, loving marriage, and now it's all gone."

I didn't know what to say. "Why do you feel it's all your fault?" I finally asked.

"It's not all my fault. David has his own issues, but my controlling nature drove him away." Kay opened up. "I can see it now, but I could never see it before. For seventeen years, I had to have it my way. To not have things go my way produced a kind of panic in me — I felt out of control. David felt that giving in to me was to love me, so I never had to face it. He resented feeling controlled all the time — always giving in — and yet his compliance just exacerbated my insecure feelings. We built up a wall of separation, brick by brick, year after year from unresolved conflict."

"It seems like you're being awfully hard on yourself, Kay. He still made the decision to be unfaithful — it wasn't all your fault," I reminded her.

"I feel so angry, and yet so sad. I just feel like the bottom has dropped out and I'm free-falling." Kay's honesty bled out in a way that I suspected felt freeing, yet unnerving. "I want to hurt him back for hurting me, and yet I don't want to give up — I want to fight for my marriage. But it's over ... he's divorcing me. The papers are filed. He is a lawyer; fighting's futile."

Kay paused, reflecting. "But you know what? I never understood God's grace until now."

"But you've been in churches your whole life," I contended. "How could that be?"

"I knew the words, but not the *experience* of grace," Kay explained. "For the first time, I'm experiencing love and acceptance in the middle of facing my greatest failure and insecurity, and in a weird way, it feels freeing and hopeful."

Three years after that breakfast conversation, despite the seemingly hopeless situation — nearly two decades of relational dysfunction, built-up resentment, and an affair — I couldn't believe my ears as I met with Kay and David together.

"We're more in love today than we ever imagined we could be," David said. "It has really been miraculous." To see them together, holding hands and looking at each other like teens in love felt nothing short of a miracle.

"What happened?" I asked.

"You know, I was in the middle of this affair," David began. "I knew it was wrong, but I just didn't care. I felt so rejected year after year, trying to love Kay — I thought this would get me what I wanted. Of course, it didn't — it caused a ton of pain. Kay left the church we were attending and started coming to your church, and something started to change in her. I could see it. Something began to grow in her that I'd never seen before. I know now what it was — God's grace."

"What did you see?" I asked.

"I don't know how to describe it," David said, "except you'd have to know Kay before to see the change. It was something strong and confident and secure that grew up within her that felt loving and accepting. All I know is that I wanted to find out what she was learning — it was that attractive. So I left our old church and started coming to yours."

"Were you still in the affair?" I asked.

"Yeah, it was messy for a while," David admitted. "I needed grace — the knowledge that despite all my screw-ups, God would still meet me and help me move forward — and I saw it in Kay and what she experienced in this community."

"We desperately needed that grace," Kay explained. "We had to learn to undo the patterns of the past and learn to communicate and love each other in a new way. But it wasn't easy. Both of us have had to die to old ways we thought would work — that's painful."

David piped up, "If only we'd seen these patterns early on, but honestly, we were blind to them. I think both of us secretly hoped that we could change the other person and find life, either by controlling or by giving in — but neither strategy worked. Finally, we learned how to do conflict in a healthy way, in a way that builds intimacy rather than walls — it made all the difference."

CONFLICT HAPPENS

Why is there so much conflict? Family conflict, marriage conflict, roommate conflict, business partner conflict. The reality is: conflict happens. This is the story of humanity. Wherever we humans go, conflict goes with us. Fighting, dividing, and separating come naturally for us.

After explaining how to live connected to God's Spirit, one of Jesus' last recorded prayers was about this new way to be human: "My prayer is not for them alone. I pray also for those who will believe in me through their message, that *all of them may be one*, Father, just as you are in me and I am in you. May they also be in us so that the world may believe that you have sent me" (John 17:20 – 21, emphasis added).

We are unique individuals with different gifts, passions, temperaments, races, and genders, but Jesus' prayer was that we would be like God, who is one. When the world sees people uniting rather than dividing over differences, it reveals God's reconciling work through Christ because it's so unnatural. Unity is probably the most important work of God's Spirit, but as the history of the church demonstrates, it's also the most challenging for us!

Why is conflict natural? The short answer is that it's a byproduct of our broken, messed-up world, filled with self-centered little kingdoms that don't appreciate our God-given differences. God intended all our kingdoms to work in unity, under the loving direction of the One whose will is perfect. Not all conflict is bad, of course, but unresolved conflict is treacherous.

We must contend with three human problems that make conflict inevitable and responding to God's Spirit essential. They are the problems of communication, heart, and perception.

1. COMMUNICATION PROBLEMS

We all desire to be understood, and to understand, though usually to a lesser degree than we want to be understood. This would be easy if we could just fully understand other people's thoughts and motives, but we can't. We're limited, finite creatures who sometimes don't even know what *we're* thinking, feeling, or wanting.

Have you ever said something and afterwards realized, "I didn't say that right," or "That's not what I meant; it came out wrong!" In a world of imperfect people, even with the best motives and intentions, we miscommunicate.

And we're all different. We have different ways of communicating but don't always value these differences. In a study of preschoolers, some researchers at Harvard recorded the sounds kids made on a playground. They found that 100 percent of the girls' sounds were audible words. They loved to talk. Little girls talked to each other, themselves, the swing set, anything! Little boys were different, however; only 68 percent of their sounds were understandable words. The rest were sound effects: grunts, growls, booms, bangs, car sounds, train sounds, you name it![1] That explains a lot doesn't it — like the success of three *Terminator* movies! Big sounds, big explosions — that's all it takes to speak deep into the heart of a man.

The fact that we're different people with different thoughts, ideas, and desires makes communication even more vital. It's why a natural byproduct of every close relationship is conflict. If you can't communicate about differences, you can't be close, because you can't be known. Intimacy requires knowing and being known. There will be differences, so there will be miscommunication, so there will be conflict.

2. HEART PROBLEMS

We all come from imperfect families and have imperfect friends. We've all been wounded, and we all wound others. In other words, we all have heart problems. Scripture puts it like this: "The heart is deceitful above all things and beyond cure. Who can understand it?" (Jeremiah 17:9). "Everyone has sinned; we all fall short of God's glorious standard" (Romans 3:23 NLT).

Sin is when our deceived hearts go their own way rather than God's way, thinking we know what's best. At its core all sin is relational. It destroys the right-relatedness God intended between us and him, us and each other, us and ourselves, and even between us and his creation. Sin is the misuse of our kingdom power.

Jesus' whole purpose boils down to reversing the effects of this heart problem. God says, "I will give you a new heart and put a new spirit in you" (Ezekiel 36:26). "Therefore, if anyone is in Christ, the new creation has come: The old has gone, the new has come! All this is from God, who reconciled us to himself through Christ and *gave us* the ministry of *reconciliation*" (2 Corinthians 5:17 – 18, italics mine).

Jesus demands that making amends with one another take priority over every other religious act or deed: "Therefore, if you are offering your gift at the altar and there remember that your brother or sister has something against you, leave your gift there in front of the altar. First go and be reconciled to that person; then come and offer your gift" (Matthew 5:23 – 24). "For if you forgive others when they sin against you, your heavenly Father will also forgive you. But if you do not forgive others their sins, your Father will not forgive your sins" (Matthew 6:14 – 15). Do you see how central relational reconciliation is to everything God wants to do in us? Yet we so often resist his Holy Spirit.

Years ago, I attended a church where the senior pastor decided to move from a Sunday school model to a small-group model, thinking that this would help people grow and develop. The associate pastor, who had been there twenty years (four times as long as the senior pastor), disagreed about the new direction. But instead of talking it out face to face, either working a compromise or agreeing to disagree, the associate pastor just subtly undermined the new direction. Sides began to form as "discussions" about the new direction turned into outright gossip. As the lies about each side's motives simmered beneath the surface, outright slanderous, hurtful comments made their way back to the senior pastor and his family. Confrontation finally erupted due to the built-up hurt and anger, and a stand-off ensued. Those who sided with each pastor felt confident the other side was deceived by Satan. In the end, the church split, and many people left feeling wounded and bitter.

The truth is, we can all be deceived — especially when we think we're right — because we all have a heart problem. Jesus once said to Peter, "Get behind me, Satan! You are a stumbling block to me; you do not have in mind the concerns of God, but merely human concerns" (Matthew 16:23). If Jesus' most zealous follower fell prey to deception, we can too! We must all realize that we can think we're absolutely right when we're actually wrong. And we grieve God's Spirit when we resist his reconciling work: "And do not grieve the Holy Spirit of God. . . . Get rid of all bitterness, rage and anger, brawling and slander, along with every form of malice. Be kind and compassionate to one another, forgiving each other, just as in Christ God forgave you" (Ephesians 4:30 – 32).

3. PERCEPTION PROBLEMS

I'll bet you've had the frustrating experience of trying to get someone to see what you see so clearly, yet they just can't see correctly because they only see from their perspective. People can be so hopelessly self-centered, can't they? Isn't that frustrating? It's a good thing *we're* not like *them*.

Several summers ago, our family visited friends in Santa Barbara, California. I got up early one morning and ran down to the beach, where I walked and prayed for about an hour. It was a beautiful morning, and I'd been thinking about how powerful the God who created the mighty ocean and majesty of the mountains must be, and yet to think Jesus revealed this same God. A God who loves me enough to lay down his life for me — mind-boggling!

I thought, "Lord, if we could just love like that — married people I counsel have a hard time sacrificing a point in an argument, much less laying down their lives for the good of another." And I was overwhelmed with a feeling of gratitude that God loved me personally enough to do something most lovers won't do for each other — lay down their lives. And I finished my walk on the beach on a spiritual high.

About an hour later, I went back to the place we were staying. Kathy was up, but I could tell she wasn't in a good mood (not normal for her). Being in such a spiritually good place, I asked her if anything was wrong — bad question. I was the problem! She explained that something I said the night before in front of our friends had hurt her. Ordinarily, I would have empathized, apologized, and asked questions to try to understand; the only problem was that *she* wasn't seeing things correctly (as I did)!

So I decided to help her understand my intent more accurately . . . which she said hurt her more because it proved I didn't understand. But I *did* understand; she just didn't understand that I understood! And as we went back and forth, I started thinking, "I was feeling really peaceful and loving before talking to you!" A defensive wall of pride had built up inside me.

Then I had a brilliant idea! See, she had hurt me a while back in a similar way, yet she didn't understand, so I brought up this old wound and said, "Well maybe now you can understand how I felt back then!" For some strange reason, that didn't help either. About thirty minutes into this, it was like a bell went off in my head.

God's Spirit brought the thoughts of that morning right into my mind's eye, "How hard it is to lay down your life, even sacrifice a defensive point, for someone you love." I realized, it's easy to feel spiritual and loving and peaceful alone with God on a beach, but truly loving other people when I can't see my own self-centered tendencies — I've got a perspective problem that I can't get beyond without God's help. Finally, I apologized. We were having a perception problem.

Stop and ask yourself some important questions and listen to the Spirit's promptings:

Is there anyone I'm at odds with right now?

Whom do I avoid during the course of a day?

If I ran into that person at the grocery store, could I look her or him in the eyes and truly want the best for that person?

Is there anyone I resent, have not forgiven, or feel bitterness toward?

As you continue your 60-60 Experiment, ask God to show you whom you have communication, heart, and perception problems with, and ask to follow his will so that "if it is possible, as far as it depends on you, [you can] live at peace with everyone" (Romans 12:18). If you ask, he will show you the path to reconciliation.

INTO THE RING WITH TRUTH AND LOVE

We live in a broken world where conflict happens. We must face it in order to love God and each other, but we can't do it alone. God wants to climb into the ring of conflict with us, to teach us how to fight for what's right, how to fight not to win the argument but to win the relationship — with truth and love. There *is* something worth fighting for in this broken world — relationships full of truth and love. We are commanded to follow his Spirit into this new way:

> *Do not lie to each other, since you have taken off your old self with its prac-*
> *tices and have put on the new self, which is being renewed in knowledge in the*
> *image of its Creator.... Bear with each other and forgive one another if any*
> *of you has a grievance against someone. Forgive as the Lord forgave you. And*
> *over all these virtues put on love, which binds them all together in perfect unity.*
> *(Colossians 3:9 – 10, 13 – 14)*

When we find ourselves in the ring of conflict, we must put off falsehood (game-playing) and speak truth in love. God is in the ring with us. He wants to teach us to stop fighting each other and instead fight for the relationship — with both hands! Think about it this way, you have two hands to fight with. In your left hand is love — care and respect for the person. In your right hand is truth — concern for honesty and integrity and forthright communication about what's right according to God. As we respond to God's Spirit, he will lead us.

THE OLD WAY TO BE HUMAN

God wants us to fight for relationships with both hands, but first we must understand which hand we favor — love or truth. Both are necessary. David Augsberger defines four common fighting tactics we use in the ring of conflict.[2] Which do you favor? Think about this question as you find yourself in the ring during this 60-60 Experiment.

1. GOING FOR THE KO: "I WIN, YOU LOSE"

Those who come out swinging for the knock-out punch favor truth with little love. When you assume you're 100 percent right and the other person is 100 percent wrong, you're in KO mode. When the goal is to prove you're right, to win the argument, you cease trying to understand what circumstances might have led to the actions that hurt or offended the other. You're in a win-lose stance. We win the argument but lose the relationship. We always fight for the wrong thing when we fight to be right. We lead with the right fist of truth, but don't use the left hand of love. Lucy's story illustrates how this tactic fails to get us what we want:

> My first attempt at seeking God came when I was twenty-seven. My marriage was in shambles, I was an alcoholic, drug addict, workaholic, and rage-aholic. Looking back; so many of my broken coping mechanisms came from messed-up conflict management. My dad and I fought constantly while I was growing up. Give and take never seemed an option; it was always win or lose, so I learned to fight. The problem is I never felt loved or valued, so I always ended up fighting the people I loved in order to prove myself worthy of love, and my relationships kept imploding.
>
> When my marriage ended, I started to explore God's solutions to life, though my first place of seeking was not in the words of Jesus. My drug use and sexual escapades escalated, but I was also becoming more spiritually aware. I met a guy at a bar who was all I ever wanted in a man (granted my wants were not based at all on God's values). Even though our lives revolved around alcohol, drugs, and co-dependency, we often talked about God.
>
> As the "romance factor" wore off after a year, we began to see each other's "warts." The fighting escalated. One night when he got drunk, a fight ensued. Criticisms, spite, hate, envy spewed out of me — that's what I had nurtured. It was not long before my anger and desire to control his behavior got completely out of control. I

resorted to violence. I hit him and threw things. During the scuffle, the cops came. I went to jail and was sentenced to take an anger management class.

Like many of the seemingly "terrible" things in my life, this became a stepping stone toward becoming who God intends me to be. In that class, I learned some simple rules of fighting fair: No violence, no name calling, no stockpiling past hurts, no minimizing, no power-play walk-outs, no arguing after 9:00 p.m. I got into recovery and started truly seeking God's will. Looking back, I see God's merciful guidance through all the mess. Finally, I came to faith in Christ, and I began to find guidance from God's Word. I started learning how to follow his Spirit, listening to thoughts and "stirrings" that prompted me not only to stop and evaluate ways I react, but to respond to God's will in ways I had never considered.

All truth and no love is a pretty typical reaction to confrontation. The problem is, we never possess *all truth*, and this posture never allows for true understanding and intimacy. Ever seen yourself respond in this way? Someone hurts or wrongs you and you immediately go on the attack; you feel the need to defend yourself and prove yourself right. This kills relationships — with friends, in marriages, and in churches.

God wants to lead you to fight for the relationship with truth and love. In the ring of conflict, you must listen and respond to the Spirit to teach you how to put your right hand behind your back at first — so you don't KO with truth. First fight for understanding the full situation, valuing the person with the left hand of love, then the real truth can be known.

2. RUNNING FROM THE RING: "WE BOTH LOSE"

At first, running seems like a godly option. You avoid the conflict. But it's actually a lose-lose solution. Some Christians think that when someone hurts them, the best thing to do is to avoid the person, leave the church, quit the small group, or just ignore the topic because conflict would be *bad*, right? The problem is, when you run, you lose both the truth and love. You lose the relationship and the chance to find understanding and unity around truth.

Running hurts everyone because we lose relationship. Conflict is an opportunity for both sides to grow in love and understanding by seeing how each affects the other — which is what love is all about. But if you run, neither person grows as a result of the conflict.

If running is your typical response, listen and respond to God's Spirit, who wants to give you the courage to stay in the ring! If you follow his lead, he will lead you to fight with both hands engaged, truth and love, so that you and the other person both win.

TAKING A DIVE IN THE RING: "I LOSE, YOU WIN"

Another common tactic for dealing with conflict is to give in. We often think it's the loving thing to do — all love, no truth. This happens when we're afraid of saying what we feel or what we desire. We fear that it will end the friendship, that things will only get worse, so we decide to give in, to do whatever it takes to keep the peace.

If the other person hurts us, we just swallow the pain and pretend we don't hurt. If asked, we just say, "Everything's fine — nothing's wrong." We think that to admit our hurts and needs and wants would not be a loving thing to do.

But you know what we're really doing? We're lying! "Do not lie to each other," Paul instructs us in Colossians, "since you have taken off your old self with its practices and have put on the new self." This could be translated, "Don't continue to live a lie [being false] toward each other."

You may think that taking a dive in conflict is love, but it's a falsehood. It is not a way to love people, because it lacks truth. You need both love and truth before a relationship can mature and bring unity. People who take this approach preserve their relationships only superficially. In reality, they have little relationship at all.

Taking a dive to avoid conflict plunged David and Kay, whose story was told earlier, into chaos. David recalls,

Though trained as a trial lawyer, I hated conflict. I grew up learning that keeping the peace at all costs was right. So I spent my career trying to help others work out their conflicts, but when Kay would insist on her way or the highway, I'd always give in to keep the peace.

Looking back, it was the most unloving thing to do. I would never voice my opinion or strong desire, so she never had to face her control issues. But Kay was living out of a lie she inherited from her parents that said, "If I don't have everything under control, no one will love me." That's a cruel prison to live in. In fact, the more I gave in, the more insecure she felt because it reinforced the lie that said she'd lose everything if she didn't control me.

When I began to speak truth and voice my differences and desires, at first it was hell. It tripped Kay's junk that made her feel unlovable, and she'd try to control me, which tripped my junk. But as we both put practices in place to respond to God in the moment, rather than to those old voices in our heads, he took us down a new path.

If you tend to take a dive in the ring, remember this: unity comes when each distinctly different person can love despite differences, express needs and wants, and work toward compromise. If you always take a dive to preserve the relationship, you need to seek the power God gives to speak truth in love and not hold back on either.*

4. FIGHT FOR TRUTH AND LOVE: "WE BOTH WIN"

God wants to lead you to speak truth in love. As I've said, when you find yourself in the ring, respond to God's Spirit by fighting *for* the relationship and not *against* the person. When you hear lies or when your pride gets in the way, God wants to teach you a new way through conflict: "Instead, we will speak the truth in love, growing in every way more and more like Christ" (Ephesians 4:15 NLT).

As you fight with the left hand of love, moving in closer, valuing the other person, affirming the importance of the relationship, remember to use the right hand of truth as well. Talk frankly about your thoughts and feelings, about concerns or issues that need to be addressed, remembering to attack the issue rather than the person. That way, you will grow more like Jesus.

But how do we really do that? Nothing in life is more difficult than to love the way God wants to teach us to love in the moment of conflict. We all think we know what love is, but we don't. Remember Jesus' definition of love:

> *But to you who are willing to listen, I say, love your enemies! Do good to those who hate you. Bless those who curse you. Pray for those who hurt you.... Love your enemies! Do good to them. Lend to them without expecting to be repaid. Then your reward from heaven will be very great, and you will truly be acting as children of the Most High, for he is kind to those who are unthankful and wicked. (Luke 6:27 – 28, 35 NLT)*

---

* If you find yourself in a dangerous or abusive situation, speaking truth will probably not help. Seek help from your church or a professional counselor or nonprofit organization specializing in domestic violence issues.

Wow! Do I love like that? That's a question worth asking, and it is what God wants to teach you how to do. Are you willing to learn? In the next chapter, we'll talk about how God wants us to love like that in the ring of conflict.

THE 60·60 EXPERIMENT

Conflict is unavoidable in close relationships. Conflict isn't bad, but unresolved conflict is treacherous. As we learn to follow God's Spirit, he will teach us how to live clean and at peace with all people. To do this well, we must be aware of our own tendencies when we're in the ring of conflict with others.

1. **Stay connected and emotionally aware.** As you practice turning your thoughts toward God throughout the day, monitor your emotions and body language. They tell us a lot about our spiritual state. Do you tense up around certain people? When certain people come to mind, do you feel anger, disdain, judgment, fear, anxiety, or defensiveness? Do you avoid certain people? Talk over with God what you notice and ask for insight. Stay in honest conversation about everything, but keep reflecting on your relational world.

2. **Memorize Romans 12:18**: "If it is possible, as far as it depends on you, live at peace with everyone." Ask God's Spirit to show you this week if there's anyone you are at odds with—due to something they did to you or you've done to them.

3. **Make a list of amends.** List in your journal any people God brings to mind whom you are not at peace with. Don't worry about how you'll handle it yet; just write their names and ask God throughout the week, "Show me what your will is with this person and help me be willing." Focus only on willingness to bring these relationships before God. Write down any action steps that come to mind.

4. **Journal about your conflict style.** Ask God to help you see your tendencies in conflict, and write down what you notice about communication, perception, or heart problems you face, as well as how you balance truth and love. Take risks to share with your Spiritual Running Partner(s) your list and discoveries.

Reconcile 2—
LIVING CLEAN WITH PEOPLE

In Matthew 18, Jesus clearly laid out what Christ-followers must do when they feel wronged:

> *If a brother or sister sins, go and point out the fault, just between the two of you. If they listen to you, you have won them over. But if they will not listen, take one or two others along, so that "every matter may be established by the testimony of two or three witnesses." If they still refuse to listen, tell it to the church; and if they refuse to listen even to the church, treat them as you would a pagan or a tax collector.* (Matthew 18:15 – 17)

IF WRONGED . . .

Jesus says, if someone really wrongs you — really sins against you according to God's Word — *go to them*. The first, and often the most difficult, step is deciding if we've really been sinned against and if we should do something about it. You need to ask: "Why am I angry and hurt? Did they really sin against me? Or did they just do something I didn't like?" You need to figure out the real issue.

Right after 9/11, America had an anthrax scare, when white powder kept appearing in unmarked letters, causing pandemonium. One night during that time, I woke up with a weird headache and uncontrollable nausea. Kathy wanted me to see the doctor, but I was sure it was just the flu. I tend to be a minimizer: "It's no big deal; let's wait and see." Kathy's a better-safe-than-sorry type.

The next day, Saturday, Kathy found a suspicious-looking letter in our mail pile, hand-addressed to "John and Kathy Burke" with no return address! Instead it had strange religious stickers on it. It met the criteria the news told people to report. She said, "Maybe it's an anthrax letter. Maybe it caused your headache and nausea!"

Mr. Minimizer held it up to the light — "Doesn't look like anthrax" — and took a big whiff — "Doesn't smell like anthrax" — and said, "I'm sure it's nothing."

But Kathy felt we should call the police and ask what to do. Next thing I knew, there were two police cars, a fire truck, a hazmat unit with a paddy wagon behind it, the fire chief's car, and other vehicles lined up in front of our house with their lights whirling.

All our neighbors came out of their houses to see what trouble the pastor guy had gotten himself into. My mom was due to arrive any second from out of town, and I knew if she pulled up to that sight, we'd need an ambulance too! As our backyard filled up with all the public service personnel Austin could muster, standing in a circle wearing masks and rubber gloves, looking at a little white envelope on the grass, Kathy could see that I was angry.

I asked (probably with an edge), "*Whom* did you call?"

"Just the police. Why, are you angry?" she countered.

Yes, I was angry. Why? Because I'd been wronged? Because a great injustice had been done? Because someone had sinned against me? No! Kathy had done no wrong. She simply made a choice out of love and concern for our family. I was angry because I felt embarrassed and knew we'd have to explain it to the neighbors. It wasn't what I'd planned for our Saturday morning, but who said life is supposed to go my way anyway? Fortunately no anthrax was discovered; just a bunch of tracts about Halloween. No poison.

When we're angry or hurt because we didn't get our way, we need to listen and respond to God's Spirit. If it's not a sin, then either let it go or talk it out to find a compromise solution. As Jesus instructs, get rid of the log in your own eye before dealing with the speck in your friend's eye (Matthew 7:5).

But what if someone really does wrong us? Jesus says to expect just that in our imperfect, sin-filled world. When that happens, here's what you must do: listen carefully; do not pass go, do not collect $200, *go directly to the person.*

GO IN PRIVATE

"Go in private ... just between the two of you," Jesus says. The way of Christ is simple: if someone wrongs you, go to that person in private. Don't gossip, don't check it out with three or four friends first, don't stuff it or ignore it. Go talk one-on-one first.

Simple, yes, but it's also the hardest thing for people to do. I don't care how long someone's been a Christian, most people stink at this! I'm convinced we do more damage to the community that God wants to create because we just can't get this one right. Why? Because we don't rely on God's Spirit to lead and guide us as we go to talk over what's wrong.

HUMBLE YOURSELF BEFORE GOD

If loving our enemies were humanly possible without God's help, every marriage would survive, every friendship would flourish, and every partnership would thrive. But we can't do it without help from above, and that requires humbling ourselves.

I know that when I fail to humble myself before God when I'm in a conflict, I almost always get defensive or say something I later wish I could take back. And I know I'm not alone. Why is this so common? Because pride is our biggest enemy in every conflict. "Fighting comes only from pride, but wisdom is with those who listen" (Proverbs 13:10 NLT).

Remember, that other person is not your biggest enemy — your pride is! Your pride says, "I'm right." "No, you listen to me!" "I always do what you want." "You're so stubborn." Pride defends, puts up walls, sees only its own point of view. Pride will be your biggest enemy in any conflict because it won't allow you to humble yourself and seek God's help. Pride says, "I don't need God's help; I *am* a loving person — you idiot!"

Of course, we don't define love like God does, do we? That's why Scripture says, "Clothe yourselves with humility toward one another, because, 'God opposes the proud but gives grace to the humble.' Humble yourselves, therefore, under God's mighty hand, that he may lift you up in due time" (1 Peter 5:5 – 6 NIV).

Once during the 60-60 Experiment, our family went on an overnight getaway to Padre Island. We played too late, swam too long, and no one got enough sleep, so we all woke up grumpy. With four of us crammed into a tiny beach-shack hotel room, the kids kept getting on each other's nerves, which got on my nerves. I had planned what we were going to do that day — it was "The Plan," the right plan, because we only had a short amount of time. According to "The Plan," we were supposed to be on the beach by 10:00 am, enjoying the day. But by noon, we were still floundering around in a tiny hotel room, getting on each other's nerves.

I was getting more and more impatient but doing a good job of holding it in — so I thought. Kathy mentioned, however, how impatient she thought I was being, and we started arguing about whether I was being impatient or whether I had a *right* to be impatient, since I had been *sooo* patient two hours past "The Plan."

The conflict escalated, and I declared, "All right, if we're not gonna go have fun on the beach, I'm packing the car and we're heading home." Of course, I didn't really mean it — it was just a manipulative threat to get my way in a conflict, but right in the middle of my sentence, the stinkin' beeper on my watch went off for the 60-60.

My first thought was, "Give me a second Lord — I can't talk right now. I'm in the middle of something." But I knew I needed help. I was stuck, unable to compromise, and my manipulative tactics weren't working. Everybody was miserable. I honestly didn't want to let God have his way at that point, and if it hadn't been for the 60-60 beeper, I wouldn't have considered it for a second. Why? Pride!

That Scripture popped into my head: "God opposes the proud but gives grace to the humble. Humble yourselves, therefore, under God's mighty hand, that he may lift you up." I remember thinking, "It's not fair, Lord! I should never have memorized that verse! My family was wrong first. I was patient while they were cranky and uncooperative." The more excuses I made, the heavier that Mighty Hand felt, until finally I left and took a walk.

About twenty minutes later I was able to humble myself and ask God for help. "You're right; I was wrong. Whether they were wrong or not, I'm not being loving or patient. Give me the power to do your will — I'll do it for you, Lord. I can't do it for them, but I'll do it for you." I apologized to Kathy and the kids, and it helped us all apologize and make up, and we went to the beach and enjoyed the day together.

When you're right in the middle of being overcome by pride, when you don't have it in you to make amends, when there's no way to forgive — just call out, "God, help me." He wants to help you, but he *will* oppose you if you hang on to your pride. So humble yourself before him.

Humbling is the first step as you work out your conflict with another person, but the next step is to listen as much as you speak.

LISTEN TO UNDERSTAND

Did you notice how Proverbs 13:10 contrasts pride with listening? Listening communicates to the other person that you care, but it certainly doesn't come naturally. I'm convinced most of our conflicts would resolve themselves quickly if only we would commit to listening. "Everyone should be quick to listen, slow to speak and slow to become angry" (James 1:19). Pride is usually what makes us quick to speak and slow to listen.

There's actually a good reason why this is so difficult. Do you know the average person thinks at 400 words-per-minute (wpm) but only speaks at 100 wpm?[1] That means we think four times faster than we speak.

Look at it this way. Let's say you and I are arguing. All 400 of the words I'm thinking make perfect sense to me. They have meaning to me, but every minute I can only get 25 percent of those words out to help you understand what I mean. You may hear my 100 words, but you've got your own 400 words' worth of thoughts going on in your head, which make perfect sense to you. But you can only tell me about 25 percent of your meaning each minute. See the problem? So neither one of us really understands fully what the other person is thinking by words alone.

KEY LISTENING PRINCIPLE #1:
MEANING DOES NOT RESIDE IN WORDS BUT IN PEOPLE[2]

Humble listening is the key to resolving most conflicts. One of our biggest communication blunders is assuming that what a person *says* conveys everything that person means. You can choose to react to what you *think* she means, when in fact, she never meant it that way at all.

We've all had the frustration of saying to someone, "That's not what I meant," and they respond, "But that's what you said!" If we really want to understand a person's meaning, we must be slow to react until we listen to more than just the first words we hear. How do you do this? It's simple.

KEY LISTENING PRINCIPLE #2:
ASK, "IS THIS WHAT YOU MEAN?"

We all think we know what the other person means, but humility requires us to admit that we may be mishearing, misinterpreting, or misunderstanding. Lots of things get in the way of our understanding each other — we only hear 25 percent of each other's thoughts, our past histories color our interpretations, we may misread cues of emotion or non-verbal expression, our own additional thoughts distract us, or noises and other distractions may cause us to miss what is said. Ever had an argument about what specific words *were* or *were not* said? That's a fun one! "No, I didn't say 'You always,' I said, 'People tend to.'" "You did not! You accused me!" "I didn't accuse you; I was making a general observation." "Yeah, but you specifically meant me — that's manipulative." See how it happens?

The only way past this is to listen until the other person agrees that you do understand her. To mediate conflicts counselors often ask two people to set up "Listening Rules" — a way to train them to listen to each other. Each person gets to talk while the other just listens. The speaker tries to describe what she is thinking until she feels completely understood. The listener can't interrupt and can only answer questions. When the speaker feels the listener understands, the roles are switched, and the listener gets time to speak until he feels understood. It may take going back and forth many times, but it will ensure that both parties feel understood.

SPEAK TRUTH PERSONALLY

In addition to humbling yourself and really listening, you also need to be heard. As you confront someone, you need to speak truth in order for conflict to be resolved with greater unity. The problem is, none of us has an entirely accurate view of what's true — except God. So when we communicate our truth, we need to do it in a way that humbly acknowledges our limitations. This is where the first speaking principle is helpful:

KEY SPEAKING PRINCIPLE #1:
MAKE "I" STATEMENTS, NOT "YOU" STATEMENTS

Communicating as calmly as you can with "I" statements such as, "I think..." or "I'm feeling..." express your meaning without verbally attacking or blaming the other person. This is hard to do, and again requires that we humble ourselves before God and acknowledge our limitations.

When we accuse others, we are, in a sense, putting ourselves in God's place — pronouncing judgments based on our limited knowledge of truth. So instead of saying, "You're always late!" — which is a sweeping, untrue judgment because no one is "always" anything — say instead, "I feel upset when you're late." Instead of stating, "You make me feel stupid" — no one can *make you feel* anything; the other person is not responsible for your feelings, you are — speak a personal truth like, "I think I have something to offer, but I don't feel I'm being heard." "I" statements communicate: I know what I feel and think (kind of), but since I'm not God, I won't judge you.

KEY SPEAKING PRINCIPLE #2:
AFFIRM THE PERSON AND POSITIVE OUTCOME

"Reckless words pierce like a sword, but the tongue of the wise brings healing" (Proverbs 12:18). As you speak truth, remember your words have power — to harm or heal. Start with how you feel, and do all you can to say positive, affirming things about the other person, your friendship, and the positive outcome you hope will result from talking about the issue. Give them the benefit of the doubt.

Even if someone has sinned against you, Jesus said the goal is to win back that relationship. You do that by striving to be other-centered. Pride will say, "Don't give in . . . he doesn't deserve anything positive! Make him hurt!" Humble yourself before God and ask him to help you affirm the person and potential outcome.

Once I went on a four-day planning retreat with the staff I worked with at a former job. We were out at a secluded little house on a lake. The afternoon of the first day, we were sitting outside talking before dinner, and I had an idea I was really excited about. I wanted to run it by a senior coworker I really respected to get his thoughts. When the conversation died down, I started telling him about my great idea. He fired several questions at me, and I defended my idea. Still, he disagreed with my approach. About then, we were called in to dinner. As he walked past me, he said, "Well, I'm glad I'm not you, because I'd feel really screwed up right now," and then he walked inside.

I was boiling! I didn't want to sit through that dinner. As everyone sat there laughing and joking, I tried to force a plasticky smile to hide my anger. I thought, "What a jerk — how could he be so flippant? He claims to follow Christ. Why did he do that?" I was deeply hurt. For the next two days, the cancer of unresolved conflict grew within me.

I knew I needed to say something, but instead, I punished him mentally. I fantasized about implementing my idea. But after I'd indulged in these punishing schemes for a while, I came to my senses and thought, "What's that all about? That's not from God." Yet my pain wouldn't go away.

All weekend I had to be around him, but emotionally I was avoiding him at every turn. I'd find ways not to be near him, and I'd avoid eye contact for fear that my eyes might betray my hurt and anger. I just wanted out of there! It felt easier to run, to mentally throw chairs, than to follow God's Spirit into courageous confrontation outlined in Matthew 18.

On the final day of the retreat, it was announced that we were going to do a team-building exercise in which we paired up with each team member to share what we need from that person to effectively do our jobs. "Oh, great," I thought, "I've got to sit down face to face with this guy. I can't fake it. I've got to confront it. Lord, I need your help!"

Before sitting down, I prayed through the principles discussed in this chapter, and I asked God for guidance. I told my friend, "Before we do this exercise, I need to talk to you about something. When you said, 'I'd feel really screwed up if I were you,' I was really hurt. And I don't want to carry this hurt and anger around any longer, because I respect you. So can we talk about it so that we can continue to be friends?"

He apologized for being cynical and coming at me sideways rather than telling me directly what was on his mind. It turned out, I had hurt him by something I had done, and that unresolved hurt had driven him to make his comments. We both apologized and affirmed one another. It was a God-moment. It unified us, but it could easily have driven a wedge between us.

COMPROMISE OR INTERVENTION

Even after you humbly listen and speak in ways that allow for true understanding, you still may not agree. For instance, you may fully understand that your wife thinks you should parent one way, while you still think you should parent another. Or your husband thinks you should take the big risk and bet the company, and you think slow growth with no debt is the right path. You just disagree. In those cases, you need to remind yourself that every relationship requires compromise.

If it's not an issue of sin, we must be willing to humbly lay down our rights, our preferences, and our desires to find a middle ground. Jesus laid down his life for you — that's love. Sometimes God's Spirit will lead us to lay down our positions, our rights, our preferences for the sake of the relationship. God will never lead us to compromise our morals, our standards, or our integrity, but in matters of preference, compromise is necessary.

If it's a clear sin-issue and that person is unwilling to reconcile, change, or get help, however, Jesus goes on to say in Matthew 18 that you take it up a notch. You do an intervention by finding one or two other people, preferably people the offender respects and trusts, and you confront him again with why this is against God's will in the Scriptures. (This assumes the person claims to be following Christ.)

If, after the intervention, the person is still unwilling to change, you ask the church leadership to get involved. The intent of all this is to restore this person into healthy relating patterns with God, himself, and others. If the hardheartedness persists, though, then you must assume this person is not truly following Christ, so don't expect anything (treat him as someone who doesn't follow God, Jesus says). Protect yourself by drawing reasonable boundaries; you've done all you can to live at peace.

So when you find yourself in conflict, determine if it's a preference issue or a sin issue, and go talk in private. As you go, humble yourself to respond to God's Spirit, listen to understand, speak truth in love, be willing to compromise if it's a preference, or take it up a notch if it's sin and you're getting no response. When you are in the ring of conflict and emotion is heating up, ask yourself, "What is it that I'm fighting for?" The answer is: the relationship! Respond to God's Spirit and fight with truth and love.

THE 60·60 EXPERIMENT

Jesus made it clear that we will sin against each other, but he wants to teach us to live relationally clean. He doesn't want to let walls of unresolved conflict or hurt divide us. His will is our unity. But following Matthew 18 and living clean consistently challenges the most seasoned Christ-follower. Use this experiment as a time to radically do what Jesus says, and you'll be amazed at the powerful new ways of relating that will grow naturally.

1. **Don't grow 60-60 weary.** Now's the time when many start to fade and go back to old habits of ignoring God most of the day. God really honors perseverance, so stay mindful, talking over every thought, every emotional reaction, every work challenge, every daily need, and stay responsive. Remember, "No

discipline seems pleasant at the time, but painful. Later on, however, it produces a harvest of righteousness and peace for those who have been trained by it" (Hebrews 12:11).

2. **Make a plan**. If you made a list of people you can't look in the eye and say, "All is clean between us," ask God which person you should first make amends with. Then pray for wisdom and write down a plan to go and pursue peace. Consider the principles in this chapter of listening and responding. Share your plan with your Spiritual Running Partner(s) and ask for feedback.

3. **Go direct with God**. As you stay connected and responsive, ask for courage and the right timing to go direct. Seek to make amends with one person on your list. Debrief with your Spiritual Running Partner(s).

4. **Journal and blog**. Write down what you learn through this experience, and make plans to keep following the Spirit until all amends have been made. Then keep living at peace following the Spirit. Blog to share insights with others. (*www.Soul revolution.net*)

PART 4

BUILDING CHARACTER

Reformation 1—
HOW PEOPLE REALLY CHANGE

The warmth of the summer sun mixed with the sounds and smells of the Mercado, triggering memories of the past. "Reynosa, Mexico! I can't believe I'm back here with a church group!" Jeremy flashed back to the many times he had come to Reynosa to party, get crazy with his friends and whomever they'd met, and stock his bar until the next trip. As he looked out over the Mercado now, he could see those memories through new spiritual lenses.

"Even in my most self-absorbed frenzy of lustful drunkenness, I always got a sense of deep despair and desolation when I would wander a block from the town square. But I just hardened my heart and ignored the hurting of others," Jeremy recalled. "That's why I'm here."

Jeremy had opened his heart to Christ at age fourteen, but he never learned to follow Christ. For decades, he walked away, turning down every path under the sun that promised fun. He started coming to Gateway Church at the invitation of a friend. But years of living for the next high, the next buzz, the next thrill, the next lustful encounter did not just go away by sitting in a church service. Still, the hope of truly feeling close to God again inspired Jeremy, and in his heart he was searching for ways to get back in tune with God's Spirit.

Sitting in church one Sunday, he heard an announcement about a Gateway Compassion trip to Reynosa — to serve a local church and an orphanage ministering to kids in Mexico. "You called me out that morning, Lord," Jeremy reminisced as he walked with his new friends through the Mercado, praying for the people they passed. "It was your gloves-off, face-slap kind of challenge issued directly to my heart — I would go back to Reynosa and give something back.

I would go to give, not just to take. So here I am God, but I have no idea what I have to offer. What can I do, Lord?"

Jeremy's confirmation to go felt like nothing short of a miracle. After deciding he would go to Mexico to serve, he knew instantly he had a problem. His twenty-five-year addiction to nicotine would not allow him even one day of freedom without "wigging out" from withdrawal symptoms. He knew this too was God's Spirit calling him out. He declared his last cigarette, stated matter-of-factly to God that he was not strong enough to quit, and issued a challenge back to God: "If you want me to go to Mexico, you have to take this addiction from me."

"Wow," Jeremy thought as they passed a fruit stand manned by a guy puffing on a cigarette, "no cravings, no withdrawal symptoms, no patch, and I haven't had a cigarette since that moment of turning it over to you, God. You truly set me free! So here I am, in Reynosa, and I'm willing. I have no real idea why I'm here, but I'm here and willing. And I'm willingly ignorant!" Jeremy laughed as he thought about it.

He spent the week doing building projects for a local church, playing and talking with the kids in the orphanage and juvenile detention center, and praying for people. As teams went out to serve in different areas, one team would take three-hour shifts praying for the other teams and those they were serving. During Jeremy's prayer shift, something broke through his hardened heart, and he found himself weeping as he prayed for Reynosa — realizing the troubles and evils of life that plague so many people and this new understanding that Jesus longs to set us all free. God was doing something new in Jeremy.

At the nightly debrief of the day's events, the team that had prayed for Jeremy's team mentioned that several of them had "10 percent" stick in their minds as they prayed. One person actually wrote down "the last 10 percent." They shared this with Jeremy's team saying, "We don't honestly know what the '10 percent' is about," but Jeremy's heart started pounding.

Jeremy knew exactly and immediately what the 10 percent was about. He felt shocked and scared and amazed all at once at how clearly it all came to him. "The 10 percent is what I'm holding back from the Lord," Jeremy thought to himself. "It's my last 10 percent I haven't been willing to submit to God: my struggle with a twenty-year habit of smoking pot, and my struggle with lust." It scared him to even admit it to himself because these were his dirty, dark secrets he even tried to hide from God, yet suddenly the light shined into his conscience, and he knew there was nothing he could hide.

Several days later, Jeremy gathered with the group before breakfast to spiritually prepare for the day. He had hurt his knee playing ball with the boys in the detention center the day before and found he couldn't concentrate on anything the leader was saying — the pain distracted him from praying, and it angered him. Suddenly, it dawned on him how this simple little pain in his knee could block his ability to listen, pray, and focus on anything else — and it was killing his joy. In that moment, the thought came to his mind, "You must give up your last 10 percent to really hear me and follow me." Jeremy began to weep, realizing God's Spirit had revealed what he needed to.do, and God was patiently waiting for Jeremy's decision.

"I need to say something," Jeremy's voice cut off the team leader's. "I know what the last 10 percent is about. God's calling me to let go of something that's blocking his Spirit, blocking my joy, and deafening my ears to hearing his guidance. For over twenty years, I've smoked pot almost daily, and I've allowed lustful thoughts to control my mind. I'm ready to let them go." As Jeremy confessed, he felt a burden lift and a peace come over him — just as he did when he gave up cigarettes. The group circled around in encouragement and support and prayed for his freedom.

The rest of the week, Jeremy felt free like he never had before. But on the way back, even before the van crossed the Mexican border, those old feelings started poking at him. He felt rushed, impatient; he snapped at a team member, cussed, a lustful thought crept in. At a gas stop, Jeremy got out of the van and walked to clear his head. He noticed a man sitting on a brick wall with his head down. Feeling prompted to go see if he was okay, Jeremy touched the man on the shoulder. He flinched and sat up straight. On the man's shirt was a picture of Jesus on the cross with the words, *Vaya Con Dios*, "Go with God," written above it. In that moment, Jeremy felt his spiritual tanks refueled as he realized the message was for him. He realized, "I'm not going to win this battle alone; I must go with God."

More than a year later, I ran into Jeremy in the hallway at church. He had told our whole church his story of God leading him to give up pot. He had become involved with our Compassion ministry, serving the homeless in Austin, going on serving trips to Mississippi and New Orleans to rebuild after hurricane Katrina. But something had been gnawing at me for a while.

In a meeting several months before, I heard Jeremy tell his story to our new director of Compassion Mobilization. He told her God took away cigarette smoking for good. Not knowing about his nicotine addiction, but aware of his pot-smoking past, I wondered why he didn't say "marijuana cigarettes." I figured it was a shame-induced half-truth, saying "cigarette smoking" instead of "pot smoking." That day in the hallway, I asked him the question. As he blushed and began to explain, I realized it was God's Spirit that stuck that nagging question in my mind.

"God did totally remove every urge to smoke cigarettes," Jeremy explained, "but honestly, I'm still struggling once in a while with the other stuff."

"Jeremy, do you have any pot right now?" I asked.

"Not on me, but at home," he admitted.

"Jeremy, you've got to decide right now — will you go the way of Christ or the way of pot? Which way do you want to go? Which master do you want to follow? You've got to decide, and then you must put people and practices in your life to respond to God's Spirit until a new habit is formed within you and you are truly free."

HOW DO PEOPLE REALLY CHANGE?

To his credit, Jeremy drove straight home, flushed the pot, and put people and practices in his life to help him truly be "re-formed" in these areas of addiction to pot and pornography.

But this brings up an important question: How do people really change?

Sometimes God does seem to miraculously remove a behavioral problem, but more often, he leads us in ways that force us to grow up, to become spiritually stronger, that require our willing cooperation in a more relational, daily way. I'm convinced that if God simply removed the behaviors, we would soon turn back to the same beliefs or practices that formed those behaviors. We'd be no better off than before. Instead, God leads us down a path of growth that deals with the inner disease of constant disconnection from God (sin), not just the outward symptoms.

Maybe over the past few weeks, as you've experimented with a radical willingness to follow God and love people, God's Spirit has pointed out an area in which you need growth. Maybe you've caught a glimpse of a fuller, freer life, but you also see things that need to change. Until now, you may have had good intentions to change those old, nasty habits or the way you relate to your family and friends or the way you habitually react. But how do we really change in life-giving ways? How can peace replace anxiety, and kindness replace sarcasm in a way that flows out from us naturally? We have to do more than break old habits; we have to become life-giving people.

In chapter 3, we talked about how simple spiritual growth is; by staying connected to God's Spirit, God causes growth in us. So critical is this concept that we find reminders throughout the New Testament. Paul puts it in gardening terms:

> *I planted the seed, Apollos watered it, but God has been making it grow. So neither the one who plants nor the one who waters is anything, but only God, who makes things grow. The one who plants and the one who waters have one purpose, and they will each be rewarded according to their own labor. For we are God's co-workers; you are God's field. (1 Corinthians 3:6 – 9)*

How do people change? *God* causes the growth! I can't emphasize this enough. If you try to change yourself or another person — someone's gonna get hurt! Everyone will be frustrated. Only God can grow us into who he intended us to be.

You may say, "Well, if God causes the growth, then why doesn't he grow and change more people?" The answer is this: God needs our willingness. He needs us to stay connected, open to do his will in our moments of struggle, and this is precisely where we need to help each other.

Notice the passage says we *do* have a role to play! We are God's coworkers in this growth. What's our job? We're the soil, the environment. Think about a garden. You don't cause tomatoes to grow, do you? But if you don't create the right environment — fertile soil, proper sunlight, and so on — you won't eat tasty tomatoes in your salad.

The same is true for spiritual growth. We cannot overcome bad habits, sin patterns, and addictions by ourselves, but we can create the right environment where God can cause the growth.

We can help in the process in two primary ways: (1) by creating the right relational environment, fertilizing the soil with grace and truth (this chapter); and (2) by putting Intentional Practices in place that allow God to grow us up especially in our weakest places (as we'll explain in chapters 11 – 12). Here's the model:

Spiritual growth happens as we stay connected to God's Spirit by:

1. Spiritually *Running Together* with Grace and Truth (this chapter)
2. Putting *Intentional Practices* in Place to Help Us Respond to God in an Area of Growth (chapters 11-12).

RUNNING TOGETHER

Team Hoyt is a father-son team that does marathons and triathlons together. What's amazing is that the son, Rick Hoyt, can't walk, and the father, Dick Hoyt, wasn't motivated to run, bike, or swim. An accident at birth confined Rick to a wheelchair for life. When Dick discovered that his son wanted to compete in races, he found the motivation for them to run together, with Dick pushing Rick in his wheelchair for the past twenty-five years. Team Hoyt has competed in 65 marathons, 216 triathlons, 6 Ironman races, run and biked across America, and brought awareness, value, and opportunity to physically challenged people worldwide. They have accomplished things together that neither alone would have been able to do.

We too accomplish more by spiritually running together than we could ever accomplish alone in this race of life. Because spiritual growth is relational, grace-giving relationship is the soil needed most. In fact, God chooses to use us in each other's lives in the healing, forming process by demonstrating his grace to one another.

There's a story in Scripture about four men who brought their paralyzed friend to Jesus. The paralyzed man had long been confined to a mat When his four friends heard that Jesus was in town, they carried their friend on his mat to the house where Jesus was staying, but the crowd pouring out of the house would not permit them access. Mark tells us, "Since they could not get him to Jesus because of the crowd, they made an opening in the roof above Jesus by digging through it and then lowered the mat the man was lying on. When Jesus *saw their faith*, he said to the paralyzed man, 'Son, your sins are forgiven'" (Mark 2:4 – 5, italics mine).

Rather than removing the paralysis immediately, Jesus began with what the paralytic needed most — the removal of the barrier between the paralytic and God. Jesus provided soul healing — forgiveness. The religious leaders protested that Jesus was taking the authority of God, for God alone can forgive sins, but Jesus replies that he has the power to heal the whole person, and to prove it he tells the paralytic to get up and walk home. The man walks and everyone is amazed.

What often gets overlooked in this story is that the man would never have been healed without his friends! Jesus sees *their faith*, the text says, and heals the man. John Ortberg points out that we all have mats (things that hold us back from becoming all God intended), and therefore we all need friends who will pick up our mat and carry us to Jesus. And we need to be that kind of friend for others.

That is the power of running together. That is the soil God uses to grow people.

Early on in this 60-60 Experiment, I asked you to find one or two people (Spiritual Running Partners) to meet with every week during this 60-60 and to risk a new way of relating. As you meet together, the goal is to motivate, encourage, and support each other to stay connected in the one area where God's prompting you to grow. Let's look at how to create the soil, or environment, in any group so God can cause the growth.

ACCEPT AND ENCOURAGE

When you meet, use the Spiritual Running Partner's card (below) to help you create the soil of growth. Read over the "Rules" of Running together as a reminder of the soil of grace and truth needed for growth: Accept and encourage each other as often as possible. "Encourage one another daily, as long as it is called 'today,' so that none of you may be hardened by sin's deceitfulness" (Hebrews 3:13). The soil of encouragement and hope gives us the ability to face our sinful patterns, knowing we're not alone, providing hope to become more. Without this encouragement, we often give up and give in to the lie of finding life apart from God's ways.

"RULES" OF RUNNING

Accept and give encouragement as often as possible.

Ask questions often; give advice only with permission.

Give reproof or correction only when absolutely necessary.

Never give judgment.

Always protect confidentiality.

NEXT-STEP RESOURCES

Find resources for taking your next step at

www.Soulrevolution.net

RUNNING PARTNER QUESTIONS

1. What do you think God is trying to do in your life right now?
   - How have you experienced the Fruit of the Spirit lately? (love, joy, peace, patience, self-control, etc. Galatians 5:22)
   - How have you treated those you do life with?
   - What sin have you been conscious of this week?
2. If there's an area you need to focus on to better love God, love people, build character, or build Christ's Church, what would it be?
3. What's one thing you will intentionally do to take steps of growth?
4. Have you said the "last 10%" or have you held back today?

ASK QUESTIONS OFTEN

Ask questions often, but in addition, you should give advice *only* when asked for it. What we need most from each other is not advice, as valuable as it can be. Like the paralytic's friends, what we need most is to help each other get to Jesus, who alone can heal us and help us grow. If we will simply slow down and help each other listen with a willing, open heart to what the Spirit of God is trying to do in our lives, we will hear. Questions force us to reflect on our actions, and they help adults take responsibility for their own growth. Discussing the questions listed on the right side of the Running Partner's card can do wonders in the soil of grace.

GIVE REPROOF ONLY WHEN NECESSARY

Listening and asking questions can produce growth as we run together. But sometimes our friends just can't get there without hard truth, what is sometimes called "reproof." Like the guy on the mat, we all need friends to carry us to the One who can heal us, but if we are spiritually blinded and even thought-provoking questions don't help us see, we need someone to tell us plainly the dangers we're walking into.

Our culture defines love as, "Don't intervene. Whatever path a person sincerely chooses is right for him. There's no right or wrong way." But if you saw a blind person walking near the edge of a steep cliff, would it be loving to say, "Whichever way you decide to walk is just fine. Just be sincere"? No! Some paths are truly dangerous and destructive.

At times true friends must speak hard words — not in exasperation or anger, but out of love and desire to walk with the person on the path toward freedom. Scripture says, "Better is open rebuke than hidden love. Wounds from a friend can be trusted, but an enemy multiplies kisses" (Proverbs 27:5 – 6). When speaking truth, we must realize that if our friend does not choose to walk God's way, we can't force her. So we speak truth in love, then we do all we can to bring her to Jesus in prayer, continuing to show the grace and patience God demonstrates to us all.

NEVER JUDGING — ALWAYS CONFIDENTIAL

Jesus told us, "Do not judge, and you will not be judged. Do not condemn, and you will not be condemned. Forgive, and you will be forgiven" (Luke 6:37). Running Partners must learn not to judge or "look down their noses" at someone's repeated offenses. They must remember their job is *not* to fix, heal, or change, but to demonstrate grace as they love and speak truth, bringing one another to the only One who causes growth.

This is different than the classic Christian accountability group model. Author and counselor Henry Cloud points out the flaws of what this kind of "accountability" has come to mean for many: asking each other if they are living up to the standard, offering forgiveness if they've fallen short, then encouraging each other to try harder. Cloud says, "This common evangelical mode of operation is a good picture of the law at work."[1] This style of accountability can expose problems but it doesn't fix them.

What we need instead is a relational "atmosphere" of grace and truth, where we are not condemned, even in failure, and where we hear the truth that we can never become all that God intends just by trying harder. This kind of relationship continually inspires us to deepen our moment-by-moment dependence on God, rather than causing us to fix it for ourselves. It's only through our connection with God that we receive the power to genuinely change.[2]

Creating this grace-truth environment is critical because it's hard to stay connected to God, as the 60-60 Experiment has revealed. Old habits take over, and we're hardly aware that we're falling back into old patterns. Asking ourselves, and others, reflective questions helps us slow down and listen to God's Spirit. God will show us what he's trying to do to shape our character into what he intended, but we must also understand that who we are today evolved from early beliefs that drove us to practices that became habits, forming our character. Can we reverse that process? That is what we will consider next.

THE 60·60 EXPERIMENT

The longer you seek to stay connected to God's Spirit, the more you'll become aware of sinful habits, character defects, and blind spots that get in the way of you fully loving God and people. God wants to reform you into a more life-giving, self-controlled, joy-filled person. He will cause the growth, but we need Spiritual Running Partners to run alongside us and help us stay connected to God who causes the growth. And we need to learn to be this kind of trusted, life-giving person to others.

1. **Notice stuck spots**. As you continue to connect with God throughout the day, think through where you keep getting stuck. What is it that keeps disconnecting you most from the Source of life? Look back over your journal, if you've been keeping one. Do you see patterns? What areas are you avoiding talking with God about because you resist change? What do you fear about change in this area? Talk honestly with God about it and ask for insight and willingness.

2. **Encourage 60-60**. As you are reminded every sixty-minute beep, consider how you can better encourage those around you. Take risks. "Encourage one another daily," Scripture says, so practice it.

3. **Ask questions**. Meet with your Spiritual Running Partner(s) or group, and use the questions on the Spiritual Running Partner's Card (p. 147). Without offering advice or condemnation, practice listening and asking guiding questions to inspire and awaken their desire to yield to God's Spirit (listen for God-prompts as you listen to each other). Discuss a next step you each think God wants you to take, and pray for each other.

CHAPTER ELEVEN

Reformation 2—
TAKING SPIRITUAL INVENTORY

The other day, I was driving to work in heavy traffic while having an intense conversation on my cell phone. Sometimes I take Highway 1, sometimes Burnet Road, depending on traffic. After forty-five minutes, I arrived at the office, snapped the cell phone shut, and realized I'd chosen Burnet without thinking about it! While talking on the phone, in fact, I had stopped for coffee, eaten breakfast while driving, navigated my way from road to road choosing Burnet, steered and accelerated and braked in traffic without hitting anybody, and I hadn't thought about *any* of it! I had been thinking about my forty-five minute conversation — which is a scary thought if everyone else on the road had been doing the same thing!

Most of life is like that. It's lived out of habit — on autopilot.

We have a hard time curing ourselves of bad habits because we lust or overspend or distrust others or lie or feel envious or judgmental — all without thinking. We automatically drink too much or automatically respond with impatience or anger or worry. We respond by habit.

The key to developing deep character is not trying harder. Rather, we must start with our beliefs and practices so that we can form *new* habits that can overcome our autopilot responses.[1] We can focus on *new* beliefs that lead to *new* practices that form *new* habits that keep us *responding to God* who will grow us and change us!

Let's look at how Spiritual Running Partners can help each other do this.

QUESTIONING OUR BELIEFS

"You know, I've never really been at peace." The statement hung in the air as Brett, Rick, and Gary simply listened. The clamor of the restaurant filled the space between my awkward admissions: "I want to love my little girl and my wife. I want to be able to relax and spend time with them, but I feel guilty for just enjoying life with them. For some reason I always have to be accomplishing something or I get anxious."

Why was it so difficult to admit my powerlessness? My lack of peace? Was it because I'd grown up wired to the idea of having to prove my worth, to play the game of life to win, even if it costs me the peace and love and enjoyment of my life? Admitting failure had never been part of my definition of success, and doing so now felt like emotional bungee jumping. And yet, this honest transparency felt sweet to my soul.

It was 1995, and these three men had become like family to me over the course of a few years. Every Tuesday I eagerly anticipated hanging out with my Spiritual Running Partners, experiencing spiritual transparency like never before. As I'd walk into the restaurant from the bitter Chicago cold, my friends' presence somehow gave the place the warmth of a family kitchen. It felt like coming home.

"As I was studying the fruit of the Spirit in Galatians 5," I continued, "I realized I'm not growing in peace — I never have! I live in the future, always needing to climb the next hill, accomplish the next goal; always taking on a little more than is humanly possible. I know enough to realize that I might accomplish a lot in ministry yet destroy my family and God's work in me in the process. I've heard too many horror stories of well-meaning pastors who fell into that trap."

"Well, why don't you start saying no to some things?" Brett asked.

"I can't. I've thought about it, and there's nothing I can cut out right now," I argued.

"Then why don't you feel at peace if you're living as you think God wants you to?" Rick countered.

"Because I have no time for my family, and I can't seem to relax when I'm spending time with them."

"So what do you get out of these other things?" Brett asked. "They must give you something or you wouldn't keep saying yes to them and no to your family. What do they do for you that enjoying time with family doesn't?"

"Nothing," I volleyed back in defense. "But if I don't study for my finals, I'll fail! If I don't do my job, I'll get fired!"

"Who says you have to get a master's degree, much less *two* master's degrees?" Brett pushed on me to force my thinking in a new direction. "So what if you fail? What does that mean?"

"Fail? I'm not going to fail!" I couldn't even conceive of it. The thought of not accomplishing my goals, not succeeding, seemed so foreign that I couldn't even imagine it. It just wasn't possible.

"Well, I think Brett's right," Rick chimed in. "How many times have we had this conversation where you're frustrated and anxious about all you have to do, but you won't say no. You say you hate it, but you keep doing it. You've got to figure out what you think you'll get out of it."

"Seems to me you're frustrated," Brett interjected, "because what you want to value doesn't match how you actually live. Maybe you ought to pray for clarity on why trying to do so much is so important."

Normally, I'd have resented questions like this, but I knew these guys really loved me, and besides, I knew all their junk too! I didn't feel the need to pretend, even about things I did over and over again, because I didn't feel judged or alone. We had all been incredibly honest about all our struggles in living the truths of Scripture, and we had built up a deep reservoir of trust. I knew confidentiality was sacred to them. They cared. They were on my side.

WHAT IS GOD TRYING TO DO IN YOUR LIFE?

Socrates declared that "the unexamined life is not worth living." A regular spiritual inventory is the first order of business for Spiritual Running Partners. It's the prayer of David: "Search me, God, and know my heart; test me and know my anxious thoughts. See if there is any offensive way in me, and lead me in the way everlasting" (Psalm 139:23 – 24). We do this by reflecting on our behaviors, our habits, who we are, and who God wants us to be; then being honest about reality with at least one trusted person. It can be as simple as asking each other, "What's God trying to do in your life right now?" When we slow down, reflect, and listen, it will become obvious.

Growth starts by regularly examining our lives. Of course, most of us lead unexamined lives. Why? Because we fear pain, or we fear facing judgment or condemnation. Again, this is why grace is the foundation for all spiritual growth, a truth that allows us to open our lives before God to face reality and

HIDDEN PAIN

I've been a Christian most of my life. On a compassion trip to Mexico, I was at an orphanage playing with Monica, a little girl whose stepfather could not care for her. She asked me, "Do you ever see your father?" I said, "No, he left when I was young, but I have a wonderful stepfather." Several days later, a group of us were praying together, and several people prayed for the healing of issues with their fathers. Nate said, "We obviously have a father-theme going here." I thought, "Huh, interesting, but it obviously doesn't relate to me." I'd been struggling with a different issue—how to hear God clearly and this idea of forgiving our enemies. Little did I know, they were all related in God's eyes. All my life I had trained myself to ignore my father's rejection so successfully that it didn't bother me at all.... I had no idea of the pain bubbling in my heart. Suddenly all the "father themes" of the past week struck me. I needed to see my father as a person, and to pray for him rather than hate him (like Jesus said we should pray for our enemies). So I prayed for God to show my father truth and love. I thought I was finished, but as the group continued praying, I couldn't hear. A noise in my ears was deafening until I finally cried out, "Okay, okay! It hurts." I confessed to Jesus that it hurt that my father rejected me and never loved me. I admitted that I'd been lying to myself all these years. All the pain and shame came out through my tears as my friends comforted me and reminded me that the most important Father loves me very much ... enough to lead me to this so I can heal. —Kathleen

move forward. But we need Spiritual Running Partners to reflect God's grace so we can bring our real behaviors into the light. Most people don't *experience* God's grace until someone responding to the Spirit shows it.

TASTING THE FRUIT?

One way to do a spiritual inventory is by reflecting on what God is trying to produce in our lives — spiritual fruit. Galatians 5 says,

> So I say, let the Holy Spirit guide your lives. Then you won't be doing what your sinful nature craves. The sinful nature wants to do evil, which is just the opposite of what the Spirit wants.... When you follow the desires of your sinful nature, the results are very clear: sexual immorality, impurity, lustful pleasures,

idolatry, sorcery, hostility, quarreling, jealousy, outbursts of anger, selfish ambi-
tion, dissension, division, envy, drunkenness, wild parties, and other sins like
these. Let me tell you again, as I have before, that anyone living that sort of
life will not inherit the Kingdom of God. But the Holy Spirit produces this kind
of fruit in our lives: love, joy, peace, patience, kindness, goodness, faithfulness,
gentleness, and self-control. (Galatians 5:16 – 17, 19 – 23 NLT)

In other words, we don't have to try hard and change ourselves; we just need to live moment by moment, willing to follow God's Holy Spirit. In time, the old things will pass away and new fruit will grow. As you reflect on that list in Galatians, celebrate with a Running Partner where you see progress. Start by acknowledging your progress. It's vital that we acknowledge and thank God when we find we (or others) have more patience, taste more peace, have stayed sober for ten days, or have grown in other ways. We need to point out the first signs of fruit budding in our lives and others' lives.

Don't skip over this important part of creating the soil for growth. All of us need encouragement that progress is being made, because we all tend to see only what is wrong or needs fixing. If Running Partners fail to take time each meeting to celebrate progress, no matter how small, they will soon give up and give in to sin's deceitful discouragement.

And we need to be honest about the main place of ongoing struggle. Reflect on the fruits of the sinful nature (our old natural way without God) and how they contrast with the fruit God's Spirit promises to grow in us as we stay connected. Since most of these qualities are relational, and spiritual maturity is relational, talk about how you are treating those closest to you. Talk about ongoing sin patterns of which God is making you aware — and then you should be able to discern one main area on which to focus.

FOCUS ON ONE MAIN THING

Too often we get overwhelmed with all the things that need fixing. But remember that God is patient, so we must also be patient with ourselves. When I was just starting to follow Christ, if God had rolled out the list of all the things he needed to change in me over the next decades, it would have been miles long and incredibly discouraging. But he didn't do that. Instead, he took just one or two issues at a time and asked me to focus on letting him do his will in those areas. Step by step, I became more aware of what he intended, and I liked it!

So what's that one main thing God wants *you* to focus on? Tell your Running Partner(s).

When I first started doing this, the one main thing I needed to focus on was my lack of peace, as I described before. Acknowledging my inability to fix this problem by myself, combined with my friends' insightful questions, helped me begin to see root beliefs driving my behavior. Recall that spiritual character is developed by *responding* to God, which is influenced by *habits*, which get formed by *practices*, which emerge from *beliefs*. It all starts with what we believe, which is why my Running Partners' questions about what I really valued, or believed, helped me.

WHAT DO I REALLY BELIEVE?

Jesus said, "If you hold to my teaching, you are really my disciples. Then you will know the truth, and the truth will set you free" (John 8:31 – 32.) If our beliefs are in line with reality according to God (which is truth), our beliefs will lead us toward freedom. But our stated beliefs are not always our actual beliefs. The way to discover what we actually believe is to look at what we actually do: our practices and habits.

Jesus asks a most penetrating question about practices: "Why do you call me, 'Lord, Lord,' and do not do what I say?" (Luke 6:46). It's not what we claim to believe, but what we *do* that reveals our deeply held beliefs. So the first order of business for spiritual growth is to take an inventory not only to celebrate progress, but to identify the one main pattern of our behavioral struggle. Then we need to ask questions and pray for each other. Ask God's Spirit to reveal lies we believe that keep leading us into habitual, broken patterns of behavior. Pray for truth to replace the lies.

A FULL INVENTORY

Kathy and I have this thing about cleaning out the refrigerator. We're good about not wasting food. The only problem is we sometimes don't eat what we save. Then one day we start noticing a foul odor, and we'll wonder where it's coming from. We both know the truth — and know what we need to do. We just don't want to face it. You have to unload everything that could possibly rot, every carton, the fruit drawer, every Tupperware container, opening each one to smell and see if it's the root cause of the odor. If you don't do this, you never get rid of the smell.

In the early days of our marriage, I was the gallant knight who would rescue Kathy from the monstrous-smelling Petri dish lurking in the back of the fridge. But I'm glad to say that we are now becoming a liberated couple, where roles like this one can be easily interchanged with a simple game of Rock, Paper, Scissors. Nobody wants to clean the fridge because it's a pretty unappealing job.

Many people never have the courage to do the dirty work of digging back through the nasty stuff on the dark moral shelves of their existence to find out what keeps causing a stench in their lives. If you don't have the courage to haul it all out, take a full spiritual inventory, and locate the root cause of the smell, it will end up stinking up your life year after year after year. It's only going to get worse. It won't go away on its own. We all have moldy, stinking lies that God's Spirit wants to clean out from our past. For God to do this, we must courageously take a full spiritual inventory. Things that stay hidden have power over us. Things brought into the light can be conquered, and the resulting freedom of living in the light is exhilarating. So I want to challenge you to do what every successful business does when they take inventory, what every successful football team does when they watch game films, what every successful person does when she is serious about lasting spiritual growth.

In the exercise at the end of this chapter, I've included an outline for taking a full spiritual inventory. There are many ways to do this, but these categories I've listed in the outline can be helpful. Sit down with paper and pen, or at a computer, and ask God's Spirit to help you bring everything from your past that was not his will into the light of his grace. Write it all down. This brings the stinking lies underlying toxic or rotten behavior into the light. Only then can God clean them out and replace them with his truth that leads you toward the life you've wanted.

As you write, confess each one to him. Admit it and face it in the light of his forgiveness, asking him to remove it. Then take your written inventory and read it to your Spiritual Running Partner (or whomever you trust most to demonstrate God's grace and love without judgment). If you will find the courage to do this for one another, you will be amazed at the release, the joy, the peace, and the hope for new life you will experience.

WHY MUST I TELL A RUNNING PARTNER?

Civil War historian James McPherson writes about a plantation owner named James Hammond, who served as both congressman and governor. Besides being insatiably ambitious and an ardent defender of slavery, Hammond also indulged a voracious sexual appetite. In 1839 he purchased an eighteen-year-old slave named Sally and her infant daughter, Louisa. He made Sally his concubine and fathered several children by her; then when Louisa reached the age of twelve, he installed her in her mother's old role and fathered several more children. His political career was halted — but only temporarily — when his wealthy brother-in-law, Wade Hamilton, threatened to reveal publicly that Hammond had been sexually abusing Hamilton's four daughters, ages thirteen to eighteen. Most remarkable, though, are Hammond's own reflections made in his diary after his wife left him and epidemics took the lives of many of his slaves and livestock: "It crushes me to the earth to see everything of mine so blasted around me. Negroes, cattle, mules, hogs, everything that has life around me seems to labour under some fated malediction.... Great God, what have I done? Never was a man so cursed.... What have I done or omitted to do to deserve this fate?"[2] How about *denial*? It's so pervasive and deceptive, we can damage ourselves and others and not even see it. All of us are capable of this spiritual blindness.

Without a doubt, telling another person about our deepest, darkest secret, our ongoing struggles, our hypocritical behavior, or our sin patterns is probably the hardest thing to do in this 60-60 Experiment — but it's the most important! Most likely you'll find yourself making excuses: "Why can't I just confess to God?" "What good will it do to air my junk to another person?" "My stuff is no big deal — it's not worth talking about." Or "My sins are so horrible, no one can handle them." All our excuses are part of the denial mechanism that keeps us stuck, and this is *exactly* why Scripture says, "Confess your sins to each other and pray for each other *so that* you may be healed" (James 5:16, italics mine)

Darrin set his sixth beer down on a nearby table and looked out from his back patio across the beauty of the rolling hills; but he saw nothing beautiful in life. "God, this just isn't working. I feel empty and emotionally bankrupt. I need help." Two divorces, losing connection with his kids, and the pressure of managing a sixty-million-dollar high-tech operation led Darrin to a habit of nightly "relaxing with a few beers." The truth is, Darrin started drinking at age sixteen and quickly developed a daily habit that escalated over the next two decades. Darrin explains the power of confessing all:

No sooner had I prayed that prayer than a good friend of mine invited me to this new church he'd found. Once I started going to Gateway, I found a spark coming back into my life. I did the Investigating the Way of Christ study, and I became intrigued with the idea that Jesus really lived. I had no idea. Then to consider the possibility that he was Messiah—it was unbelievable. I'd been so naïve about the whole thing. The more I studied, the more convinced I became.

Back on the same back patio, I opened my heart to Christ's forgiveness and asked him to come lead me. I read the New Testament and other books, and I started turning things over to God. I got baptized and joined a small group, and my life was starting to hit on all cylinders. I felt huge worries and anxieties at work, but as I turned them over to God, I found peace and saw tangible evidence that God was working if I was willing. This experience of turning things over and seeing God meet me felt like a world of heaviness lifted off my shoulders.

Part of this Investigating the Way of Christ involved sitting down with another person and talking about your spiritual assessment of where you've been and whether you really want to follow the way of Christ. I was not fully honest with Gary about my drinking. I told him I sometimes drank too much. He asked the hard questions, but I wasn't honest.

About a year later, Kenny invited me into a more intensive men's group. But I saw it had a moral code I couldn't sign because I drank every night. I had no desire to quit drinking. Kenny asked how much I drank, but again I wasn't really honest. Pride kept me wanting to hang onto it. "I'm in control—I can handle it."

I'd lie to myself so much. I'd leave church and go pick up a six-pack and say, "I can just have one." But once the first was opened, they were all as good as gone. I'd rationalize, "I've never had a DWI; it's never been a problem at work." I was just lucky.

I didn't want to quit drinking, but, one night I finally told God, "If I gotta quit drinking, show me a sign or help me learn to drink responsibly." The next Sunday, my Gateway serving team had a lunch. Somehow the conversation turned to drinking, and the woman hosting the lunch said to the group, "There's nothing wrong with drinking, but if you're getting drunk, then you're turning away from God, and you can't have a relationship with God drunk."

I was quiet as mouse. I was getting drunk every night (though I was a very functional alcoholic), and my relationship with God mattered. The next few weeks, I started going through all the Scriptures about drinking. It was painting a very bleak picture for me, but I still wasn't ready to quit. I always told myself I'd "stop tomorrow." But little by little my denial got chipped away.

My thirteen-year-old daughter stayed with me that summer. She confronted me: "Dad, I just wish you wouldn't drink so much." Nothing matters more to me than my kids. This all happened within a couple months of saying, "God if I need to quit, give me a sign." I made a mental commitment to not drink so much around her, and I found myself sneaking around her to get a drink. I caught a glimpse of my true behavior pattern.

When I prayed to God, he led me to people and circumstances that showed me I needed to stop. I got what I prayed for, but now I realized I couldn't stop. That same month, our church did a 60-60 Experiment, during which I became much more aware of God's presence and guidance. I knew about his grace, but I still didn't experience it fully. As I stayed willing, it became clear to me that I had a problem. I had an ongoing prompting to go to Gateway's recovery meeting and tell someone.

One day in our worship service, we had a silent meditation talking to God. I told him, "I don't know what to do." I was arguing in my head. I thought, "I should go to the recovery group and admit this." But I'd hear, "You can still limit it. I'm sure if you just made a commitment, you could stop on your own." A spiritual battle raged in my mind. But a strong thought kept whispering, "Just go, just go."

That Monday night, I admitted my addiction to another person for the first time. I felt relief and support as the group prayed for me, but as I left that night, panic set in. I remembered the customer I had to see that week in Florida, usually a week full of heavy drinking. The temptation was going to be huge. I remember thinking, "How am I going to pull this off?" Then it hit me between the eyes. So many things I had turned over to God—work pressures, financial pressures—I had seen the positive outcome every time I willingly followed his will. I realized, I don't have to figure it all out! I got people praying for me, I stayed connected and willing to respond moment by moment, and I've been alcohol-free for three years, starting the moment I told that group.

NO DENYING IT

We all have an uncanny ability to skim over the surface of things we need to confront directly. We are good at not seeing things for what they are. Jeremiah said, "The heart is deceitful.... Who can understand it?" (Jeremiah 17:9). We can so easily see the wrongs, the blind spots, the character defects of others, but it's hard to look at ourselves courageously.

The purpose of this inventory is to try to see ourselves honestly. Writing everything down puts it all concretely before you and God, and telling one other person makes it real and brings it into the light, so that denial gets broken once and for all. Then we know we're not alone. Then others can pray for us and support us, and we can keep being honest. Will you courageously follow God's Spirit so he can clean out all the moral rot from the past? Will you courageously tell one other person in order to break all denial and bring everything into the light?

Although it took another year of soul searching and spiritual prodding, God used my small group of Spiritual Running Partners to lead me to an awareness of the truth that has set me free in amazing ways. But it only happened because I felt the confidence that they loved me, despite the fact that I kept on doing what I didn't want to do. During a two-day retreat, still feeling like God's Spirit was trying to teach me to live with his peace, I talked openly about my ongoing struggle.

"So think about this," Brett suggested. "Jesus said when you know the truth, it will set you free, right? I think many times when we're stuck and enslaved to destructive patterns, it's because we've believed lies that may be buried deep within from things we learned in our families growing up. What messages did you guys get about your worth or accomplishments growing up?"

"I felt totally built up by my dad and mom," I chimed in. "They believed in me like crazy. My dad really valued work. He'd have me out working in the yard and say things like, 'My son will never be lazy; he'll know the value of a buck.' I think it's because he grew up so destitute in the wake of the Depression." Then something else came to mind. "Growing up in the sixties and seventies, I remember my dad would get visibly angry when he spotted a hippie, and he'd say to me, 'Son, you'll never be a bum like that.' Come to think of it, he said that a lot: 'You'll never be a bum; you know the value of hard work.'"

"Maybe that's a clue," Brett suggested. "Do you feel like you're not worth enough unless you prove something to your dad?"

"No," I said honestly. "I felt totally loved and valued by my dad." It didn't seem to connect at all. I never had to doubt how much my dad loved me and believed in me.

Three months after that conversation, my grandmother on my dad's side passed away. Sitting at my grandmother's old house, talking to my aunt about my grandmother, it hit me that I knew nothing about my grandfather. My father never talked about his father because he hated him so much for abandoning the family. And since my father died when I was a teenager, my aunt was my only connection left to my grandfather. "What was your father like?" I innocently asked my aunt.

A look of intense anger and pain transformed her naturally pleasant face into an expression of long-buried rage. I remembered times when the fleeting shadow of that look darkened the face of my father. Her forceful words hit me like a knockout punch: "He was a bum!"

The phrase reverberated in my head, "He was a bum." *He was a bum.* She had used the exact phrase my dad used with the same boiling anger. Convergence! It was as if God's Spirit had led me down this path, preparing to rip back the curtains of my psyche to show me something so ingrained that I was blind to it: I had lived subconsciously afraid of being a bum. That's why I could never do enough. That's why I could never find peace. I had to prove I wasn't a bum — by doing more and more!

Back home, I told my small group about my discovery. The pain my father's father inflicted on his family through his alcoholism and irresponsibility had somehow transferred through my father's unresolved anger, right into my soul. I didn't understand how, but it made sense. I knew my dad loved me, but would he love me if I became "a bum"? What if I didn't work hard enough? What if I didn't succeed like he thought I would? The problem is that no amount of accomplishment was ever enough. Once I understood the lie I had swallowed, my Spiritual Running Partners helped me begin to purge that hidden fear of failure with God's truth. I experienced a breakthrough to peace and love and enjoyment with my family that has continued to give me a life no amount of accomplishment could ever match.

Creating the rich soil of grace and truth allows us to take a courageous look at our true patterns and behaviors. In this environment of grace, we can help each other reflect on the lies we believe that keep us stuck, as opposed to the truth that God says leads to life. This marks the beginning of authentic change, but not the end. There's still another essential nutrient needed in the soil of our lives to develop strong character — it's the nutrient of Intentionality.

THE 60-60 EXPERIMENT

What stays hidden in the dark has power over us, but what gets brought into the light gets removed. There is an amazing freedom that comes from taking a full spiritual inventory, putting the hidden things down on paper before God, and asking him to remove them (clean out the past rot). But even greater freedom comes when we do what the Scripture says and "confess our sins to one another, that [we] may be healed." Go all out in this experiment, and trust God to protect you as you risk doing a full inventory.

1. **Do a full spiritual inventory**. The goal is to bring everything into God's light so that he can remove the hidden things fully. Take something to write on and find a quiet place to be with God. Pray David's prayer, "Search me, God, and know my heart; test me and know my anxious thoughts. See if there is any offensive way in me, and lead me in the way everlasting" (Psalm 139:23 – 24). Then put these headings listed below on the top of a page and write down anything that comes to mind that you need to confess and ask God to forgive and remove.

   - *Resentments*: People, institutions, and ideas you feel resentment toward. "I resent my father for being harsh and critical." "I resent the government for taking my money."

   - *Fears:* List all the fears you can remember since childhood. Write why you are afraid. "Perfect love casts out all fear," so ask God to show you where you need to trust his unfailing love.

   - *Moral Behaviors:* List all the immoral behaviors you've done against God's will. Ask God to show you, and write down whatever comes to mind (dishonesty, sexual impurity, taking what's not yours or cheating [even on taxes!], hoarding greedily, seeking revenge, and so on.) You could use the Galatians 5:19 – 21 list to reflect.

- *Pride and Selfishness*: Ask God to show you where pride or selfishness has hurt others or separated you from God's ways, causing you to act unloving or hypocritical. (Neglecting responsibility, blaming, boasting, being critical, judgmental, unwilling to compromise or reconsider, consumed with your agenda, and so on.) List whatever comes to mind.

- *Relational/Emotional Struggles*: List all relationships where you've had ongoing emotional struggles. Beside each person's name write the feelings their name calls up (fear, pain, anger, shame, guilt, sadness, envy). Ask God to show you what you need from him to give this over to him and clear out these negative feelings.

2. **Respond to God's Spirit.** The goal of the inventory is to break denial and see our desperate need for God's help in becoming the people we are meant to be. Only as we admit our need and become willing to let him help us will we find his cleansing help available. Thank God for his grace, forgiveness, and unconditional love demonstrated through Christ and receive it—take it in. Ask him to remove all this old, rotten stuff and replace it with his ways. If there's something you don't want to let go of, focus on being willing to let him replace it with something better.

3. **Tell one person.** Find one person you can trust (usually other than a spouse) and simply read everything you've written—confessing all until nothing remains hidden. You will be amazed at the sense of relief and freedom and even joy that God produces as a result. Spiritual Running Partners can do this for each other. If the person has not done this before, explain that you've done this inventory, and you want to confess it like the Scriptures tell us to do. Ask the listener to read these guidelines.

Rules for the Listener:

- *Commit to Complete Confidentiality*—tell the person you will never share this with anyone.

- *Don't Interrupt until They Finish Reading*—don't try to make the person feel better by minimizing or telling him what you've done; just listen and care and empathize. You are not there to fix, change, or play God, so avoid giving advice. You're there to allow him to fully bring this into God's light and let God break all denial and remove the effects of the past.

- *Ask before Giving Feedback*—After she's read the inventory, ask if you can give feedback. Remind her of God's love, grace, and forgiveness. Describe positive feelings you have for the person as a result of her trusting you to listen. Describe what you see her becoming as God forms her into his masterpiece. Then share your own inventory if you've done one, or share from your own life.

This inventory was adapted from Keith Miller's book, *Hunger for Healing*, chapters 5 – 9, which I highly recommend for better understanding this confessing/listening process.

CHAPTER TWELVE

Reorder—
HABIT-BREAKING INTENTIONALITY

Spiritual formation shaped Mother Teresa into a saint and Hitler into a devil. Dallas Willard notes that the formation of the spirit is not optional, it happens to everyone. The only question is "formed into what?"[1]

We all get shaped by outside influences, but we have the power to reorder our lives to be shaped by God. As we said in the last chapter, spiritual growth happens when we stay connected to God's Spirit by spiritually running together with grace and truth, and by putting Intentional Practices in place to help us respond to God in an area of growth. Let's look at how Intentional Practices help us break old habits and grow.

The Scriptures tell us it was for freedom that Christ set us free, but can we really be free following Christ? What would that look like? What if you could look back two to three years from now and be truly free from fears, anxieties, or worries that naturally come out when you get squeezed by life? What if you could be free from bitterness, envy, lust, or comparisons? What if you could be free from fear of rejection or from living for people's approval or from feeling easily hurt or angered? We all desire to become people who experience this kind of life, but when the pressure's on, often we show just the opposite. What comes out when we get squeezed reveals who we are deep inside.

One Sunday I asked our band to stay on stage after I came up to speak. Most of our musicians used to play on Sixth Street (Austin's younger, more rockin' version of Bourbon Street) before they came to faith at Gateway. Now they use their talents to serve God in Gateway's band. J. J. Plasencio, our music director, toured the world with Sixpence None the Richer, the Smithereens, and Plumb.

I told our church, "Today, we're gonna squeeze these musicians and see what oozes out — and you're going to help me. Think of a band, from the sixties through today, and we're gonna see if they can play a song from that band. No random underground bands that sold five albums; pick well-known bands. Shout it out; we'll see what they can do when the pressure's on."

Our church consists mostly of formerly unchurched people, so they were shouting out Green Day, Dave Matthews, the Ramones — whatever band they called out, our musicians cranked out a song — not just the chords, but a full-blown arrangement — we were all amazed.

I asked for a show of hands to see how many people played some kind of musical instrument at some point in life — most raised their hands. "How many of us, when the squeeze is on, could effortlessly make music like that on the spot?" I asked. Only a few hands stayed up. "Why can these musicians so freely and effortlessly make music, and we can't? A lot of intentional practice — right?"

J. J. spent hours learning to position his fingers to make simple chords. At first it felt unnatural, even painful, but eventually it became a habit. All these guys disciplined themselves to practice scales, study theory, and do speed drills, all of which felt forced at first but in time became second nature. Now, in terms of music, they are truly free.

SPIRITUAL FREEDOM

Paul says, "It is for freedom that Christ has set us free. Stand firm, then, and do not let yourselves be burdened again by a yoke of slavery" (Galatians 5:1).

So how do we become spiritually free? It starts by understanding that "free" is a relative term. You can be free to do drugs or drink as much alcohol as you can consume, but you may not be free to live without it or the consequences of mistakes you made when you weren't free to think clearly. You are free to smoke, but you may not be free to stop — and you may not be free of cancer. You can be free to have sex with whomever you want, but you may find you aren't free from STDs, unplanned pregnancy, or painful, soul-tearing breakups. You're free to lust after whatever you want to look at, but you may find you aren't free to experience a deep, trusting, contented love with one person. You may be free to lie and cheat in business to get ahead, but you may not be free of the fear of being caught or the consequences if you are caught. Freedom is a relative term.

WHO WILL SET ME FREE?

I always thought my husband and I had a solid marriage, until the day I discovered his six-year history of seeing "escorts," a nice term for prostitutes. It was a hidden life that no one suspected—especially me. When he told me the whole story, he wept uncontrollably and told me how empty and alone he had felt. He begged me to stay. For the sake of my children, I tried, but my soul was an open wound. I would cry all day until it came time to pick up the children from school. We needed healing. We got into counseling, and I asked my husband to go to church with me, though I knew how opposed he was to Christian churches in the past. Willing to do anything to save our marriage, he came to Gateway. From the moment the music started, I knew we had found a place of rest in my unbearable storm. The lyrics of the first song spoke of how God is with you in your darkest day. I cried as I felt those words pierce me to the core. The message talked about coming as you are, but not staying that way, rather becoming the person God intended. Tears rolled down my husband's face as he saw hope for a brighter day. We both knew that was no coincidence. Leaving church that day, we no longer felt alone.

It's been a year, and from the depths of my pain has come hope. My husband and I are both in therapy, each learning to take responsibility for

So what kind of freedom does God want for you? He wants you to be

free to do the things that lead to a fulfilling, purposeful life
free to love deeply in a lasting, content way
free to experience peace and joy and self control
free to live life wide open, unafraid to take risks

But how does that happen? Over and over again Scripture tells us that God causes this growth and that our only job — the only thing we need to do — is to stay connected. As mentioned earlier, creating the right soil, the environment, where we can best stay connected is critical, and it starts with grace-filled, authentic relationships that help us reflect and discern the one main thing God's Spirit is trying to do in our lives. But then we need practices — that is, exercises and disciplines — that help us stay connected and responsive to God's Spirit in those moments when our habitual responses threaten to take over.

ourselves. My husband has learned to understand how his thoughts, emotions, and unwillingness to work through resentments fueled his sexual addiction. The emotional and physical abuse of his childhood sowed lies deep within that kept him desperately needy. His compulsion to act out sexually came from a desire to escape pain and the stresses of marriage and family life. Through his newfound faith and connection to God, he's learning to love himself as God does despite the shameful acts of the past. My husband has truly changed. The man I'm married to today is a better person than he has ever been before.

He recently wrote in a letter to me, "I turned away from you and our love. I withdrew and turned to a part of myself (an evil part) that I never realized was within me. I am ashamed and truly sorry. I betrayed our marriage. I won't go into the sadness and pain of those dark days, but I will say how grateful I am to still be with you and the kids. I have learned from our time in church that through these struggles God speaks to us if we will listen. I truly believe that by God's grace, I have been given a chance to redeem my soul and make my life right with God and you. I have stepped out of the darkness and into God's light. I pledge my life to love and cherish you as God has always intended." —Sarah

Remember, spiritual character is developed by *responding* to God, which is influenced by *habits*, which get formed by *practices*, which emerge from *beliefs*. So the key to deep character development is to interrupt those autopilot responses with new beliefs and practices, so we can respond to the Spirit and allow God to grow us up in that area. That's why we need Intentional Practices .

THE SIN CYCLE

Most of us get stuck in habits and patterns we want to be rid of. If we could wave a magic wand and make them go away, we would, right? But try as we might, nothing seems to help. Why? Because we're not *intentional* enough about making ourselves available to God in the *critical* moments.

Let me take you on a quick theological tour of Romans 7 and 8 to see how we get unstuck. Think for a moment about one of your bad habits that you know you need to stop. You may be impatient or easily angered. Perhaps you drink too much or too often, are constantly stressed out, or struggle with impulsive lust or envy. We've all got bad habits. Think of one.

In Romans 7, Paul talks about the struggle we feel when we try to change without God's help. Here's his color commentary: "I do not understand what I do. For what I want to do I do not do, but what I hate I do.... For what I do is not the good I want to do; no, the evil I do not want to do — this I keep on doing" (Romans 7:15, 19 NIV). Can you relate to that? Have you ever vowed to "stop doing something" or "be better next time," only to find yourself doing it again without flinching? It's become a habit.

You know how it works. You constantly vow, "I'm gonna break the habit this time," but in your own power, you can't do it. You fail again and again. Then you get into a cycle of guilt and shame — beating yourself up over it, vowing to try harder next time, and when you fail again, you sink even lower, feeling a greater weight of condemnation heaped upon you. We go around and around and around, until finally, some of us just give up. We give up on God because we mistakenly think he's the one heaping guilt, shame, and condemnation on us while we try harder and harder only to fall harder the next time around.

But look at what else Paul says, "Now if I do what I do not want to do, it is *no longer I who do it*, but it is sin living in me that does it" (Romans 7:20, italics mine). This is profound! Basically Paul is saying, "Stop beating yourself up!" Instead, beat up on your sin-propensity. If you desire to do what you know God wants you to do but still don't do it, then it's not you doing it, is it? It's something else inside of you. Confused?

What Paul is saying is that we all have this sin nature that is not a part of who God intended us to be — we inherited it. We all developed the habit of living mostly on our own, disconnected from God in a fallen world. We respond to this inherited tendency of humanity to go our way instead of God's way. That's what sin is — going our way instead of God's way — and it's habitual for us. It keeps us from doing life with God, the Source of life. So Paul says, "Oh, what a miserable person I am! Who will free me from this life that is dominated by sin and death? Thank God! The answer is in Jesus Christ our Lord" (Romans 7:24 – 25 NLT).

How does Jesus help us when we're in this sin cycle of failure, shame, trying harder, and failing again? Because, as Paul explains, "There is now no condemnation for those who are in Christ Jesus" (Romans 8:1). Through Christ's substitutionary payment for our wrongs God delivers us from condemnation.

If you've told God, "I want what Jesus did to count for me," then it will count. You will not be condemned.

Here's why this is important. Unless God has access to our hearts and minds, we can't grow. God does what he does in Christ, so that if we're willing to receive it, we can know that even as we fail, he doesn't leave us or condemn us. That allows us to open our minds to God's Spirit, even as we are failing and falling — as we get squeezed in life — because that's where we need help the most. God causes the growth. But if we are afraid God condemns us, we will hide from him and fall farther. See it?

Here is where intentionality comes into play: "Those who live according to the sinful nature have their *minds set* on what that nature desires; but those who live in accordance with the Spirit have their *minds set* on what the Spirit desires. The *mind controlled* by the sinful nature is death, but the *mind controlled* by the Spirit is life and peace" (Romans 8:5 – 6, italics mine).

Paul's point is this: it's all about where we set our minds! It's like sailing. The boat and its sails have no power of their own. They are completely dependent on the wind. So what you have to do is set your sails to align with the power of the wind. Every time the situation changes, you have to intentionally adjust your sails to maximize the power of the wind — the wind causes you to move.

If we keep setting the sails of our minds to the old thoughts that lead to old practices and habits, we won't change. If we do not put Intentional Practices in place to reorder our thoughts and

---

THE MIND SET ON SELF

I thought you might be interested in hearing from someone who has *not* been participating in the 60-60. I didn't necessarily decide to not participate; I just didn't feel strongly that I needed to do it. Now, I'm beginning to believe God's using this to remind me that every time I try to handle things on my own, I end up miserable. Instead of focusing on God every sixty minutes, I've spent hours focusing on myself — my loneliness, my depression, my hopelessness, my desperation, and on occasion, my rage. I'm gonna start making an effort to check in with God every sixty minutes — if nothing else, to ask his protection against this mental attack. —Hurting Inside

subsequent responses, we will continue to be people who do the opposite of what we desire. But we have the ability through Christ to grow into the people God intended us to be because God is with us — even in each temptation, and he will grow us up toward life and peace, as we *set our minds* on what he wants hour by hour each day. It's where you set your mind moment by moment that makes the difference.

REORDER ALL OF ME

We are to love God with all our heart, mind, soul, and strength (Mark 12:30) — every aspect of our being. As Dallas Willard points out in his book, *Renovation of the Heart*, this means the will, imagination, thoughts, feelings, and body must all be considered in how we get formed spiritually. Let's take a real life example and see how Intentional Practices can work to reorder the whole person.

Let's say you struggle with lust or envy (two common struggles in our culture). Paul notes they're both natural to our old ways: "We were misled and became slaves to many lusts and pleasures. Our lives were full of evil and envy" (Titus 3:3 NLT). Let's say you find yourself responding automatically to lustful thoughts or behaviors, or you find yourself envious of what others have, or look like, or the position they hold. Consider the "parts" of you that are involved.

MY WILL

The will forms the active response of the heart, or spirit, of a person. What it means to be created in the image of God, in part, relates to this creative will we possess. Like the Creator, we can will things into being. Willard notes that

> The will is the executive center of the human self. From it the whole self or life is meant to be directed and organized.... That is why we recognize the will to be the same as the biblical "heart" or *center*.[2]

The heart, or willingness, constitutes the center of our being from which we choose either God or self. That's why God needs the heart most. "But the LORD said to Samuel ... 'The LORD does not look at the things human beings look at. People look at the outward appearance, but the LORD looks at the heart'" (1 Samuel 16:7).

Before God will do his work in us, he must have our willingness. That's why Jesus asked the man who had been unable to walk for thirty-eight years a question of the will: "Do you want to get well?" (John 5:6). Sometimes the honest answer is "No — not really." As C. S. Lewis points out, sometimes the old nasty Lizard of habitual behaviors, though slowly destroying us, has become like a comfortable companion sitting on our shoulder whispering, "You can't live without me." So we fear freedom. Willingness becomes central to our healing and growth, and so we must be willing to let God slay the Lizard.

The enjoyment of lustful thoughts may actually feel like a friend that comforts you when feeling down or makes you feel alive when bored. For some, there is a genuine fear of letting God slay the Lizard. How will you find pleasure or comfort; how will you feel alive without it? With envy, you may not want to let go of comparison because it's the only way you've known to feel good about yourself. Comparing beauty — or stuff or talents or position — has given you the only measure of worth and value you've known, yet it also created this character of envy.

Jesus said, "My teaching is not my own. It comes from the one who sent me. Anyone who *chooses* [wills] to do the will of God will find out whether my teaching comes from God or whether I speak on my own" (John 7:16 – 17, italics mine). Willingness is the lever God can use to change us, but willpower alone cannot do it.

So let's say you become willing (and wanting) to be free of the lust or envy controlling your heart and mind and actions. But in the moment you get squeezed, you find a barrage of thoughts and feelings cascading like a waterfall into your mind, and your will feels so weak and powerless — you cave in to the old ways almost instantly. That's because habitual thoughts and feelings exert pressure on the will.

Jesus told his followers, "Keep watch and pray, so that you will not give in to temptation. For the spirit is willing, but the body is weak!" (Matthew 26:41 NLT). If our memories are loaded with pornographic thoughts, or we habitually dwell on all we don't have, our will might not have the strength to yield to God. Instead we get washed away in the cascade of thoughts and feelings. And our will often gets confused with our feelings, and we let our feelings override our will. So reordering our willingness to change is the beginning, but thoughts and feelings must also be retrained.

LYNN'S LETTER TO HER ADDICTION

Dear Addiction,

Where oh where do I start? We've been through so much, you and I, to heaven and hell. I've been fooled by you and put faith in your strength instead of the strength of my Creator. In my teens we had some good times. You got me out of my shell. I don't know if I will ever enjoy dancing the way I enjoyed it with you. We were free to not care what people thought. I'm surprised I fell for you, the devil in sheep's clothing. It was you who kept my dad in the bars until the day he died. You that took the father of my child and turned him into a drug-addicted monster before you killed him. I was so desperate to find rest and you told me you could help me. You lied! Oh, how fooled I've been by your deception—the moral lines I crossed when you were in control. Nothing we did together turned out restful—life became more chaotic the longer we were together. I want the dream you promised. The dream of freedom and joy. Only God can make these promises and fulfill them. I was stubborn to believe that you were my best friend, and I will be just as stubborn in my belief that you are the enemy. God has taken the driver's seat from you and he is strong. Where I have failed, he will succeed. So all I have to say to you is, "In the name of Jesus, get behind me." That's where you belong and where you will stay. —Lynn

MY THOUGHTS AND FEELINGS

Thoughts and feelings provide the material for the will to work *within the moment*, but the will can choose to reorder thoughts and feelings (choose to dwell on new beliefs) so that new thoughts and feelings are available for the will to use *in future moments*.[3] That's why Scripture tells us, "Don't just copy the behavior and customs of this world, but let God transform you into a new person *by changing the way you think*. Then you will know what God wants you to do, and you will know how good and pleasing and perfect *his will* really is" (Romans 12:2 NLT, italics mine). We can direct our wills to meditate on new thoughts (setting our minds on thoughts of the Spirit — beliefs based on truth).

For instance, rather than exposing your mind to pornographic images or thinking, "I can look and fantasize and it's no big deal," dwell instead on truthful thoughts. Jesus said the truth is, "Anyone who looks at a woman lustfully has already committed adultery with her in his heart" (Matthew 5:28). It *is* a big deal because it creates the character of sexual discontentment and unfaithfulness. No wrong is committed in the body until it's first conceived in the mind, so is it any wonder that — as some experts say — nearly 40 percent of marriages experience adultery?[4] Our society has trained well for it!

Dwell on truthful thoughts, like: "Lust is not going to give me what I ultimately desire," "I want more than anonymous sex with someone I don't even know or love," "If this lustful fantasy *really* happened, think of how unfulfilling it would be without loving commitment; think of all the possible negative consequences." Think, "I don't want to train myself to be constantly looking and comparing and unable to feel content with one person." Dwell instead on the positive aspects of what you deep down want.

In the case of envy, rather than thinking, "I need that" or "I must have what she/he has," dwell instead on what is true: "Look at the lilies of the field. . . . Solomon in all his glory was not dressed as beautifully as they are. And if God cares so wonderfully for wildflowers that are here today and thrown into the fire tomorrow, he will certainly care for you. . . . Seek the Kingdom of God above all else, and live righteously, and he will give you everything you need" (Matthew 6:28 – 30, 33 NLT). So a new truthful thought is, "I don't need more things to make myself into someone of worth and value. I have enough right now to be fulfilled and content!"

Choosing to meditate on new beliefs retrains the thoughts the next time you get squeezed. But thoughts get closely tied to feelings, and if you're in the habit of responding automatically to feelings (hurt, anger, jealousy, sexual desire), you must put Intentional Practices in place to break that auto-response.

Lucy, whose story you read earlier, realized she had become a slave to her feelings — feelings of anger, or wanting to "feel good" for a minute. These feelings drove her into addictions to drugs, alcohol, and rage. Lucy recalls an Intentional Practice she put in place to retrain her auto-response to these feelings.

One day I heard a phrase that revolutionized how I responded to things: "Do what you don't feel like doing, and don't do what you do feel like doing, and you'll be right most of the time." I realized that "my best thinking got me here," so I needed a new way to think about my reactive feelings. I started doing the opposite of my first instinctual "feeling." I called it the George Castanza principle. In a Seinfeld episode, George realized his life stunk despite his best attempts at making it good, so he started doing the opposite of his first instinct. As I began to be aware of my first instinct, I'd consider the opposite approach.

As I was overcoming a drug addiction, the Intentional Practice of ninety meetings in ninety days [attending a recovery group daily] was critical. But I'd often feel strongly that I didn't want to go. So I'd choose against my desire to take the path of least resistance, because I'd decided in advance to choose the opposite of what I "felt." If I had an issue I needed to tell to my sponsor [who is like a Running Partner], my prideful feelings would resist, so I'd choose against my feelings and tell her. After trying this many times, it was uncanny how well things turned out. Eventually, as I grew in Christ, I found spiritual principles in God's Word that gave more direction than just "do the opposite of what I feel."

As Lucy learned, our feelings can lead us astray when they've been shaped by false beliefs and broken patterns of relating. So we may need Intentional Practices to stop our first response to those feelings of sexual arousal or feelings of jealousy or discontentment.

Just as negative feelings can move us to negative behavior, positive feelings can powerfully propel us in the right direction. The words *emotion* and *motivation* derive from the same root, not just etymologically, but experientially. When we feel strongly in a positive direction, it gives motivation to the will to choose that direction. This is where the imagination comes into play.

MY IMAGINATION

The imagination often gets neglected in the spiritual formation process, yet it has powerfully shaped who we are currently. Beliefs take concrete form in our imaginations (we literally form a picture of what we believe to be true, even if it's false).

When Mindy first came to Gateway, everyone knew she was in trouble. She was anorexic. She weighed about ninety pounds and never ate anything but salad. As I later learned in counseling her, not only did she believe false thoughts ("God thinks I'm a fat slob"), but she had a false image of herself. She would look in a mirror and literally see (through distorted spiritual eyes) someone who looked fat and needed to lose weight, even though she was dangerously close to malnutrition. Imagination is powerful.

Imagination can work for us or against us in spiritual formation. It's a gift from God that brings pictures to mind, either pictures of past memories or pictures of future possibilities. These images then often produce feelings that can motivate or demotivate the will's response to God. For instance, imagination can bring to mind a painful memory of an abusive past. That memory triggers feelings in the present of fear, anxiety, distrust, along with thoughts (often lies about us and God) that have been stored as a result of that unhealed memory. All this interacts to motivate how we feel and think in the present unless we allow God to heal and reorder these memories.

One summer, my wife and I led a project for college students. A girl named Megan, one of the students Kathy got to know, opened up about her struggle with anorexia and suicidal depression. They spent time praying, asking God to reveal to Megan's mind the lies driving the behavior. Once as they prayed together, Megan recalled a memory when she was in kindergarten. Her family was driving somewhere, and Megan got upset and started crying uncontrollably, as five-year-olds sometimes do. Next thing she knew, her father pulled over on the side of the country road, opened the car door and said, "Get out. This will teach you." As a vulnerable five-year-old, she watched in terror as her family drove away to "teach her a lesson." Tears flowed as Megan experienced the gut-wrenching, out-of-control feelings of fear and helplessness *as if it were happening again*, just by recalling the memory. The lie, "You're vulnerable, helpless, out-of-control, not worth keeping" still lived active in her mind attached to that memory.

Kathy encouraged her to replace the lie with the truth about her. "Jesus was there with you," my wife reminded her. "What does he want you to hear and see as the truth?" As she kept praying for truth, Megan pictured Jesus standing with a protective arm around this little five-year-old girl by the roadside. Kathy encouraged Megan to picture the sins of her parents hanging on the cross with Jesus, already paid for so that Megan didn't have to keep paying. As Kathy and Megan prayed through other memories of her abusive childhood that summer, Megan's anorexic struggle and depression began to subside. She found such freedom and healing that the following year she confronted and forgave her parents, which set in motion their change of heart that led to reconciliation and healing. Megan's life changed so dramatically that after graduation, she went into ministry working with kids in the inner city of Chicago, helping other wounded children heal.

Imagination is powerful. It can hide hurtful lies buried in memories, or it can picture the healing truth. Imagination can be used to fuel fantasies that motivate lustful feelings, or it can be used to picture sexual fulfillment in a loving, soulful marital commitment. Imagination can be used to picture ourselves

GIVING MY BODY

I spent nine years in a lesbian relationship, trying to run from what my dad created. My father and I never connected on an intimate level. We had no father/daughter love. He was a minister, and I loved and admired him, but I found myself jealous of the attention he gave his congregation. As I later found out, it wasn't the church that kept my father from drawing close to his daughter; it was his sexual compulsion for women. Over the years, he had nine affairs while married to my mother. When I learned this, it all started to make sense. I battle with opening myself to God (and to men) because of the influence of my father. In my journey back to the Lord, I realized I must heal from the effects of his (and my) sexual decisions. I started with a decision three years ago to give my body back to the Lord to do his will. Since then, God has been amazingly faithful to guide me through emotional and spiritual healing. —Ann

finally possessing what we envy, or it can be used to picture what God already sees: a person already of great worth and value, "given every spiritual blessing, his adopted child, heir to all things" (Romans 8). As you use your imagination, focus on what God says is true about you and what he promises as you follow him. This will produce new feelings of security, contentment, and gratitude that motivate the will's response toward self-control and contentment.

MY BODY

The thoughts and feelings and imagination all work together to help or hinder our will to respond to God. But spiritual formation doesn't only happen inside us, our physical body itself plays a critical role. As Willard explains, the body has a "knowledge of its own." Our willful choices settle into our character and are then "outsourced" to the body to automatically carry out what we keep willfully choosing.[5] That's why I can drive to work, stop, start, and eat, all while paying attention to my cell phone conversation — my body has a built-in knowledge that can bypass my conscious thoughts and will.

Understanding this is critical to forming new habits because our bodies too have been trained by a world that has strayed from God's intended ways.

That's why Paul says, "Do not let any part of your body become an instrument of evil to serve sin. Instead, give yourselves completely to God, for you were dead, but now you have new life. So use your whole body as an instrument to do what is right for the glory of God. Sin is no longer your master, for you no longer live under the requirements of the law. Instead, you live under the freedom of God's grace" (Romans 6:13 – 14 NLT).

That's also why we are told that true worship of God is to "give your bodies to God" as instruments of his will (Romans 12:1 – 2). But we may need Intentional Practices in place to break in and reprogram our body's habitual response to the old nature. Lust causes a physical reaction, which creates a desire for action, but our body's instincts or hungers do not have to control our spirit any longer — God intends it to be the other way around. We literally can tell our body, "No — you don't *have to* have that right now." As we give our bodies to God, and reorder our thoughts, feelings, and will, our bodies will stop controlling us. In time we'll find freedom.

When the body's instincts rule, children get sexually molested by fathers or brothers or uncles who "just can't control themselves." When the tongue has been trained to lash out from feelings of hurt or anger, damaging words flow naturally even though we "didn't mean to say that." But the body can be reprogrammed and held in check so that it once again becomes obedient to the spirit submitted to God's powerful will.

With envy, the eyes can have a force all their own — that automatically looks up and down, sizes up, and compares. But those eyes can be retrained to bounce off the objects of our envy or lust so they look for what we *do have* rather than what we *don't have*.

The body, the will, thoughts, feelings, and imagination all work together in the formation of our character. And Intentional Practices must be used to reorder the old ways we've responded against God's will, so that we can willingly respond to God's Spirit in new ways. Let's put it all together in a spiritual workout.

THE 60·60 EXPERIMENT

God causes the growth as we stay connected to his Spirit. Our job is to yield to him when the moment of temptation beckons, when the temper flairs red hot, when the addiction screams for our attention. These habits only change when we plant ourselves in the soil of Running Partner relationships and put Intentional Practices into place to help us respond to God instead of responding out of habit.

1. **Assess**. What's one main area in your life that's ripe for growth? Read over the "fruit of the Spirit" in Galatians 5:22 (or take the assessment on *www.Soulrevolution.net*) if you need help assessing.

2. **Pay attention to your main growth area**. As you keep doing the 60-60, with every beep of the watch or reminder, think back over the last hour. Ask yourself, "When I disconnected from God's Spirit and gave way to an old sinful habit or character defect, what happened in my body, thoughts, feelings, and will?" Ask God to help you see Intentional Practices you could use to strengthen your will's ability to respond to God next time.

3. **Discuss**. Journal and talk over what your main growth area is with your Running Partner. Discuss how the "parts of you" come into play and consider Intentional Practices that can help you better respond to God in that main growth area.

CHAPTER THIRTEEN

Retrain—
DEVELOPING A SPIRITUAL WORKOUT

A woman wrote me saying,

> Sex and money have been two areas that I've historically avoided thinking about but tend to indulge in until I'm completely overwhelmed. I knew I couldn't live as I was living, but I didn't know what to do about it. In my own insanity, I wanted God to make my wrongs right by giving me what I wanted. After taking your classes on Singles and Sexuality and Financial Freedom, I now have a plan. I know I don't have to do it alone. I'm still learning about God's grace as I go, but I know I can trust God to help me obey. Once I would have run out of the room if I even heard the word "obey," but I now realize following God's will over time is the only way to experience true joy and peace.

All of us need spiritual training before we can actually do God's will. Paul writes to the Corinthians, who lived in the region where the Olympics originated: "All athletes are disciplined in their training. They do it to win a prize that will fade away, but we do it for an eternal prize.... I discipline my body like an athlete, training it to do what it should" (1 Corinthians 9:25, 27 NLT). Like Olympic athletes, we won't succeed in our spiritual contest without time and training.

But here's the problem: we don't *want* it to take time or training. We want the fast-food version of deep character — with a side of fries, please!

Just as musicians and athletes excel in their fields, we can only form deep spiritual character with Intentional Practices. These disciplines train us to stay connected to the Source of life, so that when the squeeze is on instead of doing what we've always done, we respond to God who causes growth. To do this, we need a spiritual workout.

I started going back to the gym a number of years ago when I wanted to get back in shape. I decided to work out before work, but when I arrived at 6:00 a.m. on the first morning, I was blown away. I couldn't find a parking space anywhere! The sun wasn't even up yet, but the gym was packed. Why? Because people see the value of physical exercise. It helps them stay in shape, feel better, look good, and so on. In short, they believe it will bring them a better life.

The Scriptures say, "Train yourself toward godliness. . . . For physical training is of *some* value . . . but godliness (spiritual training) is useful and of value in *everything* and in *every way*, for it holds promise for the present life and also for the life which is to come" (1 Timothy 4:7 – 8 AMP, italics mine). Think about what that last line means: spiritual training benefits us in *this* life *and* the next! What if when you die, your experience of eternal life is determined by the spiritual capacity developed in this life? I don't know if that's what this verse means, but think of the implications!

So let's talk about how to develop a spiritual workout plan. The goal is to put Intentional Practices in our lives to help us better respond to God's Spirit moment by moment. Dallas Willard defines a discipline as "any activity within our power that we engage in to enable us to do what we cannot do by direct effort."[1] God alone grows us into what he intended. These disciplines help us respond with our heart, mind, feelings, and body.

SPIRITUAL CARDIO ROUTINE

Some spiritual exercises are like cardiovascular exercise — they need to be regular and ongoing before they can help your whole self stay spiritually fit. Some examples of spiritual exercises are regular prayer, reading and studying Scripture, and solitude. Other exercises work on strength-building in specific areas of weakness, like rehab exercises work for a damaged knee.

So let's look first at reordering your life with some regular, ongoing spiritual training. Then we'll look at focused strength-building for weak areas needing special attention.

KNOWING GOD'S WILL IN SCRIPTURE

If we don't know God's will, how can we respond to it? If we don't know the truth, how can it set us free? Reading, studying, memorizing, and meditating on Scripture form a basic spiritual cardio exercise that everyone needs in order to be spiritually fit. During different seasons of life, I've had different regular practices in the Scriptures. At first, just reading and considering what it revealed about God, about me, and about life was enough. But I soon realized that there was so much I didn't comprehend. I needed time for more intensive study, which helped me better understand what I read. I even memorized important truths to have them with me always as I battled lies.*

Now, I'm back to a very simple practice of nightly reading through a 365-day Bible. As I read, I ask God's Spirit to highlight anything he wants me to see. I chew on the thoughts that stand out in my mind, asking God to teach me and use the Scriptures as his spiritual mirror to help me see my life and his vision for it.

For instance, you may find it hard to stop worrying and stressing. But you may not even know that worry is not God's will until you read Jesus' command, "Don't worry about these things.... Seek the Kingdom of God ... and he will give you everything you need. So don't worry about tomorrow" (Matthew 6:31, 33 – 34 NLT). Knowing his will, you can write it down and keep it with you. When worry hits, instead of dwelling on it, you can read and meditate on this verse and pray, "God, show me what I can do about this today. Help me give you the worries of tomorrow that I can't do anything about." You can't make yourself stop worrying, but you can do that spiritual exercise. As you train in knowing God's will and interrupting that old response to worry with a new response of seeking God, soon it will feel natural to take wise action, then let go of things you used to worry over incessantly. But first, you must know God's will.

PRAYER

Ideally, prayer should be a turning of our mind toward God's Spirit continually — at every decision, at every interaction, at every choice. But this takes training, because our habit is to ignore God most of our days. We also need focused, regular times to pray. Instead of waking up and just getting sucked up into the whirlwind of the daily schedule, take a few minutes to pray and meditate. You can start by simply letting your first thoughts when you wake up be directed toward God: "God thank you for another day; I give it to you. Help me to listen and do your will each moment today." This sets your trajectory for the day.

---

* Check out *www.Soulrevolution.net* for what God says about what you're facing.

Then find a time and place to talk through the day ahead with God, imagining how it might go, picturing yourself responding to his will in every situation and interaction. This focuses you in a positive way. Tell God how you are feeling: "God, I'm stressed about this decision," "I'm still angry at my boss," "I'm feeling really lonely." Then remind yourself before God of the decision you made (if you did) to turn all aspects of your life — your will, thoughts, feelings, body — over to his care. Let this be a surrendering again if needed. Ask him to show you his will today in each moment, giving you ears to hear his promptings and the strength to respond.

MEDITATION

Meditation is a way of listening more deeply to truth. It is not emptying our minds, but positioning our imaginations to spiritually see and picture God's reality. It's tuning our minds to listen through silence or through the words of Scripture, so that we experience what is true about God, about us, and about others. It helps us guard against spiritual selective hearing.

Now, a lot of people who have grown up in traditional Christian churches balk at the word *meditation*. But it's really just semantics. Scripture affirms its importance: "[Isaac] went out to the field one evening to meditate" (Genesis 24:63); Joshua says, "Study this Book of Instruction continually. Meditate on it day and night" (Joshua 1:8 NLT); the psalmist says "Oh God, we meditate on your unfailing love.... [I will] meditate on all your mighty deeds" (Psalm 48:9, 77:12). Scriptural meditation is all about focusing our minds on what is true about God and about us. It's letting these thoughts roll around in our minds, utilizing our powerful, God-given imaginations to picture what God says real life with him is intended to be.

A study done at the University of Chicago took randomly selected people and divided them into three groups. One group went to the gym and practiced basketball free throws twenty minutes a day for three weeks. The second group went to the gym, but instead of practicing free throws, this group was told to simply visualize shooting free throws successfully. The third group was told to forget about basketball for the entire three weeks. At the end of the study, the group that had physically practiced free throws improved by twenty-four percent, the group that did not practice showed no improvement, and remarkably, the group that *just visualized* also had an improvement of twenty-three percent.[2] Meditation on God's truth utilizes the imagination to prepare us to

SOUNDS FROM THE SILENCE

I've heard you say that people need extended time to be quiet and alone to be able to hear and respond to God during the noise of our busy days, and I couldn't agree more. Since coming to faith two years ago, I have changed so much. It hasn't been without its difficulties, but I feel more alive than I ever have. God had healed me of the porn issue as I learned to take captive each thought and respond to him to show me what I really longed for, and that changed the way I related to my girlfriend. But in those quiet times alone with God, I began to see fears, habits, and wounds that kept me hanging on to an old way, not in sync with God. My relationship with my girlfriend was now sexually honoring to God but still based on all the wrong principles—fear, desperation, and self-esteem issues, yet I couldn't let go. Holding on hurt us both. The lesson I've learned is to truly seek and actively respond in spite of whatever feelings churn inside me. I'll be happier that way. Over the last two years when I have responded, everything has really worked out for the best. I really believe now this is the best path for me, and I understand what my role is—to take every thought captive as I seek his will and respond. —Juan

make spiritual free throws when the game of life is on. Meditation on Scripture can also set us free from those condemning, judging, harsh thoughts that punish us with guilt or fear or feelings of worthlessness.

I asked the woman who struggled with anorexia to write down the thoughts that went through her head and drove her to starve herself. I took those thoughts, which were all lies about her worth and significance, and I put down God's truth about her from Scripture. I asked her to form a mental picture of what God says, meditate on it, and imagine him telling her these truths, and try to accept them as reality. She called me in tears saying, "This is unbelievable; I've been believing lies about myself and it's killing me, and yet I didn't even realize it. I thought the lies were what God thought about me, but Scripture tells me just the opposite." She started down the path toward healing as she meditated on God's truth.

SOLITUDE

Our biggest challenge to hearing and experiencing reality according to God comes from our noisy, busy, overcrowded lives. For this reason, solitude must be a regular practice for spiritual health. We must set aside regular times, monthly if not weekly, to be alone and quiet for three hours or more — no iPod, radio, TV, people, books — just you, quiet enough to get past the static noise and truly hear God's quiet whispers. Often we fear solitude because noise and busyness have become the habit we use to run from something toxic inside that God wants to clean out and heal. Karen explains what she discovered in forced solitude:

> *I moved from the city to the country. At that time, I was a Pharisee, a religious hypocrite who did church really well. I made sure I always looked like I had my act together, but the truth is, I was full of pain and fear and doubt. The way I handled my abuse from the past was through self-protection. Show you're strong and need no one! In this small town, without the noise and distractions of the city, the sounds of silence began to tear me apart. I couldn't understand how God could have allowed so much pain in my life. I became suicidal and addicted to drugs. It was reading books by Dan Allendar that helped me begin to face the painful memories of my past, so God could show me truth and healing. I began to envision a life where God could be at the center, and even use the pain of my past to discover my calling.*

Though Karen ran from silence and solitude, trying to deny the pain of her past, it was in silence and solitude that she found God's healing. Today she helps others who have been through the same abuse. Solitude must be a regular practice if we will truly learn to hear and see and experience the life God intended.

There are other regular practices like journaling, reviewing the day with God, and reading spiritually helpful books. You need to figure out what a regular spiritual cardiovascular workout will look like for you to maintain spiritual fitness in the different seasons of your life.

FOCUSED STRENGTH-BUILDING

Just like rehab exercises focus on building strength in a weakened joint, we sometimes need focused spiritual exercises that build our strength to respond to God in our personal area of weakness. This is where you and your Spiritual Running Partner can get creative. Let me give you a few examples of focused, strength-building Intentional Practices.

Maybe you struggle with road rage. As you discuss it with your Running Partner, the two of you can come up with focused exercises, like listening to worship music as you drive. Perhaps you decided to memorize and meditate on a couple of verses each day as you're driving — such as "Vengeance is mine says the Lord." These are things you *can* control, and they will help you better respond to God in an area you *can't* control.

So imagine you're in your little 1995 Mazda and one of those new model SUVs (like the Ford Exhibitionist, or whatever it's called) cuts right in front of you — as if they're taunting you, "Go ahead, little Samurai car, and try to stop me." But instead of responding by trying to ram your Mazda right up his tailpipe, you interrupt that response with a new practice. You take deep breaths and say, " 'Vengeance is mine says the Lord'; Give it to God — I don't need vengeance.... Lord, give me patience." The new practice turns to a habit, the habit shapes your character — and soon you'll habitually take a deep breath, put it in perspective, and respond to God by letting it go (just feeling good knowing you get better gas mileage!).

Experts in dealing with addictions have found that people need ninety meetings in ninety days to break an addiction effectively. In other words, you don't have the strength yet to resist the gale-force mental and physical winds that alcohol, drug, tobacco, or sexual addictions slam against you. You need focused strength-building by being with others *daily*, having a sponsor available 24/7 (like a Running Partner), and hearing stories of success. The recovery movement's habit-breaking "ninety in ninety" simply helps people stay connected — as God causes the growth. Before long, their minds and bodies and wills have gained the strength to respond to God's will instead of the will of the addiction.

Maybe you struggle with a critical spirit. A creative spiritual exercise might be to take a pad and pen with you, and try to fill a page by writing down good things you notice that God brings throughout the day. You're interrupting this critical mindset by focusing on finding ways to be thankful. You're reordering your mind to "give thanks in all circumstances, for this is God's will for you in Christ Jesus" (1 Thessalonians 5:18 NIV). So you practice looking for the good, you write it down, and you use it as a prompt to reconnect to God's Spirit and be grateful to God. You'll be amazed how, over time, you find gratitude, peace, and joy actually coming out naturally — fruit happens.

As you continue this 60-60 Experiment, discuss with your Running Partners what a regular spiritual cardio workout might look like for you. Then take that one main area of weakness God is prodding you to focus on, and get creative about focused spiritual strength-building exercises. But don't forget the point.

You're not doing the exercises to be a "good boy" or a "good girl" for God. You're putting Intentional Practices in place to interrupt auto-response habits, and instead, you're responding to God who causes the growth.

That's how people grow. Running together in the environment of grace and truth, you put Intentional Practices in place to help you respond to God's Spirit moment by moment. Do this, and you will look back years from now amazed! You'll find you're living more and more of the life you've been searching for but could never grasp. You'll realize God is at work, forming you into a truly life-giving person. And as he forms us all to be more like him, we actually become his Body in our world. This mystery is the most profound, compelling, exciting truth of all — you are his Body.

THE 60-60 EXPERIMENT

Developing a Spiritual Workout is a way to train ourselves to better stay connected and responsive to God when the "game is on." But there are also specialized Intentional Practices we can get creative with to help us interrupt old habits and better respond to God in weak areas.

1. **Design a regular workout**. Think through a regular spiritual workout that can best keep you "in shape" spiritually. Make it something you can do consistently for an extended period of time. Write it down and share it with your Running Partner(s). Keep this 60-60 Intentional Practice in place, staying in constant contact with God throughout the day as part of this regular workout.

2. **Get intentional**. Think of that one main growth area you've identified, that one place in which God seems to be prompting you for growth. Discuss with your Running Partner one or two key Intentional Practices to help you strengthen your thoughts and will to better respond to God instead of the old habit. Get creative! [Check out *www.Soulrevolution.net* for helpful practices.]

3. **Trade ideas**. Share your Intentional Practices on our blog and learn what others are doing to stay responsive in different areas of growth.

PART 5 **BEING THE BODY**

Re-present 1—
GOD HAS A BODY

"Wow, how great it is to eat something other than *kartoshka* and *agortsi!*" Stuart proclaimed as the four of us perused the menu of Zum Baren, a nice Swiss restaurant we were enjoying on our ten-day break. A year of living in the new, post-Communist Russia was taking its toll, and a little indulgence seemed in order.

Kathy had been pensive all night as Stuart, Jenni, and I joked and celebrated. Finally she couldn't keep it in. "I just can't enjoy this."

"Why? Because there are no cucumbers or boiled potatoes?" I jested. "You're not gonna eat like this for six more months — don't miss it."

"I can't stop thinking about our Russian friends," Kathy replied. "They can't even get enough milk to feed their babies. I just feel it's wrong for us to not do something about it."

Hyperinflation had Russia in a vice grip since the fall of Communism, and consequently, food was scarce. It was 1991 and everywhere we went in St. Petersburg, people stood in long lines to get bread, cheese, and milk. As Westerners in St. Pete, our dollar went far, but trying to help our Russian friends seemed like a drop of water in an ocean of need.

"I know, Sweetie, but what can we do?" I replied, feeling a little wet from her coldwater dousing of our warm celebration. I knew Kathy was right, yet making a difference seemed impossible.

"I feel we must do something," Kathy insisted. "I feel like God wants us to do more."

"I agree," Jenni said, "but it's overwhelming — what can we do? There's so much need, and just four of us."

"Maybe we could find a way to ship food from Finland," Stuart suggested.

"We could write all our friends and family in the States and try to raise money, and then truck it in from Finland," I added. "But could we even import food like that?"

"Let's pray and ask God for a way," Kathy wisely suggested. "If he wants it done, he can show us how."

We stopped in the middle of dinner and prayed that if God wanted us to be part of the solution, we were willing. The rest of the dinner there was a new excitement — not just over the meal, but over a plan forming among the four of us.

The next week, we returned to St. Petersburg. A message was waiting for me at our apartment. I returned the call — from someone in Moscow.

"There's a C – 110 military transport plane scheduled to land in St. Petersburg in a few days," the American on the other end explained. "It's loaded with over a thousand boxes of nonperishable food. Each box will feed a family for three months. A church in Ohio shipped it, but their distribution contact fell through. I think the contact turned out to be mafia related. Anyway, we heard you were Americans living there. Is there any way you could distribute the food for them?"

"Well, ordinarily I would have to say no, because we don't have the means. But I have a feeling we'll figure out a way," I replied in shock. "When is it arriving?"

"Two or three days."

I hung up the phone, blown away at God's greatness. Kathy was ecstatic. We rallied about a hundred Russian college students who had just started following Christ, and they helped figure out how to distribute over a thousand boxes of food in three days. They somehow lined up military trucks to ship it. The president of the university gave us all the storage space needed and the largest auditorium to use. Over a thousand families from married-student housing received food, including powdered milk for their infants! We held an optional meeting in the auditorium for anyone who wanted to hear about the God who was behind it all — nearly everyone who received food attended.

I learned that if we are truly willing to respond, the Greatest Mind in the universe has a plan to use willing people to do his work in this world. He wants to include you in his dream for humanity. All you have to do is stay connected, willing, and responsive, and you and your friends will be amazed at what God will do through you.

GOD'S DREAM

In 1961 President Kennedy said, "I believe that this nation should commit itself to achieving the goal, before this decade is out, of landing a man on the moon." An unbelievable dream; yet millions of Americans bought into this shared vision. Thousands of the best and brightest scientists and engineers took lower-paying government jobs to give their lives for the dream. And by the end of the decade, we put a man on the moon.

Martin Luther King Jr. stood on the steps of the Lincoln Memorial and said, "I have a dream; that my four children will one day live in a nation where they will not be judged by the color of their skin but by the content of their character." Millions caught the vision, and it set in motion a revolutionary change as people unified around this common dream, willing to sacrifice even their lives to see it fulfilled. A shared dream can catalyze people in powerful ways.

God too has a dream. Ever thought about God's dream for humanity? For you and me? Ever thought about what God might do if we all shared his dream? God's dream is no secret; it was the final thing on Jesus' mind as he prayed his last night on earth: "My prayer is not for them alone. I pray also for those who will believe in me through their message, that all of them may be one, Father, just as you are in me and I am in you. May they also be in us so that the world may believe that you have sent me" (John 17:20 – 21).

One of Jesus' last prayers was for a unified community of growing Christ-followers, who stay continuously connected to God as Jesus did, responding to God's revolutionary ways of relating with each other, unified as one. And the result? The world around us will be changed! People will see us becoming more loving, life-giving people. They'll see us learning to be openhearted, resolving conflict in healthy ways. They'll see us humbly growing past broken, hurtful patterns, to care not just for ourselves, but for others around us. As a result they'll say, "That's not natural, that's *super*natural — God must be in this. There's something to this way of Christ!"

God's dream is revolutionary! It's a dream to overthrow the kingdoms of this world that keep people alone and isolated, hurting and hating, blowing up families, imprisoned in addictions, locked behind bars of fear, destroyed by systems of greed and injustice.

People often ask, "If God is so loving, why doesn't he just wipe out all the evils of this world that hurt people?" Philosophers tell us 95 percent of the world's suffering and evil come from choices people make (even well-meaning humans)! Instead of wiping out all of us, God's plan is to undermine the kingdom of evil, one willing life at a time, and then do something about it — through you and your willing friends and your willing church and others together as One. It's a big dream, a *huge* dream, a *God-sized* dream. That's why we can't do it without God and without each other. Even God's worldwide restoration plan is relational!

Jesus' words in the upper room made this vision clear: "I tell you the truth, anyone who believes in me will do the same works I have done, and even greater works, because I am going to be with the Father" (John 14:12 NLT). As we each stay connected and responsive to God moment by moment, his dream can come true through us, and as his kingdom comes through us, we all benefit — what we experience is better than we ever dreamed.

GOD STILL HAS A BODY

Romans 12 paints a graphic picture of God's dream: "Just as each of us has one body with many members, and these members do not all have the same function, so in Christ we who are many form one body, and each member belongs to all the others" (Romans 12:4 – 5 NIV).

God wants nothing less than to represent himself through you and your group and your church and others willing to function as his Body. God dreams of a responsive, connected community that he can live in and through to tangibly show the world what he is like.

Two thousand years ago, God, the unseen Spirit, revealed himself tangibly in a Jewish, male, Nazarene body. Jesus said "God's kingdom has come near," and wherever Jesus went, the brokenness caused by the evils of this world found healing and restoration through the power of God. But look at this: "We will speak the truth in love, growing in every way more and more like Christ, who is the head of his body, the church. He makes the whole body fit together perfectly. As each part does its own special work, it helps the other parts grow, so that the whole body is healthy and growing and full of love" (Ephesians 4:15 – 16 NLT).

This is a radical concept! God who is Spirit still has a body on earth to represent himself to the world tangibly — through you and me together as we respond to the Spirit of Jesus (who is the head). And the sign of our maturity is that together we demonstrate his loving, redemptive, restorative kingdom ways to our world, working together as one Body.

Dr. Walter Penfield was the neurologist credited with mapping the human brain. He discovered which areas of the brain control which body functions. Penfield opened up a patient's skull to expose the brain and then woke the person up. The person was conscious while he probed around, sending electrical currents to stimulate different areas to determine what they controlled. As freaky as it sounds, probing the brain doesn't hurt the person because the brain has no pain-sensing nerves. What Penfield discovered about the brain shocked him and completely changed his view of humans as mere biological machines. He would stimulate the brain region that made the patient's right arm raise and lower, and the arm would raise and lower at his electrical prompting. But the patient would say, "You're doing that, not me."

In other words, Penfield discovered that you — as a spiritual being — are distinct from your physical brain.[1] It's like you use your brain and body to present yourself physically to the world, but you are more than the sum total of your body parts. When your body doesn't respond to your spirit, something's dysfunctional, and you try to correct it. When your body parts respond to your spirit's will, you present yourself to the world through your body.

In the same way, the Spirit of God wants to re-present himself to the world through us — to physically demonstrate his love and compassion, hope and healing, care and concern to a broken world. As the diverse parts of his Body respond to his Spirit moment by moment, he coordinates unique people with different gifts, like parts of a body, to accomplish his dream for the world.

GET INVOLVED

During our 60-60 Experiment, Aaron and Lindi stopped at a traffic light one evening on their way home. A violent-looking argument broke out between a couple in an adjacent parking lot. Both noticed, but neither said anything. "Better not get involved in a domestic spat when we've got two little kids in the car," was the first thought that ran through Aaron's mind. "Besides, it's bedtime; we've got to get the kids home." Before the light turned green, the guy raised his hand as if he were going to strike the young woman he was yelling at. He cussed her out instead, jumped in his car and drove off. The light turned green.

As Aaron and Lindi drove on, both felt a tug in their consciences as they noticed the woman bury her head in her hands, sobbing. Because we were doing this 60-60 Experiment, they each asked God what his will was — should they go back, or not get involved? Lindi broke the silence first. "Did you see that couple fighting?"

"Yeah, I'm thinking God wants us to go back," Aaron confessed.

"I do too, but what can we do?" Lindi asked.

"I don't know, but let's pray and ask God and just be willing to respond." Aaron pulled a U-turn under the overpass and headed back for the parking lot.

When they arrived, the young woman was sitting alone on a curb, her head in her hands. Lindi sat down next to her and just prayed. For the next twenty minutes, the young woman, Christy, spilled her guts without any prompting. As Aaron stayed with the kids, Lindi discovered that nineteen-year-old Christy was being physically abused by her boyfriend. She had made a bad decision to move from California to live with him. Now she had no place to stay, no friends to help her, no money to get back to her family in California; she felt scared and alone.

Lindi let Christy know she was not alone. She assured her that there's a God who cares about her, and he wants to help her get out of this bad situation and move forward on a better path. Christy asked, "Why are you here? Are you an angel?" As Lindi counseled her spiritually, Christy began to feel a sense of hope. Meanwhile, Aaron got on the phone to call Nate, a guy in their small group at our church who volunteered in our Benevolence ministry. Nate made some calls and gave Aaron some contacts.

Because of the fresh marks on her neck where her boyfriend tried to strangle her, the police arrested him. That weekend Aaron helped Christy contact a licensed Christian counselor who donated time to counsel people through our church. Lindi continued to spiritually guide Christy as Aaron and Nate worked with our Benevolence team to access finances she would need to get on her feet.

Because people in our church voluntarily contribute resources, we have a Benevolence fund to meet crisis needs. Our Body not only helped Christy get her spiritual footing but got her out of that situation and home to California. This young girl tangibly heard and experienced how much she matters to God — that he wants to lead her into healthy, truly loving relationships. She will still have to decide whether to follow God's kingdom ways or old broken ways, but she experienced God's heart as Aaron and Lindi responded to his Spirit, connected her to other parts of his Body, and demonstrated his kingdom coming near to restore what's been lost and broken.

IMAGINE YOUR IMPACT

What if we took God's dream as seriously as those who committed themselves to John F. Kennedy's dream? What if we committed ourselves to God's dream like those who have risked their lives for Martin Luther King Jr.'s dream? God's full dream requires your willingness to do his kingdom will in cooperation with others. Jesus taught us to pray, "Your kingdom come, your will be done on earth as it is in heaven" because God's will is *not* always done on earth. Ultimately, his kingdom will come, but it's not a given that this will happen through us as he intends. Instead, he's given us amazing decision-making power and causality to participate (or not) in bringing his kingdom to earth!

Will you choose to participate in his shared dream? Will you align your dreams under his dream? Only then will your dreams find true fulfillment. Do you realize that God intends you to be an interdependent part of his Body, connected to others in your Christian community or church?

So as you continue this 60-60 Experiment of staying connected and responsive to God throughout the day, say a simple prayer each hour as you go through the day. "God, I want to see with your eyes, reach out with your hands, and be your Body." Go all out, and just see if God's dream doesn't begin to come alive through you and your community. Journal and talk together with your Running Partners about what God shows you as you pray this way at every watch beep or reminder.

"GOD, I WANT TO SEE WITH YOUR EYES"

As you stay connected, ask God to help you see people through his eyes. Jesus traveled through the neighborhoods by the Sea of Galilee. "When he saw the crowds, he had compassion on them, because they were harassed and helpless, like sheep without a shepherd" (Matthew 9:36). When Jesus looked out on the neighborhood, he saw beneath the surface. He saw deep into people's lives — into the pain and confusion, into the disease and trouble, into the heartache and sadness, into the chains of brokenness and addiction that keep people enslaved.

Jesus saw people wandering and in danger, in need of the God who wants to lead them toward life. And Scripture says, "He had compassion." When you look out at the people you live and work around, what do you see? What I typically see are just people — they come and go, we exchange small talk, they drive decent cars in and out of their decent-size garages attached to their decent houses; they seem to have decent friends or family around them. They look like things are just fine — they don't really need anything. At least that's the game we all play.

SOBERING TO SEE

What if we could see the people we interact with every day not just on the surface, but underneath the "I have it all together" pretense? What might we see if we could spiritually see underneath it all with the eyes of Jesus? Well, just think about it statistically. Nearly one out of two people you meet spend more than they make — personal debts are still growing like a well-fed St. Bernard puppy. People are racking up debt burdens and financial struggles that weigh them down with worry. Nearly every other marriage will fail if trends continue — leaving heartache, struggle, and pain for adults and children alike. Two out of every five people you meet under age forty are chained to some addictive substance, struggling to get free, feeling helpless and hopeless. Of every five women you meet, one or two of them likely hides the devastating memories of sexual abuse, probably as a teenager at the hands of someone they knew and trusted. About one in five people you interact with have a sexually transmitted disease, and at current rates fifty percent will get an STD at some point in their lives. Most people will suffer in silence and keep being sexually promiscuous because that's the only life they've known. One-third of the women you meet will get an abortion by age forty — many experience deep regret and remorse. Fifty percent of men and thirty percent of women will likely get some form of cancer over their lifetime. Most people don't know their neighbors, and if they were honest, one in three would admit to frequent periods of intense loneliness, and twenty-five percent would admit they have no close friends.[2]

Sobering reality! And that's not half of it. More than likely, everybody you lock eyes with struggles with something, or soon will. But is there anybody who sees with Jesus' eyes — beneath the surface — who will reach out with compassion?

Without God's nudging, I'm essentially blind to these needs because I get so preoccupied with all my own concerns. Every day you and I interact with people who have spiritual and physical needs God wants to meet, but so often, we just pass right by because we don't see. But if you'll pray for God to give you his eyes of compassion, he will show you.

One Monday morning during the 60-60 Experiment, Billie was out saying goodbye to her husband on the driveway. As she was walking back into the house, she had this strong prompting to pray for her next-door neighbor. She hadn't seen the neighbors all weekend, and as she prayed, she sensed she should go knock on the door. She didn't want to — it was 7:30 in the morning! She would surely wake them up. She questioned, "Is this just my crazy imagination or is it you, Lord? I can't wake them up! Even if they're up, they'll think I'm crazy." As she prayed, she fought back fear and decided to respond. Here's an excerpt from her journal about her 60-60 experience:

> When my neighbor came to the door, I could see she had been crying. She reached out and hugged me, and asked me to come in. As we sat on the couch, she poured out her heart about their crisis-filled weekend that left her brother in the hospital. We talked, prayed together, and stayed in touch that day.

It was clear in hindsight; God was showing her a spiritual need he wanted to meet. Because she responded, she got to demonstrate his compassion. But first we must have eyes to see.

WHO ARE YOUR FOUR?

Most of us have four or more people whom we interact with all the time — at work, in sports, in the neighborhood — who have no church community. They have spiritual and physical needs God wants to meet, but they are disconnected from his Body. You probably don't see their needs because the world says, "Suck it up, no one cares," so most people hide.

Joanie sent me this email:

> Hello John: I came to Gateway at the invitation of a friend. I had hardened my heart to God, and I had distanced myself from him and other people. I had learned to protect myself from being hurt again, at the cost of having no "real life." Sure, I worked and I went through the motions and most people thought I was a "happy" person, but I was "dead" inside. I had no hope for the future.

This is the game most people play. As Thoreau wisely intuited, "Most people lead lives of quiet desperation." Joanie goes on to tell of the difference it made when someone reached out to her and walked with her toward faith:

> This is definitely a new experience for me. Every day I am blown away by the contrasts in my life. This commitment and new walk with God has just been amazing. The joy and peace I feel now is so awesome. It is like I was just

MAPQUEST TO GOD

The day my little brother committed suicide became the defining moment of my life. I have had my share of hardships ... sexual abuse as a child, neglect by my alcoholic mother and coke-head father, the loss of my grandmother who raised me. Nothing before, no matter how terrible, brought me closer to God. If anything, the incidents of my past pushed me farther away. To be honest, without God, my life was not that bad. It was livable. There were plenty of good times, but I must also confess, it was lonely. Why was my brother's suicide so different? Perhaps because his last words on the note were, "I've asked God to forgive me." I wanted forgiveness too—for failing my brother so badly.

After the funeral, I was exhausted mentally, emotionally, and physically. After a week off, I went back to work. I walked into my cube, pulled out my chair, and found a MapQuest printout for Gateway. A friend put it there with a note saying she thought it might help. At the time, I thought it was very sweet, but I still was not ready to give God a chance.

I went through the holidays depressed, alone, and self-loathing. Christmas came and went without much ado. I realized I needed something ... what that was, I didn't know. I spent January trying to figure it out. What did I need? How was I going to get through this? In early February, I was cleaning out my desk and found my friend's note on the map. I asked my friend about the church, and she encouraged me to go at least once.

I talked my husband into going, and I found the experience educational and fun. The message was "Jesus Knows What He's Talking About." When the speaker said, "Take a small step and read his teachings and you'll be amazed," I decided to do it. I went home and started Matthew. He was right, I was amazed. The dregs of society were a symbol of my brother, and I knew in my heart that I loved him as Jesus did the leper. For all the people who saw my brother as worthless, I know that God loved him and that made him more important than he'd ever been given credit for. I've been coming back every Sunday since. I'm still reading the Bible and working on figuring it all out. I talk to God throughout my day, and though I don't always get clear answers, now I'm always listening. —Shae

released from a concentration camp and I suddenly have life. The contrast from feeling oppressed to suddenly having peace and joy is impossible to describe. It is like you've said, "supernatural."

Will you do this? Write down four names and start praying, "God, I want to see these people with your eyes." These four people may not be connected to a local expression of the Body, they may be far from God, they may be skeptics or atheists, but if you will pray for them, God will show you how he wants to demonstrate his compassion toward them. Pray for them each day and write down what God shows you about their spiritual and physical needs and share them with your Spiritual Running Partner or small group. That leads to the next part of our prayer of willingness to be the Body.

"GOD, I'LL REACH OUT WITH YOUR HANDS"

God wants us to be willing to reach out when he lets us see a need. We can't do it all, but we can do something. "Seek justice, encourage the oppressed. Defend the cause of the fatherless, plead the case of the widow" (Isaiah 1:17). God takes seriously the needs around us, and he wants us to be willing.

Here's the next problem (and also the thing that keeps us from being the Body): we don't want to see the needs because they overwhelm us. We hear voices telling us, "You can't do anything about that," or "They'll think you're weird if you ask," or "I don't have time to get involved." And so we'd rather cover our eyes and not see. Or if we do see, we often throw up our hands and say, "I'm just one person. I can't solve the world's problems. I don't know how to help a struggling single mom, fix an addict, counsel a depressed person, solve someone's financial crises, eradicate poverty and injustice, answer people's spiritual questions, or give someone hope!"

Jesus said the burden he gives us is light, not overwhelming (Matthew 11:28 – 30). How can it be light if he wants us to be part of the solution to the overwhelming needs of the world? Because we are not alone! If you've opened your heart to God's grace offered in Christ, he's with you always. And remember, he is the Head of his Body. You're now connected to the Greatest Mind in the universe.

I read a book called *The Elegant Universe*. It explains how Einstein's theory of relativity elucidated much of the large-scale macro-phenomena of stars and galaxies in our universe. Quantum physics has allowed us to understand and predict what happens in subatomic particles at the smallest scale. But even the greatest minds don't understand why quantum physics and general relativity don't work together at all. There's a theory called string theory that may solve these problems in dimensions beyond time and space — but our greatest minds have struggled thirty years and still can't fully grasp it. I read books like these because they help me go to sleep at night — I understand so little. But just think about this: you are connected to the Mind who understands it all!

God knows it all, because he created it all. And he says it's not all about quantum mechanics or relativity or superstring theory — it's about loving God and loving people. And you don't have to figure it all out; you just have to reach out, and *he* will figure out a coordinated way to do the rest.

Kathy didn't know how to feed a thousand Russian families, but God had already prompted some Christ-follower in Ohio to meet these needs. That person responded, spoke up, and rallied his local church Body to raise money and ship food to St. Petersburg. We didn't have the food, they didn't have a distributor, but God had a dream! And one hundred new Russian believers got to participate with the worldwide Body. All we need to do is be willing to reach out with his hands, and the Greatest Mind in the universe orchestrates the rest. That doesn't mean hard work, mental ingenuity, and perseverance are not required to see needs met and injustices set right. It means God works in and through our willingness to coordinate his Body.

MEETING SPIRITUAL NEEDS

There are both physical and spiritual needs God wants to meet through your willingness. God wants us to tell people of the hope we've found in a relationship with him through Christ. "Always be prepared to give an answer to everyone who asks you to give the reason for the hope that you have. But do this with gentleness and respect" (1 Peter 3:15). At Jesus' last supper, he told his followers, "When the Advocate comes, whom I will send to you from the Father — the Spirit of truth who goes out from the Father — he will testify about me. And you also must testify, for you have been with me from the beginning" (John 15:26 – 27).

If you've found hope in Christ — you just have to tell people what you've found.[3] I'm convinced that every person I meet would love the life God longs to give them in Christ — I'm motivated by my personal experience to encourage people to seek the God Jesus revealed wholeheartedly. As one person said, "It's

PIERCED BY A ROSE

My neighbor came to faith after getting to know some of the women in our neighborhood who threw a welcome party for her family when they moved in. She wanted her husband to find faith too, but he was a very stoic, skeptical intellectual. For months and months, our husbands would try to grapple with his deep questions as they dialogued about faith, but nothing could convince him, it seemed. One day I was in my garden, praying for him as I knew it was his birthday. As I prayed for him, I felt prompted to pick a red rose to give to him with a birthday card. I was actually quite intimidated by him, so I took the rose early in the morning and taped it to his front door with a card that simply said, "Love you, and so does God." Shortly after that, he became a Christ-follower, and they started coming to church. Several years later, I was talking to him, and he said, "You don't know this, but the reason I opened my heart to Christ was because of the rose you left me on my birthday—I'd never been given a flower before in my life, and for some reason, God's love for me struck my heart for the first time when I got that rose. It was the factor that opened me to faith." I was awestruck at how God works in ways so unique to individuals—in ways beyond words and imagination. —B.K.

like one beggar telling another beggar where he can find bread." If you've found hope, you point others to the one who gives hope eternally. If they are hungry, they'll eat. If not, you don't need to bully or badger them, you respect them.

Before I was a Christian, I used to get so turned off by the "Prophets of Condemnation." As a student at the University of Texas, I was walking through the main mall to class one warm spring day, and a guy yelled at me through his bullhorn, "You're going to hell!" That caught my attention since I'd recently received Christ's forgiveness and grace and was pretty sure this guy was wrong. When I asked why he said that, it was because I was wearing shorts! I knew my legs looked white, but I didn't know they were that repulsive! (True story — you can see how people get very distorted messages about the way of Christ.)

That's not what Jesus had in mind for the church. Instead, if we will be a Body of people who live in a new way with each other, and show compassion for others in tangible ways, and then are willing to invite others into the hope we've found in Christ and his community (with gentleness and respect), many people will discover grace, hope, and life.

THE WAY OF POOH

Once I was flying home to Santa Barbara, sitting next to a student from the University of California, Santa Barbara, who was reading a book called *The Tao of Pooh*. I had read some Taoist teachings, so I knew it must be a book on spirituality. Not too long into the flight we got to talking, and I asked him what the book was about. It led into a really great conversation about the theme of the book, "the way of life." I had a chance to tell him what I was discovering about the way of Jesus and the life I was experiencing. He was interested, but had serious questions about Jesus. The flight ended, and Jason and I parted ways.

About three months later, I was walking outside praying one morning. I had a very busy day ahead, so I prayed for guidance for all I had to do. As I prayed, I kept thinking, "Go to campus." I was working at UCSB at the time, but I'd planned to work at home that day. I kept ignoring the thought, because I had no reason to go to campus, and I had lots of reasons to get to work. But the thought persisted. So I asked, "Lord, am I supposed to go to campus?" I didn't get any clarity, but the thought didn't go away. I wasn't quite sure, so at this point, I had to decide — do I take the risk and just go for it? Finally, after wrestling with God over all the work time I'd lose, I gave in.

As I walked on campus, I saw a large crowd of students listening to an open-air speaker. Sitting on the edge of the crowd ... was Jason. Figuring this must be more than a coincidence, I said hi to him. It turned out, Cliff Kneckle, from Yale, was speaking about the intellectual validity of faith in Jesus, and Jason had been listening.

As we talked, I could tell Jason was really seeking to understand. We decided to get together to continue our discussion and play guitars — a love we both shared. Jason found faith in Christ as a result of our interactions. I have no doubt that God saw his seeking heart and knew that day was a critical day for Jason. I got to see God's heart and meet a spiritual need.

I'm convinced that everyone would want the life God longs to give them, but they're just unaware or misinformed about God's intentions. But when they start to see them, when they hear what others are experiencing doing life with God, many will decide to follow the way of Christ. About 60 percent of the nearly 4,000 people attending our church were not following Christ when a friend first invited them, yet most say they now actively follow Christ. We keep seeing more and more people attracted to our community, finding faith, and becoming part of our Body because people long for what Christ offers — an eternal quality of life that flows from within.

Begin to pray, "God, I want to see with your eyes, and reach out with your hands, and be your Body." Think about the four people who seem disconnected from God who you already interact with — neighbors, coworkers, classmates, golf buddies, play-group parents. Will you pray for their spiritual and physical needs? Are you willing to reach out and do what you can? Remember you are not alone — you're connected to the Greatest Mind in the universe, and you don't have to have every gift or ability either because you're connected to a greater Body.

THE 60-60 EXPERIMENT

Staying connected moment by moment requires effort until it becomes a habit. If you feel like you're failing and want to give up—or maybe *have* given up—remember it's not about "doing it right" but about growing in relating to the God who loves you. Keep using those sixty-minute reminders to grow in this habit of letting God influence all of your life. This week, pay special attention to how he wants to use you to meet spiritual and physical needs around you.

1. **"Help me see with your eyes."** As you stay connected, at every sixty-minute reminder ask God to help you see the people you interact with through his eyes. As you interact with people, quietly ask God, "Lord, show me this person's spiritual or physical need you want to meet." You may not get an immediate understanding, but stay faithful this week and watch what gets revealed. Journal what you discover.

2. **Write down four.** Write down the names of four people who may seem far from God or disconnected from community and commit to praying for them. Ask God to show you what needs they have that he might want you to reach out and meet.

3. **"And I'll reach out with your hands."** As God shows you needs of the people in your life, take bold risks to respond by reaching out to them. Ask for guidance to be God's hands reaching out, and then step out in faith even if you don't have complete

clarity on how you can be of help—at least show you care and ask the person how you can pray for him or her.

4. **Share with your group**. Talk with your group or Running Partner(s) about whom you're each praying for and what you sense God's showing you or asking you to do. Be sure to blog to encourage others when you see God doing his work through you.

CHAPTER FIFTEEN

Re-present 2—
BE THE BODY

As our church grew, we developed a study called *Investigating the Way of Christ*. My assistant at the time, Becky Laswell, had a passion for resourcing people to grow, so I asked her to be on the team. As the project developed, Becky became the editor for the study. I started to see her teaching gift fanned into flame editing and writing. We came up with the idea of a web-based resource to help people find Intentional Practices to grow. Becky's past experience had been creating web resources! Her passion, experiences, and gifts really aligned better with developing the Way of Christ resources than assisting me as her primary role.

Our Body needed what Becky could bring to the Way of Christ resources, but I would be without an assistant. We both took a step of faith, and she has since done an amazing job producing both written and web-based resources. For three months, I interviewed potential assistants, struggling to keep my head above water. No one seemed like a great fit. I told my wife in frustration one day, "Man, I wish I could just get Theresa Rozsa to move to Austin — she was awesome when she assisted me in Chicago."

"Why don't you call her?" Kathy asked.

"I think Greg (her husband) took a job in Seattle a few years ago. There's no way they'd uproot for her to be *my* assistant!" I hadn't actually talked to Theresa or Greg for about five years but kept up with them through friends. With that, I dropped the thought. But I redoubled my efforts praying for the right assistant.

About a month later, Theresa was sitting at her desk at Mars Hill Graduate School, where she assisted the school president. Theresa recalls, "That whole day, I kept wondering what had happened to John and Kathy and the church they started. I didn't normally think about them, hadn't talked to them in five years, so it seemed odd that they kept coming to mind. Finally, wondering if it was a God-prompting, I Googled them to find the Gateway website. As I browsed the pages, I saw an ad for an administrative assistant for John. As a joke, I shot him an email: "Hey John, long time no see. I'd apply for the job, but the commute's a little far! ☺ — Theresa Rozsa."

When I read Theresa's email, I was blown away. I took it as a sign from God and did a full-court press to recruit her. As it turned out, Greg was just transitioning out of his job, and as they prayed for God's will, they both felt led to move to Austin and be a part of our community! Theresa's gifts of administration and service, combined with her experience and passion, are an amazing fit. I'm so grateful for Theresa's partnership, and I'm so grateful for what Becky's been able to do for our whole community. When we're willing to stay connected and respond, we can look back and see that "God has arranged the parts in the body, every one of them, just as he wanted them to be" (1 Corinthians 12:19 NIV).

God's dream is that we would no longer see ourselves as independent, isolated silos of self-will, but as uniquely gifted, *interdependent* parts of his Body. Because the needs of this world are diverse and complex, it requires a diverse and complex coordination of us working together to accomplish his dream.

God has made us all unique, and wants to coordinate us to meet needs together. To function best, we need to "PEG" our uniqueness — that is, know our unique Passions, Experiences, and Gifts — and use them to work together for God's dream.

Our passions help us know where best to serve — are we passionate about kids, about poverty and injustice, about the arts? You may have a gift of leadership, but your passion tells you whether leading students or leading a compassion ministry fits you best.

God will also use our unique experiences — good and bad — to be the Body. Most of Gateway's ministries were started by people who have struggled with a divorce or abuse or drug addiction, but now use their experience of God's healing to be wounded healers. They are living out the verse, "God is our merciful Father and the source of all comfort. He comforts us in all our troubles so that we can comfort others. When they are troubled, we will be able to give them the same comfort God has given us" (2 Corinthians 1:3 – 4 NLT).

God also gives us spiritual gifts. Have you figured out what yours are? Paul tells the church in Corinth, "Now about the gifts of the Spirit, brothers and sisters, I do not want you to be uninformed" (1 Corinthians 12:1). Paul says God's Spirit gives each of us gifts for the common good — to build up and round out the local expression of his Body. Knowing each other's gifts, helping develop those gifts, and finding ways to coordinate them accomplishes God's dream.

Scripture tells us, "In Christ we, though many, form one body, and each member belongs to all the others. We have different gifts, according to the grace given to each of us. If your gift is prophesying, then prophesy in accordance with your faith; if it is serving, then serve; if it is teaching, then teach; if it is to encourage, then give encouragement; if it is giving, then give generously; if it is to lead, do it diligently; if it is to show mercy, do it cheerfully" (Romans 12:5 – 8). Knowing the gifts God's Spirit has given us, in conjunction with our passions and experiences, is essential to function as One Body.

If you're not sure about your gifts, check out some of the gifts assessments recommended on the website *www.Soulrevolution.net*[1] This may give you some clues, but I've found the best way is to experiment and ask yourself, "Where does God use me to best serve and build up others? What energizes me and gives me passion as I'm doing it?" We're told to "fan into flame the gift of God" (2 Timothy 1:6) and to "eagerly desire the greater gifts" that most build up the Body (1 Corinthians 12:31). So spiritual gifts need to be pursued, discovered, and developed. As you do this, you'll find they energize you and build up the Body to meet needs.

◾

Carlyn and Jeremy sat listening in horror as Chad and Cinnamon relayed the tragic tractor accident that took the life of Chad's work associate. They had all started seriously following Christ through the small group they were in together. Carlyn felt she had the gift of mercy, so hearing stories like this moved her to want to help.

"Nancy's devastated," Cinnamon explained, "But I'm afraid it's gonna get worse for her. Her husband had no insurance, and she's pregnant; she has one young child and no job or money."

Even though Nancy and her husband had never been to our church, a value of this small group was to be the Body to the world around them, serving the spiritual and physical needs of their neighbors. Cinnamon and Carlyn decided to put together a care package for the family.

For the next year, Cinnamon ministered to Nancy by organizing people from Gateway to meet needs, providing meals, childcare, car repair, financial counsel and assistance. Seeing faith in action, Nancy opened up to God and leaned on him like she never had before.

One day, more than a year later, Carlyn found herself praying for Nancy out of the blue. Carlyn recalls, "My husband and I felt compelled to do something for Nancy again as she was brought to mind. We bought gift cards from several stores, and my son bought toys to give to Nancy's two young children. We had never met Nancy or her family personally but felt strongly that it was something God wanted us to do. We called and asked if we could come by, then surprised her family with our gifts. They seemed shocked but appreciative. The next day I got an email from Nancy saying: 'Last night, we sat down at the dinner table and ate our last box of macaroni and cheese. I had no money for food or diapers. No one knew of my need, but I prayed as we ate our last meal, trusting that God would somehow provide. Thank you for answering my prayers.' "

VALUING EVERY PART

As you do this 60-60 Experiment, if you will pray, "God help me see with your eyes, reach out with your hands, and be your Body," he will honor that request. God uses various parts of his Body to meet various needs. But you can't be the Body alone.

> *The eye cannot say to the hand, "I don't need you!" And the head cannot say to the feet, "I don't need you!" On the contrary, those parts of the body that seem to be weaker are indispensable, and the parts that we think are less honorable we treat with special honor.... If one part suffers, every part suffers with it; if one part is honored, every part rejoices with it. Now you are the body of Christ, and each one of you is a part of it. (1 Corinthians 12:21 – 23, 26 – 27)*

We need each other, and we need to value the diversity and uniqueness we each bring to the Body. As we stay connected to God's Spirit, we will respond to better value and coordinate in a unified way. But when we disconnect from boldly responding to God, our old sin nature tends to isolate and divide the Body. See, what sin does (self-centeredness rather than God-centeredness) is it destroys God's dream. It causes some to think too highly of themselves and look down on others (like they don't need those parts of the Body). It causes others to think their dreams are more important than God's dream, so they won't make themselves available to the Head. It causes some to doubt their worth, so they take themselves out of the game rather than developing and deploying their gifts. Sin causes us to gossip, fight, divide, and destroy the unity of the Body. It keeps us from trusting God to pool our resources and time and work together for God's dream. Sin is like an autoimmune disease — we attack and starve and destroy our *own Body*. We can't allow this to happen — it destroys God's dream! And God's warning is severe, "Don't you know that you yourselves [note the plural] are God's temple and that God's Spirit dwells in your midst? If anyone destroys God's temple, God will destroy that person; for God's temple is sacred, and you together are that temple" (1 Corinthians 3:16 – 17).

We should all take warning, pastors and leaders especially. Right before this, Paul says our job is creating the soil, the environment, where God's dream can grow in a community of people. Don't try to make God's dream serve your dream or you'll destroy it. Instead we must value and encourage each other's contribution — especially those who serve behind the scenes.

JUST A PARKING GUY?

I think about the guy serving in the church parking lot the day Brian Williams drove in. Brian was still an atheist, but he had come to a point where life didn't make much sense, so he was searching. Brian circled the lot, found no parking space and quickly said, "Good, I didn't want to go to church anyway." A crowded lot was all the excuse he needed, so he decided to head for home. A parking volunteer, serving behind the scenes, noticed Brian's car had circled several times and was now leaving. He waved Brian over and said, "Hey dude, I'll find you a spot. Follow me."

Brian sat on the back row that day, arms crossed, aisle seat, ready to run. Halfway through the service, a video created by our Arts Team came on while the band played a song he'd heard on the radio. Verses from the Bible scrolled across black and white images of people looking pensive or dejected, contemplating life's struggles alone. The message over and over was, "You're not alone ..." Brian found a lump rising in his throat that his folded arms and stiff upper body could not hold down. It ended with Jesus' words, "I am with you always, even to the end of the age.... You're Never Alone!" As the last three words scrolled, Brian fought back tears saying to himself, "I don't believe that ... but I want to."

Six months later Brian found faith in Christ and started to grow. He began to use his gifts in an area of passion — serving those in need. He had always felt a deep concern for the marginalized of society. Eventually he led our Church

Under the Bridge outreach to the homeless, then our entire Compassion ministry — mobilizing hundreds in our Body to serve the under-resourced.

I think about the many people on whom God had an impact — the homeless God clothed, the elderly God visited, the houses God built, the lives God changed through Brian and others ... and it all started because the guy in the parking lot was being the Body ... and because the volunteers who produced the *Never Alone* video offered their creativity to the Creator of life! This is God's dream — it happens all over all the time, and if it's not happening through you, you're missing out! We need each other, and the world around us needs what God wants to do through all of us together. Do you see?

ONE COORDINATED BODY

Jesus said, "The Son of Man did not come to be served, but to serve, and to give his life as a ransom for many" (Mark 10:45). So if we are his Body, he will lead us to serve those around us as One Body. But that takes immense coordination! God actually gives the pastors and teachers and leaders in your local church Body a job description: "Their responsibility is to equip God's people to do his work and build up the church, the body of Christ. This will continue until we all come to such unity in our faith and knowledge of God's Son that we will be mature [coordinated, healthy, full of love]" (Ephesians 4:12 – 13 NLT).

The job of those who lead and teach should be to communicate and organize and lead us all to function better as a coordinated Body — each part responding to the Spirit of Jesus (the Head of the Body) as he does his will through us together. Pastors, leaders, and teachers are not the Head; they are more like the central nervous system. They help all the parts respond to the Head. They facilitate communication between all the parts of the Body, so that resources get distributed, different parts work together in a coordinated way, and we all continue to respond moment by moment to the Head, so that his will gets done through us as One Body.

The way we know if our local Body is functional is measured by love — remember, it's all about loving relationship. So Paul explains, "We will speak the truth in love, growing in every way more and more like Christ, who is the head of his body, the church. He makes the whole body fit together perfectly. As each part does its own special work, it helps the other parts grow, so that the whole body is healthy and growing and full of love" (Ephesians 4:15 – 16 NLT). Love in action is the measure of our maturity.

Susan came to Gateway and got connected into Comfort and Hope — our support group for healing from sexual and physical abuse. Her friend Jessica, who was not a part of Gateway, had grown up in an abusive family. Susan started praying for Jessica, and not long after that a conversation between them led Susan to tell Jessica about the hope and healing she had experienced from her own abuse. Inspired, Jessica started coming to Comfort and Hope with Susan.

During the next few months, it became known that Jessica's husband, John, was an alcoholic and also abusive. They had several little kids who were acting out, being disruptive, getting in trouble — no doubt in response to the chaos at home. Jessica began to grow in grace and community and understand her identity in Christ, which gave her the courage to confront John. She told him she loved him and wanted the marriage to work, but he was destroying himself, her, and most importantly their children, and he needed to address his issues.

It didn't go well, and fearing for their safety, she moved out. But the Body moved in. The Prayer Team got involved praying for the family's safety and for John — that his heart would soften. Jessica's new small group brought meals and watched her kids when she needed childcare. When all finances got cut off, her small group connected her with our Benevolence volunteers who helped her make a plan. She accessed Gateway's food pantry and the clothing closet that our Compassion volunteers maintain, and our Benevolence fund helped with crisis housing. Her kids went to Kids' Quest (our kid's ministry). When the Kids' Quest volunteers heard what the kids were going through, they connected Jessica to Confident Kids, a ministry run by Gateway volunteers who help kids deal with the trauma of divorce, death, or abuse. Meanwhile, Jessica got counseling. Jesus was demonstrating his compassion through his Body.

Miraculously, Jessica's husband, John, started coming to Gateway separately and took in the messages each week. Through seeing the Body in action and receiving the message of grace, the blinders came off, and John agreed to get help for his alcoholism and anger issues. When John got back from six months of treatment, he and Jessica went through marriage counseling together, experienced significant healing, and they reconciled.

This was a family on the verge of total destruction — from abuse, addiction, codependency, and financial struggles, with kids heading the same way. But God's healing work reversed the effects of the broken kingdoms of this world — through his Body!

This is God's dream expressed through local communities called his church. This dream can be lived out to various extents through small groups, prayer groups, classes, whole churches, associations of churches, and other ministries in a city. But it doesn't "just happen" — not without the willingness of each part to stay connected and responsive to the Head, valuing and encouraging each other, working together in a coordinated way. When God's dream comes alive through us, he changes lives and restores our broken world, and in the process, makes all our little dreams much more fulfilling.

As you continue this 60-60 Experiment pray, "God I want to see with your eyes, reach out with your hands, and be your Body. I'll do what I can, but I'll also connect people to other parts of the Body, so you can do your work through us all." It's a beautiful dream for the world. But what if you're in a part of the world that doesn't know or follow the way of Christ, and struggles with just enough resources to survive — can they be the Body? That's Jaya Sankar's story, which we'll consider in the next chapter.

THE 60-60 EXPERIMENT

God wants us to function together as his Body doing his work in the world all around us. The more aware and willing we are to use our gifts to serve, the more God's Spirit will guide us to different places at different times to meet needs as local expressions of his Body.

To best do this, however, we need to know what part we play and what part those around us can play, and we need to encourage each other to develop our gifts and follow our passions.

1. **PEG yourself**. Take time to explore your Passions, Experiences and Gifts. For resources, check out the links on *www.Soul revolution.net*. Do some personal reflection as you ask for God's insight into how he's gifted and equipped you. Journal about past experiences and passions that may inform where God could use you to accomplish his purposes.

2. **Know your body**. God will use you to connect people in need to other parts of the Body. Discuss with your small group or

Running Partner(s) how each other's unique passions, experiences, and gifts might be used together as One Body to build up each other and serve others, including the four people you've chosen to pray for. Discuss the other ministries your church offers that you could connect people to. This may also show you a need your church has for a new ministry—talk to your leadership about the need.

3. **Be the Body**. As you continue in moment by moment connection, every sixty minutes pray for opportunities to be the Body. Continue praying for your four. Journal and blog about where you're struggling or succeeding.

CHAPTER SIXTEEN

Reconsider—
NOT ENOUGH

Young Jaya Sankar's legs ached from standing in the closet almost two hours, watching for the gods to appear through the cracked door. As a curious twelve-year-old Indian boy, he couldn't resist the temptation. Every spring, the families in Bhanumukkala, Jaya's village in the remote Andhra Pradesh region of southern India, celebrated the "festival of the gods." Jaya's grandfather, the village guru, explained that if the gods choose to eat the food left out, the house will gain additional blessing that year. So every year, after laying out the feast, all of the families left their houses for the day knowing the gods would not come under watchful eye.

Jaya's heart raced as he heard something stirring on the floor near the table. Of the thousands of idols they worshiped, would he really see one of the gods Grandfather said looked after them? Would his adolescent doubts be erased? If he dared to look, would he be struck down by the gods as warned? But he desperately wanted to know the truth. His heart pounding, he stretched on his tiptoes to gaze over the furniture blocking the view to the table top.

Rats! Jaya saw rats scurrying over the table, devouring the most valuable food the family could offer. When his family returned, Jaya confessed to hiding in the closet as he revealed the truth about the rats. Jaya's grandfather flew into a rage and beat young Jaya, telling him the gods can take any form, including that of rats. They had been gracious to a capricious boy by disguising themselves, so that he would not be destroyed by his spying on them.

Instead of subduing Jaya's growing cynicism, the rebuke and beating increased his doubts about the gods. One day Jaya discovered an old locked trunk, belonging to his grandfather, filled with ancient palm leaf manuscripts of the Hindu Vedas (scriptures). Still yearning to discover the truth about the gods, he broke in and leafed through the crumbling documents. One particular god of the Vedas caught his attention — the god of light! He had never heard of this god of light. Jaya read in the ancient scroll that sacrifice was necessary to take away sins, so that people could truly know the Creator. But it could not be the ordinary sacrifices of men; it had to be the sacrifice of the Creator in the form of man, dying to shed his blood for the remission of sins.[1] Something inside made Jaya determined to find out about this god of light.

Jaya asked the Hindu priest, who pointed him to a holy man in a nearby village who could guide him to the god of light. Sitting in lotus position on a stack of pillows, the bearded holy man told young Jaya that if he wanted to see the god of light, he must immerse himself in the Krishna River every night for a hundred nights and chant a special mantra a hundred thousand times. If he did this perfectly, the god of light would appear.

Undaunted by the burdensome task, Jaya, now fourteen, spent the next three months waist-deep in the filth and human sewage floating down the Krishna River. He chanted nonstop every evening, even as leeches attached themselves to his body and his skin broke out in boils. One hundred days and hundred thousand mantras later, Jaya crawled out onto the bank of the river, waiting in anticipation for the god of light to appear. No light appeared except the distant light of the rising moon. Jaya was beside himself — what had he done wrong? Discouraged, he gave up the search for two years.

At age sixteen, a holy man passing through the village came to stay with his family, and Jaya asked him about the god of light. He told Jaya he would take him to a high priest who lived eight hundred miles away, who knew the god of light. With the longing still burning within him to know the truth, Jaya decided to secretly run away with this holy man to see the high priest, willing to face the consequences when he returned.

Halfway through the weeklong train ride, Jaya discovered the holy man and his assistant had disappeared, and with them all Jaya's possessions and money. Exhausted and famished, he made it back to the train station in Rajahmundry, but discouragement overtook him as he sat by the side of the tracks and sobbed. Too ashamed to return home, too dismayed to hope, despair set in as he decided to end his misery.

Hearing the faint rumble of an approaching train, Jaya laid his body across the tracks. In one last prayer of desperation he cried, "God of light, if you are real, reveal yourself to me now for I am about to take my life." Jaya cannot explain exactly what happened in the next moments except he thought he was seeing the light of the oncoming train, but unlike any light he'd ever seen. He heard a voice say, "Jaya, I am the God you are seeking. I am the God of light. My name is Jesus." The next moment, Jaya felt the rushing wind of the train screaming past him as he stood beside the tracks — alive!

Filled with a sense of hope and purpose, Jaya declared, "Jesus is the God I have been seeking!" and hurried home to tell his family. After a tearful reunion with his family who feared him dead, he explained how he had almost committed suicide, but Jesus, the God of light, saved him. On hearing the name "Jesus," his grandfather flew into a rage and beat Jaya again, forbidding him to ever mention the name of Jesus, this god of the outcasts. As a wealthy, high-cast family, the idols they worshiped were off limits to the lower castes, and they despised the outcasts — the beggars, lepers, and "untouchables" — who often took Jesus to be one of their main gods among millions. Jesus had been known in India since the apostle Thomas (doubting Thomas) is said to have brought the message to India in the first century.

Jaya's encounter with Jesus faded into a distant memory as he grew up and went off to college, having dreams of becoming a wealthy businessman. After graduation, Jaya started a business. One day Jaya was riding his motorcycle across town and had a terrible accident that fractured his right leg. Two months after treatment, the leg had not healed, so he returned to the hospital. The doctors warned that unless the leg improved quickly, they would need to amputate it.

Jaya was distraught. Amputation was nearly a death sentence in a world where any handicap automatically conferred the status of untouchable (seen as the just consequence of bad karma). Lying on his back in the hospital, Jaya again felt his life ending. Then he remembered how Jesus had saved him. Through the intensifying pain in his leg, he cried out for Jesus, asking for his forgiveness and help. He vowed that if Jesus would heal him, he would not turn away, despite persecution, but would live for him and tell others.

As he drifted in and out of consciousness, he heard a melodious voice and felt a warm hand massaging his leg. When he awoke, the pain was gone. He asked the doctors who had come into the room what they had done to relieve his pain, but the doctors were baffled. No one had entered the room! Two days later, Jaya walked out unexplainably healed.

In 1986 Jaya started a church in Yerrakonda, a village near his home town. As a result, his family disowned him, and great resistance to his message formed in the community. After five years estranged from his family, Jaya found out his father had cancer and doctors were giving him a few days to live. His family permitted Jaya and his wife to come say goodbye.

Standing beside his father's emaciated body, Jaya and his wife boldly prayed for Jesus to reveal his power by healing his father. To everyone's amazement, days later the doctor pronounced him healed, and he went on to live five more years. One by one his father and mother came to faith in Jesus, then his brother (who also became a pastor), his sisters, and finally even his Hindu guru grandfather committed his life to Christ. Soon other villagers heard the story of the God of light, Jesus, and put away their idols to follow the living God.

I met Jaya years later, when he came to visit a Gateway staff member, Gary Foran. Gary had been a pastor at Kensington Church in Detroit when he visited Jaya's amazing work in India. Despite the fact that Jaya ministers to people who live on less than two dollars per day, God has provided the resources to accomplish his work through his growing Body. From 1986 to the year 2000, on virtually no budget, Jaya had started an orphanage for fifty-six kids abandoned to karmic justice, forced to beg to survive when they lost their families. He had started a sewing school, teaching destitute widows a trade so they could climb out of poverty. He had helped start thirty-five village churches out of a pastoral training school he set up. And when he stopped seeing miraculous healings, he asked the Lord why, and the answer he got was, "I want *you* to heal them," so he founded a modest medical clinic.

When the Kensington team visited India, Jaya took them to a vacant lot near his house. God had given him a vision to build a campus to minister to the poor, the orphans, the widows and to train pastors to go and do the same. Yet he had no idea where the resources to buy such prime acreage and build such a facility could come from. But God did — his worldwide Body!

When Kensington Church heard Jaya's vision, out of their abundant resources, they gave enough to buy the land and build Jaya's training center. With the larger Body connected and responding to God with their resources, God's dream expanded in Jaya's region. Within six years, the orphanage grew from 56 to 185 kids, 70 pastors were trained and sent out to start village churches in the region, an English school was started and 165 Hindu and Muslim kids enrolled, and in six years the eight-bed medical clinic treated almost 10,000 people who could not afford medical care.

When Jaya visited Gateway to see Gary, little did I know he had been praying for four years that God would join us in partnership! As Jaya told his story, God's Spirit was doing something in my heart. I was in awe of the amount of ministry God had accomplished through Jaya's staff of forty people amidst persecution and with so few resources (a typical pastor lives on $50 per month). As Jaya explained his vision to build a hospital to increase the capacity of the medical clinic tenfold (80 beds), the thought wedged deep in my mind, "God has blessed our Body so much. We can't do it alone, but if we team up with Kensington and people respond, we could raise the money for the hospital by Christmas." After visiting Jaya's project, our leadership team felt compelled to join him. We put it before our church, and thousands responded. Partnering with Jaya's ministry and thousands of people at Kensington church in Detroit, our church is seeing what God can do through us together as his worldwide Body that none of us could do alone. All it takes is people willing to simply listen, and respond together — even with their resources.[2]

NOT ENOUGH?

As Jaya's story illustrates, God is at work all over the world, building his kingdom through willing people. His plan is to begin to reverse the effects of this evil world as willing people function as his worldwide Body. It's his dream — it's the hope of the world. But it's also the most challenging task on earth, and one of the most challenging aspects has to do with our fear of not having enough resources.

God has a plan to resource his Body, the church, to overcome the evils of our world, locally and globally, through willing individuals whose hearts *feel wealthy*. God's desire is for you to feel so wealthy that you're filled with contentment, so wealthy that generosity comes easy, so wealthy you're overflowing with gratitude, so wealthy you need nothing more to feel satisfied. Out of that kind of full heart, we would willingly participate with God and each other to respond and resource his Body to impact the world. Who wouldn't want that?

But feeling wealthy is not a matter of money; it's spiritual. Ironically, where Western Christ-followers fear willingness the most is with their resources. We fear God wants to take from us and leave us wanting. Only as we overcome this unwarranted fear and trust God fully will we ever have "enough." Then will we see his dream coming true through us and find our dreams truly fulfilling.

DOES GOD WANT ME WEALTHY?

Time magazine ran a cover story in September 2006 titled "Does God Want You to Be Rich?" about the new gospel of wealth. Does God want you to be wealthy? Well ... it depends on how you define *wealthy*. A *Scientific American* study found if people have a choice between earning $50,000 a year while other people make $25,000 or $100,000 while others make $200,000 (cost of goods stay the same), surprisingly most people choose $50,000.[3] As H. L. Mencken quipped, "A wealthy man is one who earns $100 a year more than his wife's sister's husband." For many, it's a game of comparison.

A London School of Economics study showed more money does not equal more happiness after a certain point. Compared to the 1950s, "We have more food, more clothes, more cars, bigger houses, more central heating/cooling, more foreign vacations, a shorter work week, nicer work, and better health. Once average income is above $20,000 a year, higher pay brings no greater happiness."[4] The way we often define "wealth" is worthless — God's not interested in that comparison game; he wants to free us from it so we can enjoy what we have with gratitude and use it under his guidance together as One Body resourced to win.

The wealthiest man alive penned this in Scripture: "Those who love money never have enough; those who love wealth are never satisfied with their income" (Ecclesiastes 5:10). If being wealthy means "more than I have now" or "more than others" — God's not into that. On the other hand, if wealth is defined as "having more than enough, abundance, contentment, security, peace, lack of financial anxiety, generosity" then *yes* — that's the kind of wealth God wants you to find. But it's not usually an issue of amount, but attitude. According to God, the path to true wealth is counterintuitive. It's not by worrying and hoarding more, but by trusting and giving more.

Again, the goal of this 60-60 Experiment is to practice radically responding to God's Spirit so that we learn to hear with new ears, see with new eyes, and understand how his kingdom will and ways bring Life. But to really respond to God in this area, we must understand reality and how it works with our resources. We need to start by spiritually seeing our resources in light of a world in need and God's abundance available to resource his Body.

WHO IS WEALTHY — REALLY?

God has a lot to say through the prophets about his heart for the poor and down-trodden of the world. It's not just a footnote — over four hundred times God proclaims his passion for those in need, and how he wants his followers to exhibit his same passion. To religious people who were doing all sorts of religious acts, like fasting, but were unconcerned for poverty and injustice, God says:

> *No, this is the kind of fasting I want: Free those who are wrongly impris-oned; lighten the burden of those who work for you. Let the oppressed go free, and remove the chains that bind people. Share your food with the hungry, and give shelter to the homeless. Give clothes to those who need them, and do not hide from relatives who need your help. Then your salvation will come like the dawn, and ... when you call, the* Lord *will answer. (Isaiah 58:6 – 9 NLT)*

Our hearts must align with his heart and mission. The needs may be as close as your own relatives or neighbors or as far away as India, but we can't throw up our hands or hide behind clever defenses. As I've studied this, God has shown me how deceived I've been when I compare myself to those around me. I realize that I don't live in reality. We now live in a global village where the entire world is our "neighbor." Here's reality in our global village.

Over 20 percent of our neighbors live in abject poverty — 1.3 billion people live on less than a dollar a day. It's hard to imagine, but we need to. The book *Rich Christians in an Age of Hunger* helps us consider what we would have to give up to live like 20 percent of humanity:

> We begin by invading your house and stripping it of its furniture. Everything goes: beds, chairs, tables, television, stereo, lamps. Your family will get to keep a few old blankets, a kitchen table, and a wooden chair. Along with your chest-of-drawers go all your clothes, fall, spring and summer wardrobes. Each member of the family may keep their oldest outfit — only one. Only the head of the household gets shoes, none for the children. We move to the kitchen, and all appliances are gone — stove, toaster, microwave, dishwasher ... you can keep a box of matches, a small bag of flour, some sugar or salt. You'll have to recover those moldy potatoes in the garbage can — that will be tonight's meal along with a handful of onions and dried beans. Every other item in your refrigerator goes. Now we turn to the bathroom. We shut off the running water, take out all electricity, oh — and the house. Your family moves to the tool shed or ga-rage. Communications go next. No more newspapers, internet, books or maga-

zines — but you won't miss them because we must take your education — you can't read. There's one radio in your shantytown. No government services, no postman, firemen, one school three miles away has two classrooms. There are no hospitals, just a clinic ten miles away. If you have a bicycle you could get there in an emergency, but there's no doctor, only a midwife. Since we've also taken your savings and retirement away, and you are left with a cash hoard of five dollars, it's unlikely you'll have a bicycle or enough money to afford the clinic.[5]

This is your life if you are one of the 1.3 billion people with the bottom 20 percent of the world's resources. Half the planet, 3 billion people, live on less than two dollars a day (that's much of India, China, Pakistan, and many African countries). I've been to places of extreme poverty. I've visited shantytowns where raw sewage runs past the front doors. I've walked among cardboard homes in Mexico, lived among poverty in Russia — the reality of poverty is not new to me.

Here's what hits me like a knife through my heart. Consider who are the wealthiest people in our global village. Everyone in the top 20 percent of the wealthiest earns at least a whopping $1,800 a year! Let that hit home. If you earn more than $1,800 a year, you're in the top 20 percent. If you earn over $25,000 a year, you're in the top 10 percent of the world's wealthiest. Get this, if you earn over $47,000, then you're wealthier than 99 percent of all humanity; you're among the top 1 percent of the wealthiest people on the planet! Let that sink in for a minute.

Now, if it's true, say it: "I'm one of the wealthiest people on the planet." That's

ENOUGH ALREADY

I'm a relatively new Christian. I came to faith two years ago at Gateway. I have always felt uncomfortable about money and have worried about spending it and having enough, even though I have plenty with an engineer's salary and dual-income family. We have saved a lot, yet the lie that money is the source of security and that we need more to be secure is strong. The perspective you shared this morning helps me break free from that lie to place my trust in God rather than money. It has been a gradual process but we've decided to tithe and give more. It was startling to realize we are among the 1 percent wealthiest, and it was humbling to realize we have let fear hold us back from helping more. — Tonya

reality. For most of you reading this book, God has given you and me more personal resource power and ability to change things than 90 percent of humanity. This just rocks me to the core. And there's this thing Jesus said that I've never really liked: "From everyone who has been given much, much will be demanded; and from the one who has been entrusted with much, much more will be asked" (Luke 12:48).

When my eyes were opened to see reality, I was broken by it. Something is so terribly wrong. Though most Americans are in the top 10 percent of the world's wealthiest, we've believed lies that we aren't wealthy! Gallup Survey reports that only 2 percent of Americans think they are wealthy, 98 percent feel they don't have enough yet.[6] Think of how evil and deceptive that lie is.

God grieves over the wrongs and injustices in this world, and I must repent, turn from this lie that I'm not wealthy and that God has not blessed me enough. I must live in reality with gratitude. Gratitude is the beginning of living in reality, so that we as his well-resourced Body can both enjoy his gifts and make a difference.

WILLING TO BE GRATEFUL

Many people, when they hear these statistics, immediately go into guilt mode. They want to turn the channel, shut the book, run from God. But guilt is not the answer — *gratitude* and *willingness* are the answers. God does not say it's wrong to have wealth or savings: "When God gives people wealth and possessions, and the ability to enjoy them, to accept their lot and be happy in their toil — this is a *gift of God*" (Ecclesiastes 5:19, italics mine). The ability to enjoy and be happy with what you have is a spiritual matter, and it starts with gratitude, acknowledging your wealth as a gift from God.

Here's a great exercise to do this week. Sit down at an empty table with a pen and pad of sticky notes and begin to write down everything you have, one item per sticky note, and as you put each note out on the table, thank God for that gift. Include intangible blessings as well as material things. You'll be amazed as you see the sticky notes covering your table. Break the power of the "not enough" lie by thanking God for giving you "more than enough." Scripture does not say it's wrong to be wealthy, but it does command us to fight against the "not enough" trap by holding our wealth with an open hand, as receiving a gift, and by practicing generosity. Scripture says,

Command those who are rich in this present world not to be arrogant nor to put their hope in wealth, which is so uncertain, but to put their hope in God, who richly provides us with everything for our enjoyment. Command them to do good, to be rich in good deeds, and to be generous and willing to share. In this way they will lay up treasure for themselves as a firm foundation for the coming age, so that they may take hold of the life that is truly life. (1 Timothy 6:17 – 19)

God richly provides everything for our enjoyment — it's not wrong to enjoy all that he's richly provided. But he blesses us to *be* a blessing. He wants us to willingly, generously use it to do good. Most of us want to think of ourselves as generous people — right? I mean, whom do you admire most, people who are open-handed, sharing their blessings with you, generous and giving; or do you enjoy being with stingy, tight-fisted, greedy, protective kinds of people? Most of us resent wealthy people who are stingy, don't we! All of us want to be thought of as generous, but how do we get that way?

Jesus says it's a heart issue: "Store your treasures in heaven, where moths and rust cannot destroy, and thieves do not break in and steal. Wherever your treasure is, there the desires of your heart will also be" (Matthew 6:20 – 21 NLT). Jesus is simply revealing a spiritual truth — what you give toward reveals something about your heart. You give to what you love most, and then your heart gets more attached. Think about it — if you love golf, it's not hard for you to give money toward golf is it? You don't have to say, "Darn, I really should give money to play golf." If you love fashion, it's not hard to give money for a new outfit, is it? If you love your kids, it's not a burden to give Christmas presents to them. You give to what you love and then rearrange everything else to fit around it. So our attitude toward money and stuff reveals to us how much we really love and trust God and his purposes.

As you stay connected to God this week, begin to demonstrate your love to him with gratitude. Take time to be aware and thankful for all the big and little gifts you may tend to take for granted. This week, focus on gratitude. Sarah explains what this did for her.

Your admonition to turn from guilt and turn towards gratitude was so helpful. Since hearing that, I have been bombarded with that message from every possible venue. I have realized the importance of telling God, "Thank you" for all the things I take for granted. I will find myself saying out loud, "Thank you God for this delicious, rich cup of coffee; thank you for that sweet little furry puppy; thank you for this music; thank you for these people who care enough to point me in the right direction." It has become so obvious that we are all wealthy beyond our wildest imagination. This practice has taken away for a brief moment the "insatiable lust for more" which we Westerners must fight like warriors.

God wants us to not only be wealthy, but to feel wealthy in a way that pours out with gratitude ... and generosity. But how do we become wealthy, generous people who make a difference with our resources?

THE 60-60 EXPERIMENT

We spend so much time thinking of what we *don't* have, so this week be grateful for all you *do* have. Gratitude, not guilt. That's the path forward to a heart that's open and willing to acknowledge God's goodness and blessings, and the result is experiencing the spiritual fulfillment that comes with contentment, wealthy feelings, overflowing gratitude, and generosity welling up from within.

1. **Be grateful 60-60**. As you go through your day seeking constant contact with God, use every beep or reminder to stop and express gratitude for what you experienced the past hour. Be grateful in the moment throughout each hour. God will honor that gratitude even if you don't immediately see how. Journal what this does for your soul.

2. **Sticky note exercise**. Take several pads of sticky notes and a pen and block out thirty minutes to an hour. Write each item on a separate sticky note (income, family, talents, friends' names, couch, stereo, car with stereo, vacations ... everything) and put it on the table in front of you. As you do, simply acknowledge God's goodness for providing that item and thank him. You could tell him what you like about it and use the time as conversational prayer.

227 | Reconsider — Not Enough

3. **Read and respond to God.** God wants us to view him as an ally and provider. Read 1 Chronicles 29:11 – 14, Romans 8:32, 1 Timothy 6:17 – 19. Do you see God as an ally or adversary when you consider your finances? Is it difficult for you to trust God in this area? What do you fear? Journal and discuss this with your Running Partner(s).

CHAPTER SEVENTEEN

Resource—
RUNNING TO WIN

Joshua stared up at the sterile, white ceiling of the hospital room. "I've got everything my dad ever wanted. Financial security, career success, an amazing house on the lake, my ski-boat on the dock, a beautiful wife, and wonderful kids ... so what's wrong? I have the life I've always wanted."

The pain in his abdomen felt unbearable, yet it forced Joshua to think about things he hadn't had time to consider before. With everything stripped away except the minutes to ponder his existence, the hospital room became a delivery room for a new understanding of life for Joshua.

"I'm becoming just like my dad." The thought shot a pain through Joshua's soul rivaling the pain of the two surgeries that nearly took his life. "It can't be true."

From childhood, Joshua's dad had drilled into him the importance of hard work, saving, and above all else, financial security! His dad was an honest, hardworking, upstanding church leader who had raised his kids on a steady dose of church. Joshua had professed faith in Christ from an early age. As long as Joshua succeeded and accomplished, he felt good about himself and met with Dad's approval. It all went together: hard work, accomplishment, financial success, and being a good Christian.

With time to reflect, Joshua could see something terribly wrong. His dad lived for financial security above all else. His dad's fear-driven pursuit of money had slowly destroyed his marriage and chiseled away at Joshua's self-esteem until the relationship fractured. "But he can't see it," Joshua thought, swallowing the anger these memories brought. "Dad's blind to the pain he inflicts on those he loves, because what he loves is money — more than Mom, more than me, more than ... God!"

As the clock on the wall ticked off another painful hour, a passage of Scripture kept replaying in Joshua's mind:

> Look here, you who say, "Today or tomorrow we are going to a certain town and will stay there a year. We will do business there and make a profit." How do you know what your life will be like tomorrow? Your life is like the morning fog — it's here a little while, then it's gone. What you ought to say is, "If the Lord wants us to, we will live and do this or that." Otherwise you are boasting about your own plans, and all such boasting is evil. (James 4:13 – 16 NLT)

For days Joshua wrestled with God over that verse. He fought a deep-seated insecurity over what might result if he really tried to do God's will in everything. Joshua would rattle off all the reasons to justify his current plans, but this verse seemed to stream down unrelentingly from heaven into his brain. His helpless state forced him to realize that all his accomplishments, all he put his hope and security in, could do absolutely nothing for him. He couldn't even get out of bed. He had teetered on the verge of death. His real security could never be found in all those things. His wrestling match with God pinned him into this realization: "I feel entitled to a successful life on my terms. No one sees my egotistical thoughts of financial accomplishment, but they have led my life."

As Joshua admitted this new reality, Jesus' words flowed through his mind: "I tell you the truth, unless you change and become like little children, you will never enter the kingdom of heaven. Therefore, whoever humbles himself like this child is the greatest in the kingdom of heaven" (Matthew 18:3 – 4 NIV). "Children don't pretend they're independent," Joshua thought. "They know they need a wiser, stronger, loving Parent to guide them. I've heard it said ego means 'Edging God Out' and that's exactly what I've done. I live my life my way, and give a head nod to God, but I don't depend on his guidance. This *is* the same path my father took, but that's not the life I want." Looking back months later, Joshua reflected on his experience:

> In that hospital room, I realized I needed to surrender my ego and accept humility as the replacement. I realized lying helpless on my back that God desired for me to experience a love and security I was incapable of earning, producing, or achieving. That's honestly

what I longed for from my accomplishments, but it would only come through surrendering my entire life—including my finances. That did not happen right away, but I began praying for God to help me trust him enough to surrender my ways to his ways. All I can say looking back, as painful as it was, is that this medical crisis led me to gain something inside that nothing external could bring . . . a deep-seated security and gratitude. I'd never wish that pain on anyone, but I'm actually glad it happened to me. The depth of life and gratitude I'm beginning to experience this past year has been truly amazing.

WILLING TO THINK IT THROUGH

The Scriptures talk a lot about how we handle money. Why? Because resources are simply relational power — our little kingdom power by which we can choose to love God and others. It's relational currency! But in our fear-driven world it tends to be God's biggest relational rival. We tend to view money as a god. We trust in it for hope, security, joy, peace, the blessed life (like Jaya's family trusted in the wooden idols of their culture to bring life). When we do this, it robs us of a rich spiritual life because we take money too seriously and we take God too lightly. Feelings of wealth come when we're willing to think it through from God's perspective.

One of the most challenging races on earth is the Ironman Triathlon. Athletes first swim 2.4 miles, jump on a bike to cycle 112 miles, then finish it off running a full marathon — 26.2 miles. Chris Legh felt confident that he could not only finish the Hawaii Ironman, but finish strong and win. On that day in 1997, the gun went off and Chris dove into the Pacific Ocean. He felt good after the swim. Though he fell behind by about six minutes during the bike ride, he made up the time on his run and caught up with the leader. He was set to place first or second, when something went terribly wrong.

Only fifty meters from the finish line, Chris's body gave out. He collapsed. The one thing he had not paid attention to was what he ate and drank — the resources his body needed. Chris's body lacked the resources necessary to endure the challenge. Though his body was perfectly capable of winning, he couldn't finish. After barely getting through his first Ironman, Chris came up with a plan to make sure his body had the resources needed to win. Since then, Chris has become a two-time Ironman champion. Understanding how his body works and making sure his body had the proper nutrition to run made all the difference.

God's dream, as we explored in the last two chapters, is for his church to function as his Body and take on the challenge to mend and restore a broken world. But that requires resources to run on. Our resources are simply relational currency. We can choose to willingly participate with God to resource his Body to win. Though the choice of how we use our resources has been delegated to us by God, in reality, all we have belongs to him.

Jesus wants to give us Real Life, so he shoots straight with us about reality: all resources belong to God, he entrusts us with them, and he rewards those he can trust. Jesus used parables to teach these truths: "The Kingdom of Heaven can be illustrated by the story of a man [God] going on a long trip. He called together his servants and entrusted his money to them while he was gone. He gave five bags of silver to one, two bags of silver to another, and one bag of silver to the last — dividing it in proportion to their abilities. He then left on his trip" (Matthew 25:14–15 NLT).

Commentators estimate each bag of silver ("talent" in the original Greek) was a significant amount of money — maybe $300,000. So Jesus says, this wealthy person [God] takes what he owns and entrusts it to three people — to one he gives $1.5 million, to another $600,000, to another $300,000, then he goes on a long journey. The implication of Jesus' parable is clear — it all belongs to God first, and he entrusts us with different amounts.

IT ALL BELONGS TO GOD

It's funny that this is such a difficult concept for us, but Jesus wants us to really think it through. Jesus is saying all of life, and everything that passes through our hands, are gifts from God. God gives us life and says, "I'm going to give you some stuff to take care of. There will be varying amounts — for some, a little pile, some a medium-sized pile, some a whole bunch." But as we will see in this parable, there are some conditions. The first is, we recognize that everything belongs to God. You use it and enjoy it with gratitude — not as an entitlement!

I grew up racing sailboats with my dad. In college, I raced competitively for the University of Texas. From childhood, my dream was to own a J–24 boat and race it competitively. After a few years in business, I'd saved enough money to buy one but decided against it because I was thinking of transitioning into ministry and didn't think it wise to be encumbered with a boat. Still, after I'd made my move into ministry, I ended up near the coast and found myself racing as a crew member on a J - 24. One day after months of racing with the owner, he said, "John, I like you and trust you. I want you to be able to use this boat like it's yours." No kidding! I didn't ask, hint, or anything — it just blew me away. He gave me an extra key and said, "Feel free to take friends out, let them enjoy it. Keep racing with me, and if I'm not racing, you can race it. All I ask is that you take really good care of it — treat it as if it were your own."

So there I was, having put off buying a boat so I wouldn't be encumbered, which felt like a sacrifice at the time, yet I got this opportunity to have all the benefits without the financial burden. I saw it as a gift from God. So I took him up on it — I used it! I'd take friends out for sunset sails in the Pacific. We raced and enjoyed the heck out of it. It brought me enormous pleasure.

Now, what would you say to me if I started talking about it as "*my* boat" and even started getting stingy with it — as if I were the owner. What if I fell into the delusion that I owned it because I used it so much? What if the owner came to tell me he needed to sell it to do something else with the money (which he did), and I said, "No — you can't, it's mine!" You'd say, "What an ungrateful, arrogant, son of a . . . sailor!" Right? How deceived could I be?

Think about it! You may have worked hard for your stuff, but who gave you that ability to work and earn in the first place? God warned us long ago about the deceptive blindness that wealth can cause:

> When you build fine houses and settle down, and when your herds and flocks grow large and your silver and gold increase and all you have is multiplied, then your heart will become proud and you will forget the LORD your God. . . . You may say to yourself, "My power and the strength of my hands have produced this wealth for me." But remember the LORD your God, for it is he who gives you the ability to produce wealth. (Deuteronomy 8:12 - 14, 17 - 18)

Who gave you life? Who sustains you? Who put you in the circumstances that shaped you? Who gave you natural talents to achieve and earn money? There's so much about our lives we don't have control over, and we all have unique gifts and resources, as well as unique challenges. But all of it belongs to God, and we are responsible to develop and be trustworthy with what God's given.

HE TRUSTS US WITH IT

Notice that in Jesus' parable, the Wealthy Owner doles out different amounts to "each according to his ability," and he expects them to be good managers of it. He allows them to live off his wealth and enjoy it, but he also requires them to leverage it to expand his enterprise. So Jesus says, after a long time (implying all of life), the Owner returns and asks what each has done with what he entrusted them:

> *"Master, you gave me five bags of silver to invest, and I have earned five more." The master was full of praise. "Well done, my good and faithful servant.... I will give you many more responsibilities. Let's celebrate together!" The servant who had received the two bags of silver came forward and said, "Master, you gave me two bags of silver to invest, and I have earned two more." The master said, "Well done, my good and faithful servant.... I will give you many more responsibilities. Let's celebrate together!" Then the servant with the one bag of silver came and said ... "I was afraid I would lose your money, so I hid it in the earth. Look, here is your money back." But the master replied, "You wicked and lazy servant!" (Matthew 25:20 – 26 NLT)*

The first two guys don't start with the same amount, don't end with the same amount, but they get the same response: "Way to go! You were faithful to me. You took what I gave you, and you furthered my interests with it — doubled it, multiplied it. I'm going to entrust you with even more that I own!"

But the third guy still lived off it, enjoyed all the Owner's assets, but he didn't give a rip about using it to further the Owner's interests. He was afraid. From the comments, it sounds as if he was just self-centered and lazy, afraid he wouldn't have enough for himself. Maybe he was angry that he got less than the others, so he said, "This isn't enough to do any good — I should have been given more." He missed it — the chance to show he's faithful. The fear that led his life cost him everything.

The implications are clear. God has given all of us different amounts. He wants us to use it to provide for ourselves, even to enjoy it, but he also expects us to invest it to further his business here on earth. It's not all for us. He wants us to use our creative capacities to make it multiply for good — to leverage it for his kingdom-building enterprise on earth.

Jesus reminds us, it's not sacrificial — it's wise investing from an eternal perspective. Jesus said to be like the one who hears the Word, understands it, and bears fruit a hundredfold (Luke 8:4 – 15). That's one hundred times one hundred, a 10,000 percent return! God's return on my gifts and talents invested in *his* business is 10,000 percent, not the measly 10 to 20 percent return I can earn on my money through conventional means.

But what often gets in our way is not only our unwillingness to trust God, but also an unwillingness to trust each other. Many of us grew up bombarded by media reports of public scandals of religious leaders. As a result, our generation's default setting is to distrust all leaders, and we seldom take the time to understand the vision our local church Body has for the spiritual and physical needs of the world. All wise investments require research and risk-taking. We willingly trust people, investing with their companies to get a 10 or 20 percent return. Do we treat investing for a kingdom rate of return like we do investing for an IRA's rate of return? For some, distrust becomes a clever excuse: "I can't trust anyone with my money." So we do nothing. It's wise to make sure you're investing God's resources in trustworthy ways, but an equally good question might be, "Who can God trust with his money?" Can he trust you?

The late Peter Drucker, known as the guru of management theory, wrote about forty books about business and nonprofit leadership. In his last years he devoted himself to helping church leaders, and I had the great privilege of meeting him. He said, "Few things truly transform people's lives. Really just a couple things: local churches, twelve-step programs, and a few not-for-profit agencies."[1]

If you're motivated by meeting needs and helping people, then let me tell you, there's no other organization leveraging resources to meet needs like the Body of Christ. No church is perfect; every church has room to grow, but where else can you give and get involved with the leaders and others, leveraging resources to serve together? But to resource the Body to win, we have to trust God first, then each other.

Do you realize if those who claim to follow Christ in America actually tithed 10 percent to their churches, and used their gifts, creativity, and ingenuity to fight local and global evils, amazing things could happen? If even 5 percent of those tithes were directed toward trusted partner churches in the most poverty-stricken regions of the world (like Jaya's network of local churches),* enough resources could flow through the worldwide Body to completely eradicate the deaths of children under five due to poverty, educate every child globally, provide the message of Christ for every person on earth — and more![2] Think of the potential impact!

---

* One of the largest problems facing aid going to the under-resourced world is lack of local, connected leadership empowered by the aid. For instance, malaria nets or cheap medications can prevent the greatest cause of child deaths, but in some cases mothers do not use the nets or vaccinate their children because there is not trusted education from within the culture. Church-to-church networks form a path to bypass corrupt governments or inefficient bureaucracy by partnering with local leadership who can empower people to create local solutions.

And local churches would have the resources to meet more local needs as we all got creative together. But it doesn't often happen, does it? The average Christian gives 2.6 percent and stays largely uninvolved.[3] But if we follow God's lead, he will resource and equip his Body through us. As church-to-church partnerships and networks are starting to form across the globe, it's time for those of us who follow Christ to resource his Body.[4]

God desires to so invade and change people's hearts that they freely meet needs and work together to use their best creativity, innovation, and giftedness to make an impact — that's his vision of his church. Imagine all the good the Body could do locally and globally if we pooled those resources and got smart about meeting complex needs. We can't do that alone, distrusting one another and hiding behind our cynicism. The path forward starts with trusting God, then working together in trusting relationship.

HE REWARDS THOSE HE CAN TRUST

To the two who were faithful, the Owner in the parable said the same thing: "Well done, my good and faithful servant. You have been faithful in handling this small amount, so now I will give you many more responsibilities. Let's celebrate together!" Jesus makes it really clear — this is a test of faithfulness. No matter how much or how little we've been entrusted with in this life — it's all monopoly money. As John Ortberg likes to say, it all goes back in the box when the game of life ends. It's how we've played the game — how faithful we've been — that counts for eternity.

Jesus made this clear when he said,

> *Whoever can be trusted with very little can also be trusted with much, and whoever is dishonest with very little will also be dishonest with much. So if you have not been trustworthy in handling worldly wealth, who will trust you with true riches? And if you have not been trustworthy with someone else's property, who will give you property of your own? No servant can serve two masters....* *You cannot serve both God and Money. (Luke 16:10 – 13 NIV, emphasis added)*

It's a test of relational faithfulness!

WILLING TO TRUST

God wants our faithfulness and love. He tests our hearts with our resources to see who gets first place — God or money? What do we trust in most? We

TITHE — YOU'VE GOT TO BE KIDDING!

Tithe 10 percent? Are you kidding me? This was not the time to start tithing! My state job had been in a salary freeze the past year. I had to take odd jobs just to make ends meet. But the Ascending Leader's course I wanted to take required willingness to take God at his word and tithe 10 percent back to him. I had been okay with giving less than the full tithe, but as I sought counsel, I realized I wasn't trusting God on this one. I decided to go for it, though I couldn't see how it would work. The past month was my first official month to tithe and surprisingly, I had more money left at the end of the month than I have had in a *long* time. Only God could orchestrate that miracle ... ask my parents! Why am I writing this? Well, today was our state meeting at work. "The Vision for Tomorrow" is typically a free meal where they tell us we're great, and the salary freeze will continue another year. But surprise—we are getting merit increases in March! I couldn't believe my ears. On top of that we will get a bonus based on last year's success and a one-time appreciation bonus for hanging in during years of no raises. I don't get it, but I'm blown away with how God works things out. —Karen

tell ourselves things like, "If I just had more money," "Money can solve all my problems," "Money will make me happy," "Money will save me" — but it's all a lie! Money can't save you, fix you, secure you, or even make you happy. But it's an attractive God-substitute. When we trust in money more than in God, it produces discontentment, anxiety, greed, worry, and no more happiness. But Jesus says God trusts us with worldly wealth, which will not last beyond the grave, to see if he can trust us with things that last eternally. God doesn't force our hand open with our resources. He doesn't want us giving out of guilt, because it's a test of loyalty and faithfulness.

Thousands of years before the time of Jesus, God set out a test to see whether our hearts trust and love God more than money. It's a test of spiritual trust — a higher motivation than guilt, a higher motivation than meeting needs, and it requires the motivation of faithful obedience. Moses said: "One tenth of the produce of the land, whether grain from the fields or fruit from the trees, belongs to the Lord and must be set apart to him" (Leviticus 27:30 NLT). God says through the prophet Malachi,

"Bring the whole tithe into the storehouse, that there may be food in my house. Test me in this," says the LORD Almighty, "and see if I will not throw open the floodgates of heaven and pour out so much blessing that you will not have room enough for it. I will prevent pests from devouring your crops ... then all the nations will call you blessed." (Malachi 3:10 – 12 NIV)

For people who claim to love God, God says, "Demonstrate it by honoring me first. Take the first tithe (one tenth) of all I've given you and redirect it toward my purposes in my house." In that day the Temple, in our case the local church where we function as his Body, reaching out to serve the spiritual and physical needs of people. Why this benchmark amount? Because it seriously tests our loyalty — it's not easy, but it's not impossible. But it makes us face head-on the god of money that screams, "You need more," "Hold me tight, I'll save you," "I'll make you happy." It forces us to choose which god we will trust. And that's why God says, "Test me." This is the only place in Scripture where God says, "Test me with this one and see that I'm a loving Father who can provide all you need and more."

When my son was around four years old, we were in a mall, and I treated him to my favorite candy — Jelly Bellies. I bought him a big one pound sack. As we were walking along, he was shoving them in his mouth as fast as he could, drooling those delicious fruity flavors, and I asked him if I could have a few. He said, "No." I said, "Buddy — you're not gonna share?" He held them to the other side, out of my reach and said, "No thanks," trying with his best four-year-old manners to be polite about it. I realized my son needed a perspective check. He didn't realize those Jelly Bellies *were mine!* A four-year-old doesn't have any money. I bought them, and I could take them away if I wanted. But the more important lesson he needed to realize was that I loved him — that's why I provide good things! And I could buy more Jelly Bellies than even *he* could stand. But I knew I needed to help him reorient to an abundance perspective, so that he would trust me.

It's a spiritual heart issue. That's why if you hate hearing this, it's worth asking, "Why am I feeling so threatened, angry, and defensive? God's not making me give anything — he's letting me choose. What am I afraid of?" One person emailed me, "When you talked about giving 10 percent to God, I nearly gagged. It was a huge blow, and I'm a new Christian. But you challenged us to do it for three months, and just see if we weren't glad we did. So I took the challenge, and I have to tell you, I'm blown away with what's happened. Some of

JUST JELLY BELLIES

The message on Sunday moved me to tithe 10 percent for the first time in my life. Not out of guilt—but out of inspiration and faith. I was scared. It's a lot of money. I live paycheck to paycheck mostly. As a fairly new Christ-follower, I was pretty proud of myself for working up to 5 percent, but then Sunday it hit me—they're just Jelly Bellies. I came into the office today and my boss wanted to talk to me. I couldn't imagine what it was about. Then she told me ... she just got approval to give me a raise I hadn't even asked for! Is that crazy or what?!?! God is *good*! I thought you would get a kick out of that. —Angie

my financial messes worked out in ways I could never have predicted."

You may be thinking, "I can't afford to tithe." But see, you're still leaving God out of the accounting. Maybe the reason you can't afford to tithe is because you *don't* tithe. In the Old Testament book of Haggai, the people were finally really prospering and started getting consumed with more, more, more. But the problem was, the more they got, the more they felt they needed. The more they spent on themselves, the less content they were with the last purchase. The more they made, the less they gave toward God's business. Here's what God says through Haggai his prophet: "Now this is what the Lord Almighty says: 'Give careful thought to your ways. You have planted much, but have harvested little. You eat, but never have enough. You drink, but never have your fill. You put on clothes, but are not warm. You earn wages, only to put them in a purse with holes in it.... Give careful thought to your ways'" (Haggai 1:5–7).

Maybe the reason you constantly feel like all you make gets devoured and you never have enough to obey God is because you *won't* obey God in this area. And the only way past that is to trust — to do it, and see if God's faithful — right? That's why I always challenge people, like I'm going to challenge you — test God on this one. Tithe the full 10 percent for three months, and see if you're not glad you did.

Brad heard me teach about tithing while he was still a cynical atheist. With an engineering degree and a Harvard law degree, he peppered me with questions for nearly three years. Ironically, it was this idea of testing God with tithing that started to convince him of God's existence. Brad wrote me later to explain what happened:

I heard you say the bit about testing God by giving the full 10 percent, and I thought to myself, "Okay, that's empirically verifiable. I'll do it and see what happens. But this scam artist isn't going to get it. I'll give it to another charity." I just assumed all pastors pocketed whatever they could take in. For the next three months, I tithed, but not to Gateway. I was truly amazed. I received a totally unexpected 17 percent raise, which after taxes was just above my tithe. What's more, the raise was retroactive covering the period of my tithing (something my firm has never done before or since). I could not explain some of the things that happened, which became a major factor that led me down the path of opening my heart to Christ. Months later, after becoming a Christian, I decided to buy a house. My wife and I had always lived in an apartment because I never saw the value in the hassles of owning a house. God began to show me that the value was not about my self-centered cost/benefit view of the world; it was about my family having a gathering place to serve others. So I stepped out in faith and bought our first house.

During this time, I started following God's will at my work, which made my job extremely trying and difficult. I found myself persecuted and put down by my atheist boss. I was literally at risk of losing my job and felt it was just a matter of time. Yet at the end of the year, I was promoted to partner over the objections of my boss. With it, I received a huge jump in salary that just covered the additional monthly house expenses and a

TOO MUCH DEBT NOT TO TITHE

We've had $100K of medical debt due to an illness we've been paying off. We always give, but have never fully tithed 10 percent. This New Year's eve I finally said—alright God, it's time you took this over—and I decided to start tithing that night. I work straight commission. New Year's day at 11:00 p.m. a contract came in. My sales manager emailed to tell me because that doesn't happen on a holiday. The next day another contract came in. Wednesday the next contract, Thursday two contracts. God has continued to bless us, accelerating getting debt free—it's been amazing. —Kristy

bonus that almost exactly covered the out-of-pocket expenses. I felt like God bought me that house.

God has poured out blessings in so many areas of my life. Most notably, since opening the doors of my house, I have become a very different person. My circle of friends has grown dramatically. I used to be very self-centered, evaluating every relationship on "what's in it for me?" I find I now give with no desire to receive back. My relationship with my wife and daughter has grown deeper and better than ever. I've stopped trying to get them to give me what I want. I don't need anything back because God has blessed me with such abundance. Yet I've received a gift from all these people as I give to serve them. When I look at what God has done in my life, it brings tears to my eyes. I will always remember that Sunday when you read from Malachi, "Test me in this. . . ." I no longer need to test God, but he continues to pour out more blessings than I could imagine.

I went to lunch with Brad after he came to faith, and I asked him, "What made you think I would benefit if you gave more? Because none of us do — it just goes toward more ministry."

He said, "Even though you don't come across this way, I just figured the more you can get people to give, the more you get." I've got to tell you, that hurt me. I understand that a few church leaders take advantage of the Body, but the vast majority do not. Just look at statistics for average pastors' salaries.[5] Don't let a few untrustworthy leaders destroy God's dream by letting it undermine trust in the rest.

And church leaders, we need to go out of our way to ensure accountability and make sure our motives are not monetary. "Be shepherds of God's flock that is under your care, serving ... because you are willing, as God wants you to be; not greedy for money" (1 Peter 5:2 – 3 NIV). Kathy and I have tithed and given beyond 10 percent to ministries outside our church, and we've seen this in our lives as well as in story after story from others: when you radically respond, God is faithful. That doesn't mean you won't face trials or fears or financial setbacks. This isn't some magic money-making formula — this is not God Lotto! You don't obey God to get rich — it's a relationship, not a get-rich-quick scheme.

Since it's a relationship, God's interaction with you will be unique. Don't give to get. Give to be faithful and demonstrate loving trust in a good Father who provides for his children. God wants us to be willing to trust him — first! Even if things don't immediately work out as we want or think they should.

So I challenge you. If you claim to follow Christ, then test God by giving 10 percent for three months. Don't let any excuse get in your way. Just respond, and see if you're not glad you did. And if you don't trust your church — then give it to a church you do trust or to a ministry like World Vision or Compassion International for three months. But when God proves faithful, then decide which church you *will* trust, continue your tithe there, and get fully involved. You were meant to be part of the Body. You'll see when living off the rest that 90 percent with God's blessing ends up to be way more than 100 percent without it.

WILLING TO SACRIFICE IN LOVE

Tithing is the beginning of fully trusting God, but it's not the goal — love is the goal. "What sorrow awaits you teachers of religious law and you Pharisees. Hypocrites! For you are careful to tithe even the tiniest income from your herb gardens, but you ignore the more important aspects of the law — justice, mercy, and faith. You should tithe, yes, but do not neglect the more important things" (Matthew 23:23 NLT). Jesus reminds us that even tithing can become a legalistic, loveless act. We should do it, but the goal is that our hearts would grow so that we give out of love for God and people, not to feel self-righteous.

Picture these people and what they stood for: Martin Luther King Jr., Mother Teresa, Gandhi, Abraham Lincoln. What made them great? I'll bet most of us could picture every face and what they stood for — why? Because they were all movie stars? Because they were all powerful, wealthy, successful people? No! So what do they all have in common that etched their names and faces on the walls of our minds as great people? We all know what it is — they all *gave sacrificially* for the benefit of others. We recognize them today because each did something extraordinary — sacrificial — not to be noticed, but out of genuine love for others.

That's the character of God: "God put his love on the line for us by offering his Son in sacrificial death while we were of no use whatever to him" (Romans 5:8 MSG). Love made him do it. Sacrificial love is the heart of following Christ, and God wants to stretch our hearts until love for God and love for people cause us to not only be spiritually obedient, but lovingly generous. This shows the world the God who freely gives everything, and always has more to give.

When we become willing to follow God's Spirit moment by moment, including with our resources, he will lead us at times to make sacrifices above and beyond the 10 percent. When he does, give cheerfully, because something exciting is in store. The truth is, the greatest people — people God has used to change history — have been those who made the greatest sacrifices for others. And the more willing and open we are to respond and channel his resources toward his kingdom enterprises, the more he entrusts us with, and the more he flows our way. Ironically, as we radically respond with our resources in sacrificial ways, it never feels like sacrifice — it feels like abundant wealth!

In 1979 a man named Hugh Maclellan prayed, "God, I need you to stretch my heart in my giving." He said several things happened following that prayer. He realized that God really owns everything, and it all goes back in the end, and that he has an opportunity to participate in God's work and really make an impact that lasts. He started praying for God to really use him, an ordinary business guy, to make a difference in people's lives. He and his wife made a plan. He said, "We'd made business plans, vacation plans, retirement plans — but never a giving plan." They made a giving plan. They tithed already, but their company, Provident Insurance, and their investments kept growing. So they stretched their generosity beyond the tithe to their church and gave a greater and greater percent to feeding the poor, to starting churches around the world, and to youth programs in their city. They felt like God's Venture Capitalists — receiving more and more from God to invest in his business. For decades now they've given away 70 percent of what they made! Only love could motivate that.

Hugh Maclellan explains, "Since making that plan we've had the best years of our lives. There's no question about it, God really blessed it. For us it hasn't been sacrificial, but it has broken the power of money in our lives." Hugh and Nancy Maclellan's generosity helped Gateway and thousands of other churches get started. Love made them do it.

As you continue this 60-60 Experiment, seeking to stay continuously connected to God, ask him how you can trust him more with your resources, and make sure you listen and respond. If you've never fully tithed, test God. Take the three month challenge and give the full 10 percent, and I'll bet you won't be sorry. And before you discount your church, find out how much good your local church is doing already or hopes to do in the community. If the leadership is dreaming God's dream, use your gifts and resources to help your own church Body function to peak capacity.

THE 60-60 EXPERIMENT

As you keep connected and responsive to God, pay attention to your attitude toward all the resources he's given you. How willing are you to respond and use your stuff to love and serve God and others?

1. **Stay in 60-60 gratitude.** Keep practicing continuous connection to God, and with every beep of the watch or reminder, practice gratitude for all the blessings he gives. Ask him to show you if he wants you to use some of your resources to serve others in some way, and respond.

2. **Take the next step of trust.** Ask God to show you the next step of trust you need to take with the resources he's given. If you're not fully trusting to give anything, be willing to give something. If you claim to follow Christ but have been unwilling to trust by fully tithing, take the three-month test and see if you're not glad you did. If you faithfully tithe, has it become a loveless, religious duty? If so, ask God to stretch you to give out of the abundance he provides and see if you don't learn something new about God's goodness.

3. **Discuss.** Talk with your Running Partner(s) about what God's teaching you, where you feel fear, what your next steps might be. Share insights and stories on our blog and learn from others reading about their trials and victories.

CHAPTER EIGHTEEN

Re-imagine—
DECISIONS AND COMMITMENTS

Living in post-Communist Russia for a year gave me a gift — *time*! With no TV, radio, Internet, or transportation other than the subway, I decided to try my hand at writing. It was 1991, and as a minister to college students, I was feeling the shift from a modern to a postmodern world, though no labels had yet been applied. After much prayer, I decided to write a book to help my generation sort through these newly evolving questions about faith. With the extra time, I wrote eight chapters before returning to America.

Back in the States, I was asked to speak about our time in Russia at a little church in Solvang, California. Afterward, a group from the church took my wife and me to lunch, and there I met Carol. She mentioned she had to leave early because she had a chapter to finish. I questioned her and found out that she was a writer — and not just any writer. She was a widely published author in her own right, and had even done some writing for Billy Graham!

Wondering if this was another God coincidence, I told her about the book I'd been writing, and she asked me to send it to her! Within two months, Carol's publisher called and intimated they'd like to publish it. What a God thing! Publishers get about five thousand no-name author submissions every year. Most never have a chance, even if they are great books. I felt blown away at how God can orchestrate things as we follow his lead.

Then the phone call came. Carol's publisher had purchased another book company that flooded them with titles in my book's genre. They were really sorry but couldn't publish it at that time. Carol's editor passed the book on to two other major publishers, so the embers of hope were still alive. During that time our first child was born, my family moved from California to Chicago, and I started a new job as well as graduate school. I told the Lord, "If none of these publishers want the book, I'll take it as a sign to wait." Both publishers said no.

It's always confusing when you think God is up to something, all the planets seem to align, but then it gets eclipsed by some other events.

But that's not the end of the story. Four years later, I sensed it was time to try again. I'd been teaching a seminar on how faith works, so I put together a proposal and talked to Jack Kuhatschek, then an editor at Zondervan who published the people at Willow Creek Community Church where I worked. Jack felt the book had potential and got me working on some sample chapters and a proposal. My creative energy and excitement grew.

During this time, Brett Eastman and I drove to a retreat in Wisconsin, and on the way we talked about the way God had led each of us from California to Chicago. He asked, "How long do you think you'll be at Willow?"

"Definitely through 2000," I confidently responded. I had a great job and had just gotten a new responsibility to develop Willow's Extension partnerships in Chicago's inner city and around the world, which I had a vision to accomplish. Plus, I was only a thesis away from my master's degree, our second child was three months old, and now God had opened doors to write a book on faith. "All I know is that God clearly led us here," I continued, "but when he gives me a new vision and says, 'It's time to go,' I'll go. But I'll be here the next three years at least because I want to see this Extension effort to completion," I explained.

Two hours later and about thirty minutes into worship, everything changed! I don't get visions or hear voices. And although God's leading has always been clear looking back, it's never that clear looking forward. This time was different. As I worshiped, without a voice or a sound, the Lord said directly to my soul, "It's time."

I'm not even sure if those were the exact words because there were no words, but I knew what he meant: "It's time to step out in faith and follow my lead, just like you've been learning to do over these years." That was it. Nothing else.

It was not good timing. I've found the Lord doesn't have our sense of "good timing"; instead, he makes his own timing good. I told Kathy and reassured her that we wouldn't do a thing until God gave her the same confirmation that it was time to follow him into something new.

God confirmed it as Kathy and I prayed together over the next three months. "Delight yourself in the Lord," the psalmist says, "and he will give you the desires of your heart" (Psalm 37:4 NIV). I believe that has nothing to do with getting that mansion or Lamborghini you desire; rather, it's a promise that the more this moment-by-moment intimacy with God becomes our delight, the more we can trust that our hearts' desires are from God and in line with his will. I had a desire to see my postmodern, post-Christian generation find faith and become "the church." And as we prayed about location, "Austin" kept surfacing in conversation after conversation.

What a crazy sense of humor God has! I had lots going on at Willow, a thesis to finish, a book to write — but we left it all to start Gateway Church. Instead of wanting me to write about faith, God seemed to be saying, "No, I want you to step out in faith." Kathy was nursing a three-month-old, and we had a four-year-old at home; we had no money to start a church, no staff, no core group in Austin — but we did have faith. I asked the Lord to not take us to the edge (where he's all we have to depend on) and to give us some sense of security in this transition. He did. For a few months!

A team of close friends formed around the vision, three couples committed to moving with us to make up our staff team. A former friend from Russia called to ask if I'd help Hal and Sue Rich, who had just moved from New York, get plugged in at Willow. As Hal and Sue heard the vision, they felt God wanted them to be a part of the team, and so they committed the finances we needed for the first year! I networked with the one friend I knew in Austin, flew there, and had my first core-group meeting with ten people. God answered my prayer — we had confidence-building security!

A month later, my job at Willow ended, and we were three months away from moving to Texas. I flew to Austin expectantly for our second core-group meeting. Absolutely nobody came! Zero. No one! That same month, one by one, each staff couple decided not to move with us to Austin, and Hal had a huge job reversal and told me, "I can't promise that I'll be able to fund what I committed."

I HATE NOT SEEING

Even though the apostle Paul said, "We walk by faith, not by sight," I hate it sometimes! Trusting God when God is the only one we *can* trust gets scary, but with all our bridges burned, our family marched forward in faith (with knees knocking at times). Within three months, one door after another opened as God led us from person to person, from foundation to foundation, to provide all the money needed to start Gateway, plus enough to help start another church two years later. (Hal and Sue not only came through but opened many other doors.)

Now, nine years after starting Gateway, thousands of people have found faith and have become the Body of Gateway. I'm in absolute awe of what God has done — I can't take credit. Ironically, what I thought God wanted me to write in the book I started in 1991, God wrote into the Body of Gateway rather than onto paper. He did bring me back to writing twelve years later. Here's my journal entry from January 2003:

> When I look back at the exponential growth of Gateway, it all began the summer I spent in California fasting and praying during a four-week period, letting go of my need to control what happens, taking up the mantra, "I've been crucified with Christ, and it's no longer I who live but Christ who lives in me...."
> Now I'm fasting and praying for you to guide me as I try to learn from the past and look ahead to the future. Lord, should this be the year when I rekindle my desire to write and try to get published? I don't want to get published just to say I did; I want to write to make a kingdom difference. If so, lead me to know whether to write about the way of Christ or to do the faith book idea that's been on the shelf — I have so many stories of God's work.

Three months later, I attended a conference for the emerging church. In one of the sessions, I felt extremely troubled by all the deconstruction and the antagonistic spirit I felt there — it lacked the Spirit of unity Jesus desires. I kept thinking, "If my Buddhist friend who just found faith in Christ were here she'd say, 'This is why I've never wanted to consider Christianity.'"

I walked the grounds praying off my frustration, asking God what I should do. We were seeing thousands from our generation interested in exploring faith, yet here again, it seemed church leaders were getting mired down with internal debates and infighting. As I turned a corner, I saw Brett Eastman talking to the editor-in-chief of Zondervan. Brett called me over and introduced me to Stan Gundry. I mentioned I'd talked to one of his editors, Jack Kuhatschek, years before about a book idea.

"Jack's here. You should get together with him," Stan said. As Stan and I were talking, Jack was just leaving a meeting where the conversation centered around God's work with the emerging generation. They prayed for the Spirit to guide them, and as Jack walked across campus he prayed, "Lord, I need to be more responsive to your leadings. Lead me today — I want to be willing to listen and respond." Because of that prayer, he decided to meet me when I called.

Two hours later, Jack and I met for coffee. I caught him up on the past five years, telling him the amazing stories I'd seen of God's perfect work in imperfect, messy people.

"You'll never believe this," Jack said, "but I was just in a meeting discussing where this kind of thing might actually be happening, and now you're telling me these stories. I was asking God to lead me to this just before you called . . . Can I come to Austin and meet some of these people?"

After visiting people who found faith at Gateway, Jack encouraged me to write about their stories and the "soil" in which God caused this growth, and so *No Perfect People Allowed: Creating a Come-as-You-Are Culture in the Church* was published to help people find faith, written through people's lives in our church.

DYING TO SELF . . . AGAIN!

"Dying to self . . . again" was the title of that journal entry from 2003. It's a lesson I'll probably have to learn the rest of my life. As we get better at continuous connection and radical responsiveness to God's Spirit, we *will* see greater and greater evidence of his loving guidance. But it does take time — for me, years of faithfulness. And it does take dying to self (turning it over and letting God be God 'cause I'm not) again and again. Often God's ways and timing do not fit our plans or timing, and that gets very frustrating along the journey. Only as we stay faithful do we see increasing evidence of his faithfulness.

Sometimes, I believe his timing has more to do with what he's accomplishing in me rather than just through me — he cares about you and me that much! And I'm convinced that God sometimes leads us to places where we have the opportunity to see our broken strategies clearly and let them go, so we can experience all he intended. I noticed this line in my journal: "That's the scary part. You will let me remain blinded by my own assumptions and views if I'm not willing to humble myself before you and seek you with all my heart — and let you *undo* me to remake me." Often it takes time before I'll humble myself and let go to truly follow God.

Unfortunately, I find many people get discouraged and give up too soon. When things don't go their way, they get impatient and disconnect from God; they stop listening and responding to him and instead respond to whatever seems more instantly gratifying. Soon, they don't hear a thing (spiritually speaking). Then they complain, "God just doesn't lead me like that. I tried, but it just didn't work for me."

Hopefully you've engaged in this 60-60 Experiment consistently enough to start to spiritually see and hear and understand that there's so much more to living than you've imagined. I've prayed that your eyes would be opened to see how wide and long and high and deep is the love of God, though you could never fully comprehend it. I've asked God to help you hear his thoughts in your mind and have courage to radically respond. I hope you've caught a glimpse of life with God as you did respond, so that you've seen evidence of his goodness and willingness to make your paths straight as you trust him with all your heart. And I hope you've encouraged others by blogging what you've been learning and experiencing. But this is just the beginning! God did what he did through Jesus so you could live this way beyond sixty days.

More than anything else, I hope you realize God's will is that this experiment in continuous connection and radical responsiveness *never ends*. On Jesus' last night he said, "Now this is eternal life: that they know you, the only true God, and Jesus Christ, whom you have sent" (John 17:3). Eternal life starts now! This is the "one thing" Jesus said is necessary — to know God and stay connected, listening, and willing.

THREE YEARS FROM NOW

Imagine what life would be like three years from now if you decide to make this a way of life rather than a sixty-day experiment. You have a picture of life according to old strategies, but reimagine your life for a second. Imagine looking back three years from now with a growing love for God that brings you overwhelming joy and gratitude, retracing the many "visible" ways God has been good to you as you've trusted and responded. Imagine experiencing a growing sense of confidence that your life brings delight to the heart of God. Imagine having memories with the One you're now realizing is not only your loving parent and teacher, but also your best friend and greatest guide through all of life.

Larry came up to me with tears in his eyes at the end of our 60-60 Experiment. Every year he coordinated a worldwide conference. It never helped his ulcer. He'd been on the bubble with his boss because it hadn't gone well the past two years. He was responsible to coordinate executives across the globe whom he didn't have authority over. They would never get back to him, or he couldn't get them to agree and work together, so historically it had caused two months of ulcer-inducing stress and worry. With eyes filled with tears of gratitude, Larry shared, "This year, I kept giving my worries to God, asking for clarity on the next right thing to do, praying for things moment by moment rather than just worrying. I didn't get an ulcer, people got back to me on time, they worked with me, and my boss said this was the best conference ever! It's amazing ... when you just stay connected to God how much difference it can make."

As we stay connected and responsive, we get to know God. We make memories with the One who loves us.

Imagine three years from now finding it easier to love even hard-to-love people. Imagine growing in your ability to live at peace with everyone, able to resolve conflicts quickly instead of letting things stew. Imagine experiencing tolerance and patience with other's wrongs and faults, so that they see you as an ally for change rather than an adversary. Imagine living your life free from worry about what others think of you, and instead, increasingly able to encourage and motivate and inspire others. Imagine being completely at peace with your past, regardless of what people did to you or what you did to them. Imagine having such God-given, clear boundaries that you can choose to serve others without feeling resentment. Imagine a close group of trusted friends who know everything about you, yet see your potential and encourage you as you pursue your dreams.

Imagine having the confidence that God has a bigger purpose for your short stay on this planet, as you see your unique gifts, experiences, passions, and resources developing and expanding to make a difference in this world. Imagine what your life could be like!

But you won't just drift into this kind of maturity. Like every worthwhile endeavor, it requires a decision and commitment. That's why this last exercise of the 60-60 is the most critical of all — deciding and committing.

COUNTING THE COST OF LIFE

Jesus often talked about decisions and commitments. A large crowd was following Jesus one day when he turned to the people and said,

> You cannot be my disciple [student in living], unless you love me more than you love your father and mother, your wife and children, and your brothers and sisters. You cannot come with me unless you love me more than you love your own life. You cannot be my disciple unless you carry your own cross and come with me. Suppose one of you wants to build a tower. What is the first thing you

will do? Won't you sit down and figure out how much it will cost and if you have enough money to pay for it? (Luke 14:26 – 28 CEV)

Jesus asked, "Why do you call me, 'Lord, Lord,' and do not do what I say? As for those who come to me and hear my words and put them into practice, I will show you what they are like ..." (Luke 6:46 – 47). Then he told the story of a person, who built a house with a strong, solid foundation, and when the flood waters of crisis hit — it lasted. But the other person, who took the instant gratification route, watched his whole house wash away.

Jesus is saying, you need to count the cost and decide: will I be committed to building my life's foundation on living the way of Christ? What is Living Water worth to you? Are you willing to pay the price to decide and commit to live moment by moment in responsive relationship with God? Will you let go of old, shallow strategies that lead you away from the way of Christ? It may not always be easier, but it will bring an eternal thirst-quenching kind of life from within, and it will last forever. You have to ask, what's that life worth?

Frank Laubach, looking back on his experiment in practicing the presence of God every minute of the day (which is the real goal — not every sixty minutes, but every sixty seconds), declared: "When one has struck some wonderful blessing that all mankind has a right to know about, no custom or false modesty should prevent him from telling it.... I have found such a way of life, ... and it is very simple, so simple that any child could practice it, ... yet it transforms life into heaven.... The results of this effort begin to show clearly in a month. They grow rich after six months, and glorious after ten years."

But Laubach also notes the price we must pay. "The first price is the pressure of our wills, gentle but constant." In other words, it costs the discipline of constant willingness. "The second price is perseverance." He reminds us not to give in to poor results in the short run, faithfulness requires stick-to-itiveness. There are no losers except for those who quit. "The third price is perfect surrender." Laubach says if we hold back a remote corner of life for self or evil and refuse to listen and respond to the Lord, that small worm will spoil the fruit. "The fourth price is to be often in a group." Laubach notes that we need to be around others intent on walking closely with Christ moment by moment to keep encouraging one another.

DECIDE AND COMMIT

A spiritually fulfilling life requires the same level of decision and commitment required for any important accomplishment in life. Dallas Willard notes how this decision to follow the way of Jesus is what's lacking in much of Christianity today: "I rarely find an individual who has actually made a decision to live as a student of Jesus.... It is the power of the decision and intention over our life that is missing. We should apprentice ourselves to Jesus in a solemn moment, and we should let those around us know that we have done so."[1]

For the past sixty days, we've been doing this experiment in living the way of Christ. As the last exercise in this experiment, I want to ask you to do what Willard suggests: decide if you will continue this next year to go the way of Christ in community with those around you, as we've experimented with during this 60-60. If you will decide and commit, then tell someone. Affirm that decision with your group or Running Partner or closest Christian community, because there's power in deciding and committing.

If you have done this experiment in community with others, work through the last exercise at the end of this chapter, then make a point during your next meeting to talk about what each of you has decided and committed to for the next year. I find year-by-year decisions and commitments to a smaller community are a good way to reaffirm what you desire, and then you can help each other stay committed to that path. We all stray, so we need that yearly assessment and recommitment.

ROCK PILES

If you're committed to continuing on the way of Christ this next year, let me give you some helpful suggestions. We have short-term memories when it comes to God's goodness and faithfulness. Whenever God did a great work in Old Testament times, he'd have the people make a "rock pile" memorial as a reminder of his faithfulness: "Each of you is to take up a stone on his shoulder, according to the number of the tribes of the Israelites, to serve as a sign among you. In the future, when your children ask you, 'What do these stones mean?' tell them that the flow of the Jordan was cut off before the ark of the covenant of the LORD" (Joshua 4:5 – 7).

I have a stone in the shape of an arrowhead that I mounted on a plaque I keep on my desk. It reminds me that I can trust God with my "Isaacs" (those things most dear to me). When leaving the business world for ministry, I asked God repeatedly to let me stay in Santa Barbara and work with the campus ministry where I served as a volunteer. I was doing my ministry training at a place called Arrowhead Springs (so called because a huge rock formation forms a giant sixty-foot arrowhead in the mountain above the old resort). I had just started a plan for reading through the Bible for the first time and read Genesis the night before I heard the bad news. I would not be able to move back to Santa Barbara; my first ministry assignment would probably be in New Mexico.

Hurt, confused, and miffed at God, I took off running up the trail to the top of Arrowhead Mountain to blow off steam. At the top I told God all that was on my mind. I went through the litany of "good boy" sacrifices I'd made for him and asked him why he couldn't do this one thing for me. Slowly, despite my complaining, I started to recall the lessons I'd learned when things weren't going my way and how God's ways were always good. "Didn't I provide a job when you trusted and went to Russia?" The thought interrupted my tirade. "Didn't I provide a great roommate and friends and fun for you in Santa Barbara when it seemed inconvenient?" I sensed God whisper. And on and on I recalled the many ways God had been faithful, until I found myself in tears of gratitude, apologizing for so quickly forgetting. "Okay, Lord, if it's New Mexico, then I'll trust it's going to be even better."

I spent another hour on the mountain just thanking my Father, and as I started down the trail with the golden sunset lighting the way, I had a clear prompting to look down. Right then, I stepped across a rock in the exact shape of the giant arrowhead. "Remember my faithfulness," was what I sensed as I picked up the rock and put it in my pocket.

When I got to the conference center, I was greeted with the news — I'd be going back to Santa Barbara after all! I was ecstatic. That night I picked up reading in Genesis 22 — the story of God testing Abraham with the sacrifice of Isaac, only to give Isaac back. The arrowhead rock on my desk always reminds me: "God will be faithful with my Isaacs."

As you see God do those little (or big) "coincidental" things in your life — pile up some rocks to remember! I've kept a journal for the past twenty years as a way of recording God's faithfulness — it's been a great rock pile to go back to when circumstances look bleak and I need help trusting God's faithfulness. Find a way to pile up rocks of remembrance whenever you see or hear God's presence — it will help you stay faithful to the One who is always faithful.

CELEBRATE GOD'S LOVE

Finally, don't forget what it's all about — loving relationships! You'll know you're growing in loving God when people experience his loving ways through you. After all, Jesus said that would be the way people could spot his true followers — by their love. When you see evidence of this growing God-like capacity to love or experience his love — celebrate it! That's important. Thank God — it's his supernatural doing.

Remember, the Christian life is really simple at the core — do all of life, moment by moment, in relationship with God. When we are willing to do his will, he leads us into truly loving relationships with those around us, and gives us an unexplainable joy and contentment despite our circumstances. Then together with our unique gifts and passions, time, and resources, he helps us function like interdependent parts of his Body to express his love and compassion to the world around us.

That's the way of Christ — what we've been practicing for sixty days. I pray it will become your habit for life, and you'll experience just how wide and long and high and deep the love of Christ is for you, and you'll become all God intended through this soul revolution.

THE 60·60 EXPERIMENT

Congratulations! You've done the 60-60 Experiment. Although no one can do it perfectly, I'll bet you've seen progress — and that's the point. God's desire is that this would not be an ending, however, but the beginning of an ever-growing intimacy and daily walk with your Creator as he guides you into his life-giving ways. But this won't happen by chance. You'll have to decide and commit to continue in this way. As the last exercise in this experiment, decide where you want to go from here.

1. **Reimagine the future you**. Take some time to write down what you dream for yourself three years from now. Who do you hope to be on the inside? How do you hope to be in relationship with the people and the world around you?

2. **Decide**. What do you believe about the importance of staying connected and responsive to God in order to become who you hope to be? Count the cost and decide what it will take to grow deeper in this way of life for the next leg of the journey.

3. **Commit**. If you're willing to commit to continuing on the way of Christ as we've been exploring, pray about a reasonable time of commitment. I find a yearly rhythm of assessing, celebrating, and committing for the next year (I do this every January 1) is a good way to see progress and keep refocusing on what matters most. Decide and write down your commitment.

4. **Tell someone**. Tell your group or Running Partner(s) what you've decided and committed to so that you can pray for each other and encourage each other. Talk about whether continuing to meet as a group or as Spiritual Running Partners would be helpful. As you do, be sure to regularly assess and celebrate — make rock piles of God's faithfulness. Keep reading our blog and encouraging others continuing in the way of Christ (*www.Soulrevolution.net*), and let's see how God changes the world through us!

Special Thanks

The more I write and speak, the more I realize how my ideas are greatly formed in community, which makes it difficult to acknowledge everyone who has had a shaping influence on this book because there are too many to thank. But there are a few people whose sacrificial contributions made this book possible.

Kathy, you are my partner in everything. When I think about all we've seen God do in our lives, it's because you have been an eager partner in this faith-venture. Thanks for all the late nights and early mornings brainstorming and talking over ideas, reading and editing messages, and doing such a great job editing this book. Not only did I marry the most beautiful woman in the world, but the most talented, Spirit-filled, faith-filled too. You live out what this book is about like no one I've ever known.

The original 60-60 Experiment came out of a series we did at our church. A team of people helped shape message titles, the experiment, web resources, and small group curriculum. Becky Laswell worked tirelessly building our Way of Christ resources found on the *www.Soulrevolution.net* website. Ted Beasley, Gary Foran, John Drusedum, Betty Blake Churchill, Michael Warden, and Kenny Martin all contributed significantly on that team.

Michael Warden, you have been an amazing example of living the way of Christ in tune with his Spirit. Thanks for all your hard work writing curriculum and exercises that made it a richly textured experience for thousands. Your excellent input on this manuscript has made a huge difference.

John Raymond has given invaluable input along the way, helping me think through ideas and see things from new perspectives. Thanks for your editorial input and friendship throughout the project. Theresa Rozsa, thanks for going above and beyond helping with research and reading the manuscript. Your partnership in ministry has been an incredible blessing. Bill and Renee Curtis, you have been such an example of generosity as long as we have known you. Thanks for letting me hang out and write in such an inspiring place.

Notes

Chapter Three: Reorient — Doing Life with God 60-60

1. Brother Lawrence and Frank Laubach, *Practicing His Presence* (Jacksonville: SeedSowers Publishing, 1978), 19.
2. Brother Lawrence, *Practicing His Presence*, 2.
3. Brother Lawrence, *Practicing His Presence*, 3.
4. Brother Lawrence, *Practicing His Presence*, 5.
5. Brother Lawrence, *Practicing His Presence*, 14 – 16.
6. Brother Lawrence, *Practicing His Presence*, 22 – 23.

Chapter Four: Reconnect — Prayer as a Way of Life

1. For more on Jesus' view of the Scriptures read Matthew 4:1 – 10 (Jesus quotes Scripture as having authority from God); Matthew 21:42 – 46; 22:29; 22:41 – 46; 26:52 – 56; Mark 12:7 – 11; Luke 4:16 – 21; 24:25 – 27; 44 – 45; John 5:39 – 47; 10:34 – 39; 13:18 – 19; 19:24 – 37.

Chapter Five: Respond — Engaging in Risky Behavior

1. See Psalm 51; Ephesians 2:8 – 10; 1 John 1:1 – 2:2.

Chapter Six: Revolution — Kingdoms in Conflict

1. I first heard Jerry tell this story in 1992. It has since been published in: Angus Menuge, ed., *C.S. Lewis: Lightbearer in the Shadowlands* (Wheaton, Ill.: Crossway, 1997).
2. Dallas Willard, *The Divine Conspiracy: Rediscovering Our Hidden Life in God* (San Francisco: HarperSanFrancisco, 1998), 31.

Chapter Seven: Relate — A New Way to Live Together

1. U2, "Walk On" on *All That You Can't Leave Behind* audio CD (Santa Monica, Calif.: Interscope Records, 2000).
2. George Barna and Mark Hatch, *Boiling Point: Monitoring Cultural Shifts in the 21st Century* (Ventura, Calif.: Regal, 2001), 102 – 4.
3. George Gallup, *The People's Religion* (New York: Macmillan, 1989), cited in Randy Frazee, *The Connecting Church* (Grand Rapids: Zondervan, 2001), 24.
4. Adapted from John Burke, *No Perfect People Allowed* (Grand Rapids: Zondervan, 2005), 289 – 90.
5. Larry Crabb, *Connecting* (Nashville: Thomas Nelson, 1997), 98.
6. Crabb, *Connecting*, xi.

Chapter Eight: Reconcile 1 — In the Ring

1. Gary Smalley and John Trent, *The Language of Love* (Pamona, Calif.: Focus on the Family, 1988).
2. David Augsburger, *Caring Enough to Confront* (Ventura, Calif.: Regal, 1973). This book is an excellent resource on conflict resolution.

Chapter Nine: Reconcile 2 — Living Clean with People

1. James G.T. Fairfield, *When You Don't Agree* (Scottsdale, Pa.: Herald Press, 1977), 56.
2. Fairfield, *When You Don't Agree*, 60-61.

Chapter Ten: Reformation 1 — How People Really Change

1. Henry Cloud and John Townsend, *How People Grow: What the Bible Reveals about Personal Growth* (Grand Rapids: Zondervan, 2001), 69.
2. Cloud and Townsend, *How People Grow*, 70.

Chapter Eleven: Reformation 2 — Taking Spiritual Inventory

1. Dallas Willard has written extensively on this idea. I recommend his book *Renovation of the Heart* (especially the chapter on transforming the body).
2. James M. McPherson, *Drawn with the Sword: Reflections on the American Civil War* (New York: Oxford University Press, 1996), 44–47.

Chapter Twelve: Reorder — Habit-Breaking Intentionality

1. Dallas Willard, *Renovation of the Heart: Putting on the Character of Christ* (Colorado Springs: NavPress, 2002), 45.
2. Willard, *Renovation of the Heart*, 144.
3. Willard, *Renovation of the Heart*, 142.
4. Karen S. Peterson, "Affairs Rare Despite Rumored Popularity," *USA Today* (December 21, 1998): *www.dearpeggy.com/announce4.html* (Accessed September 24, 2004). A 1994 study done by the University of Chicago indicated about 28% of men and 17% of women admitted to an extra-marital affair. Since it was a random survey, assuming none of the men randomly surveyed were married to the women surveyed, it appears an estimated 45% of marriages were affected. Others have estimated much higher rates of infidelity. See Bonnie Eaker Weil, *Adultery: The Forgivable Sin* (Hastings House Book Publishers, 1994), 3. She estimates 30–50% of wives, and 50–70% of husbands have had an affair, but this appears too high considering research that still indicates most people are faithful most of the time.
5. Willard, *Renovation of the Heart*, 35.

Chapter Thirteen: Retrain — Developing a Spiritual Workout

1. Dallas Willard, *The Divine Conspiracy: Rediscovering Our Hidden Life in God* (San Francisco: HarperCollins, 1998), 353.
2. Alan Richardson, *Individual Differences in Imaging: Their Measurement, Origins, and Consequences* (Amityville, N.Y.: Baywood, 1994).

Chapter Fourteen: Re-present 1 — God Has a Body

1. Wilder Penfield, *The Mystery of the Mind: A Critical Study of Consciousness and the Human Brain* (Princeton: Princeton University Press, 1975).
2. For statistics on:

Spending and Debt — Kim Khan, "How does your debt compare?" Posted January 2005. MSN Money. *moneycentral.msn.com/content/SavingandDebt/P70581.asp.* (Accessed October 25, 2007).

Divorce — John Crouch, "Divorce Rates." *www.divorcereform.org/rates.html* (Accessed October 25, 2007).

Substance abuse — "Substance Dependence, Abuse, and Treatment," *Results from the 2002 National Survey on Drug Use and Health*: *National Findings.* 2003. Substance Abuse and Mental Health Services Administration: *oas.samhsa.gov/nhsda/2k2nsduh/Results/2k2Results .htm#chap8* (Accessed September 20, 2004).

Sexual abuse — Patricia Tjaden and Nancy Thoennes, *Full Report of the Prevalence, Incidence, and Consequences of Violence Against Women*: *Findings From the National Violence Against Women Survey* (National Institute of Justice, November 2000), iii-iv. *www.rainn.org /fullnvawsurvey.pdf* (Accessed September 20, 2004). Robert T. Michael, *Sex in America*: *A Definitive Survey* (New York: Warner Books, 1994): reports one out of five women had been sexually molested in 1994 survey. Other surveys indicate as high as two out of five. Whatever the actual statistics, my counseling experience is that it's way too high a percent.

Sexually Transmitted Disease — "Learn About STIs/STDs," American Social Health Association. Last Updated: October 9, 2006. *www.ashastd.org/learn/learn_statistics.cfm* (Accessed October 25, 2007).

Abortion — "An Overview of Abortion in the United States." Posted June 28, 2006. The Alan Guttmacher Institute: *www.guttmacher.org/media/presskits/2005/06/28/abortionoverview .html* (Accessed October 25, 2007).

Cancer — "Cancer Statistics 2007" American Cancer Society. *www.cancer.org/downloads /STT/Cancer_Statistics_Combined_2007.ppt#256,1,Cancer Statistics 2007*, 18 – 19. (Accessed October 25, 2007).

Friends — George Gallup Jr., *Emerging Trends*, vol. 19, no. 3 (March 1997). Also see "Americans have fewer friends outside the family," Posted June 23, 2006, Duke University: *dukenews.duke.edu/2006/06/socialisolation.html* (Accessed October 25, 2007).

3. An excellent resource for helping others find faith is Bill Hybels' *Just Walk Across the Room* (Grand Rapids: Zondervan, 2006).

Chapter Fifteen: Re-present 2 — Be the Body

1. Ministry Tools Sites: *mintools.com/spiritual-gifts-test.htm*
Chistianet: *www.christianet.com/bible/spiritualgiftstest.htm*
BuildingChurch.net: *buildingchurch.net/g2s-i.htm*
ELCA Assessment: *www.elca.org/evangelism/assessments/spiritgifts.html*
Team Ministry: *www.churchgrowth.org/cgi-cg/gifts.cgi?intro=1*

Chapter Sixteen: Reconsider — Not Enough

1. Jaya sent this to me to explain where in the Vedas he came across these ideas: "The main theme in the Rig Veda and the Upanishads is the nature and purpose of only one supreme sacrifice known as the Purush Prajapati. This name is translated from Sanskrit as "the Lord of all creation who became Man" (Sathpathbrahmana 10.2.2.1_2; Rg Ved Purushasukta 10:19) ... This Purush Prajapati is the one and only way to eternal life (" ... Nanyah pantha vidyate-ayanaya": Yajur Ved 31:18). This Supreme Creator took a perfect human body (Nishkalanka Purusha) and offered it up as a self-sacrifice (Brihad Aranyak Upanishad 1.2.8). He

was symbolized by a spotless lamb which was the animal most commonly sacrificed in those days (Maddyandiniya Sathpathbrahmana III). He is the only sinless human being, and only in knowing Him does one obtain immortality (Chandogya Upanishad 1.6:6,7). Acknowledging the sacrifice of the perfect Purush Prajapati imparts eternal life (Kathopanishad 1, 3.8, 11). After giving Himself as the supreme sacrifice, He resurrected (not reincarnated) himself (Brihad Aranyak Upanishad 3.9.28.4_5; Kathopanishad 3:15). By his resurrection, the Purush Prajapati conquered death and released sin's stranglehold on mankind. He will return to earth only once more. At this point in its account, the Vedantic history of Purush Prajapati ends. To summarize, the only purpose of the Purush Prajapati is to sacrifice His lifeblood to pay our penalty for sin and to impart to us eternal life. It is the only way to Heaven and the only way of escape from eternal Hell" (Rg Ved 9:113.7_11; Rg Ved 4.5.5; 7.104.3). Taken from the book *From Darkness Into The Glorious Light*, (Global Evangelical Missionary Society, 2004).

2. Jeff Petherick from Kensington church also recorded Jaya's story in chapter 20 of his book, *Wavelength, Tuning in to God's Voice in a World of Static* (Elk Lake Publishing, 2007).

3. Michael Shermer, "(Can't Get No) Satisfaction," *Scientific American* (March 2007). Scientific American.com: *www.sciam.com/article.cfm?articleID=C73C7109-E7F2-99DF-31EB094AF 750C3C3&chanID=sa006&colID=13* (Accessed October 25, 2007).

4. Richard Layard, *Happiness* (New York: Penguin, 2005), 34.

5. Paraphrased from Robert L. Heilbroner, *The Great Ascent*: *The Struggle for Economic Development in Our Time* (New York: Harper & Row, 1963), 33 – 36, as quoted in Ron Sider, *Rich Christians in an Age of Hunger* (Dallas: Word, 1990), 3 – 4.

6. 2003 Gallup Study indicated only 2 percent of Americans say they are rich. Sited in M. P. Dunleavey, *Just How Rich Is Rich, Really?*, MSN Money: *articles.moneycentral.msn.com /RetirementandWills/EscapeTheRatRace/JustHowRichIsRichReally.aspx* (accessed October 25, 2007).

Chapter Seventeen: Resource — Running to Win

1. I heard Drucker say this at an event in 1995, but others have noted his belief in the importance of churches and nonprofits. See Leadership Network Advance: *www.pursuantgroup .com/leadnet/advance/nov05o.htm* (accessed October 26, 2007).

2. One hundred twenty million Christians x $36,276 per capita income x 10% x 5% = $21,765,000,000 for compassion globally (with 5% left for church planting and 90% left for local church and community impact). Imagine the potential impact:
   - Child Deaths under Age 5: 6 million children per year saved for $5 billion
   - Education for all children globally: $7 billion
   - Complete world evangelization: $1 billion
   - (source of statistics: *www.emptytomb.org/potential.html*)
   - It will take more than just money to eradicate poverty and child deaths because it's a spiritual and systemic challenge, but engaging the church with resources, brainpower, and creative empowerment solutions can make an impact.
   - $29 billion would: Put 77 million children, most of whom are girls, in school. Provide access to clean water to 450 million people. Prevent more than 5.4 million young children from dying each year from poverty-related illnesses. Save 16,000 lives a day by fighting HIV/AIDS, tuberculosis, and malaria. (Source: One Campaign *www.one .org/better_aid*)

3. "Giving Research" Empty Tomb: *www.emptytomb.org/fig1_04.html*. Barna indicates only 7

percent of those professing faith in Jesus Christ to take away their sins actually tithe the full 10 percent. "Giving to churches rose substantially in 2003," Posted April 13, 2004. The Barna Update: *www.barna.org/FlexPage.aspx?Page=BarnaUpdate&BarnaUpdateID=161*

4. There are organizations seeking to network church-to-church partnerships. Red Del Camino is networking North and South American churches: *www.lareddelcamino.net*. The Empty Tomb organization has been seeking to rally Christians to meet global needs and updates on progress: *www.emptytomb.org/scg002Sol.pdf*. Rick Warren has been working to connect churches in his P.E.A.C.E. plan.

5. *www.payscale.com* will show median and average salaries.

Chapter Eighteen: Re-imagine — Decisions and Commitments

1. Dallas Willard, *The Divine Conspiracy: Rediscovering Our Hidden Life in God* (San Francisco: HarperCollins, 1998), 297 – 98.

creating a COME AS YOU ARE culture in the
CHURCH

JOHN
BURKE

chapter

1

The First Corinthian Church of America

Look around you! Vast fields are ripening all around us
and are ready now for the harvest.

Jesus, John 4:35 NLT

Do not be deceived: Neither the sexually immoral nor idolaters nor adulterers
nor male prostitutes nor homosexual offenders nor thieves nor the greedy
nor drunkards nor slanderers nor swindlers will inherit the kingdom of God.
And that is what some of you were. . . .

1 Corinthians 6:9–11

What do a Buddhist, a biker couple, a gay-rights activist, a transient, a high-tech engineer, a Muslim, a twenty-something single mom, a Jew, a couple living together, and an atheist all have in common?

They are the future church in America!

Most of them are in their twenties or thirties and became followers of Christ in the past five years. Many are now leading others in our church.

This is the generation the church must reach if it is to survive. It is an eclectic generation on a winding, wayward spiritual quest, and the church has an incredible opportunity to be a guide for the journey.

But time is running out. Unless Christians leading the church in America change, and unless the church begins living out the magnetic attractive force Jesus had on the world, the Christian church in America will be completely marginalized within decades!

So what will it take to become the kinds of Christian leaders in the kinds of churches and ministries and small groups that will truly impact emerging post-Christian America? What will it take to turn the tide that is washing the church off the map of our country? What kind of culture will captivate and compel emerging generations? How do we become the kinds of attractive Christ-followers who draw spiritual seekers into the family of God like Jesus did?

This book seeks to answer these questions. I hope painting a picture of what God is doing through his church will help you see how you can experience the invisible Jesus made visible through his Body, your local church. But I must warn you up front, doing church like this is a mess . . . but it's a beautiful mess!

Messy Lives

Lana came in late. The strained look on her face and the redness of her eyes immediately betrayed her. Something was wrong. "Brad's not coming, he's using again." The words flooded from her mouth with a flow of tears as soon as she reached the safety of our small group. Inside, Lana couldn't believe she was telling all to a church group, yet she had never found such love and acceptance. When they first came to Gateway, Brad and Lana were seeking support. In their late twenties with two kids, it felt like they were slowly unraveling on all sides: parenting challenges, job challenges, and years of drug abuse still stalking in the shadows.

Invited to our group one Sunday by a couple they met after church, they quickly jumped into our small group. From the first, Lana wanted to make sure we understood her views. "I think all religions are equally valid," she burst out one night. "Actually, I'm attracted by a lot of what Eastern religions have to say about peace, and I think Jesus was a good person—a life worth emulating—but I don't know beyond that. Frankly I don't like religious people who judge and look down on other beliefs. That's where I'm coming from, so I hope that's all right with you all."

She wanted to make sure we weren't going to judge her for being "open." As Lana and Brad got to know the group, they soon realized this was not your mama's church. The group was comprised of mostly young couples, in their twenties or early thirties. Out of twelve people, nine had come to faith at Gateway in the past two years.

Marcy and Casey, our biker couple, typically came adorned in black. Marcy's cranberry-red, elbow-length hair sported one metal spike braid in the back, extending down to her waist. Casey's scruffy, long black beard matched his pony-tailed hair. They came to Gateway in a state of spiritual seeking. Casey was tentative and distrustful at first but, over the course of a year or so, came to faith in Christ. His mother prayed a prayer of faith with me while on her deathbed, which helped open his heart to faith. Marcy would have called herself a Christian but did not seem to fully comprehend grace. Her Catholic upbringing gave her hope in Jesus, and she had seen him pull her through a very traumatic childhood. She had lived with a man before meeting Casey, and she and Casey had lived together before finally getting married.

I found out the hard way that living together was the norm. One Sunday, early in our church's history, I gave a message about commitment, which I titled "The C-Word" (due to our generation's fear of commitment). In the message, I talked about living together before marriage, explaining that although it seems like a prudent decision on the surface, it leads to nearly a 50% higher chance of divorce for those who do get married, because there's no sense of commitment. (We'll talk more about this issue in a later chapter.)

That next week I got gang-piled at my small group. All but one couple had lived together before marriage! The reason our group was so safe to explore faith is because *I* was the abnormal one in the group. This is the emerging church, not church *for* a post-Christian culture, where Christians huddle up behind the fortress walls and make forays outside into the messy culture, but a church molded *out of* a post-Christian people—an indigenous church, rising up out of the surrounding culture to form the Body of Christ!

Some group members had skeletons of drug abuse in their past. Jay and Arden were both managers with good careers, but Jay still had a ten-year probation for possession with the intent to sell lurking in his past. Jay felt the grip of addiction squeezing tight. Skeptical about church, unsure of what they believed, Jay and Arden were seeking spiritual support for their battles but had been turned off by more traditional churches. Four years later, Jay and Arden wholeheartedly follow Christ, lead a small group, and help out with our recovery ministry.

Dave, an engineer, and Kim, a teacher, came to Gateway after watching *Touched by an Angel*, which sparked a conversation about wanting to know God. The next night, a local news station aired a segment on a new church in town. Gateway was their first church experience since childhood. When they joined the small group, they had to ask if it was okay to take smoking breaks (at first a quarter of our group would have to take smoking breaks). Their marriage teetered on the edge of the abyss when they came to Gateway. Sexual dysfunction caused by early sexual abuse and promiscuity had slowly severed their marital ties. They desperately wanted to understand if God was real and if he could help them, but they had many questions and feared being judged.

Karla and Greg met in a halfway house while both were recovering from alcoholism. After living together for four years, they found Gateway on our opening day. Imagine my shock after our first Sunday service when the second couple I met said, "We want to get married. Will you do our wedding?" Karla considered herself an atheist converted to agnosticism through recovery, but the Bible and Jesus freaked her out. Greg had lived as a transient for fifteen years. After receiving our postcards and hearing an unconventional ad on secular radio for our church, they hesitantly agreed to try it once—it seemed different. But they made a pact that they would sit in the back row, on the aisle, and if I said one wrong word, they were out of there. Amazingly, they both opened their hearts to Christ during our premarital counseling appointments, realizing Jesus was the Higher Power who had rescued them from the death grip of addiction. Greg sometimes shares his story of hope when our church participates in "church under the bridge" for the homeless in Austin, and Karla, a child development specialist, serves in our nursery.

Daryl and Brianna alone came churched. They represent a bold new genre of missional Christians who are not content to play church by just huddling up with Christians. They wanted to be in a place where real, worldly people, with real messy lives, were seeing the real God in action. But unfortunately, they represent a minority of churched Christians—Christians who, like the apostle Paul, willingly venture out of their comfort zone into the messy, pagan culture of a Corinth or Austin.

Many churched Christians who came through the doors of Gateway in the early days just could not handle the discomfort of having so many seekers around them. They would hang out in the lobby after the service, strike up conversation, and slowly realize that the person they were talking to held none of their "sacred beliefs" regarding abortion, sex before marriage, evolution, or other hot-topics of Christian subcultures. After a conversation like that, they usually scared each other off.

Don't get me wrong, I am not advocating throwing in the moral towel, but why expect a secular society to act like a Christian one? First things first, and according to Jesus, loving God comes first—followed closely by loving people. But it takes a new kind of Christian to live and minister in the mess of Corinth. And that is precisely where we now live!

Our Very Corinthian Culture

As I read about the church in Corinth, I see many parallels to our situation today. Being so near the intellectual hub of Athens, first-century Corinthians prided themselves for their intellectual pursuits. As residents of a large, wealthy metropolitan port city, the people emphasized luxury and comfort. They entertained themselves at the Isthmian games held at the Temple of Poseidon, and they advocated a full indulgence in the pleasures of life.

Corinth was known for its wild party life and sexual freedom. The famous Temple of Aphrodite, the goddess of love, complete with a thousand temple prostitutes, towered above the city, beckoning all to come and feast their sexual appetites. Partying and hedonistic pleasure-seeking was so common in Corinth that they branded the name—"to live like a Corinthian" implied diving into days of drunken, promiscuous living.

Rome proclaimed religious tolerance as a great virtue. In fact, the one thing about Christians that the Greco-Roman culture detested was this antiquated idea that Jesus was the only way to God. And *Truth*? "What is *Truth*?" Wasn't it a Roman governor, raised in the same Greco-Roman culture, who asked this first recorded relativistic question to Jesus?[1] Corinth was a mess!

Yet, as Paul's letters attest, this is precisely the place where God's Spirit built this beautiful mess of a church. And though anything but perfect and tidy, it still held God's hope for the world. And his church, functioning as the re-presentation—that is, an all-new presenting again—of Christ's own Body in the world, prevailed, and changed the whole Roman Empire. And he can do it again today through his local church in our world.

The Death Bells Toll

After studying trends of church attendance in America, pollster George Barna warns of the waning influence of the church on emerging generations, calling for radical change before a postmortem is declared:

> Our goal cannot simply be a timid, powerless survival; it must be the role that Christ called the Church to play, that of a loving, authoritative, healing, and compelling influence upon the world . . . lacking such a turn-about, we may rightfully anticipate the virtual disappearance of the Christian Church in this nation.[2]

Statistically, this has already happened in England and Europe, a continent further down the post-Christian turnpike than North America. Church attendance in England averages about 7% of the population, and Europe as a whole runs a close race.[3] In effect, the Christian Church in Europe has gone the way of the dinosaur, and the North American Church tracks close behind. Barna and others note that the current generation is actually the first generation in American history in which a majority of those seeking faith begin their spiritual journey with a faith group other than Christianity.[4]

Emerging cities of America have much in common with Corinth: wealth, education, leisure, sports and entertainment 24/7, the most religiously diverse population in the world, trumpeting the value of tolerance as the highest virtue, sexually unrestrained like never before, seeking pleasure and personal satisfaction as the prime directive, rejecting absolute truth absolutely!

But much like the church in the pagan, pluralistic, promiscuous city of Corinth, the twenty-first-century church will be messy if it's to be effective. The emerging generations represent the first post-Christian culture in America. Unlike the generations before them, they have no predisposition for Christian faith. Not only do they lack an accurate understanding, but many have a distorted view of Christianity from what they've seen.

What I like to call the "Postmodern Experiment," which we will explore in depth in the next chapter, began in the sixties in America and had a much broader effect than merely the relativistic way people think about truth.

The pragmatic effect of this experiment has been widely missed in the debate about ministry in a postmodern world. But this experiment has undoubtedly spawned a generation of wounded, broken, spiritually hungry people. These people seek spirituality with an openness not seen in decades, and yet the church has completely gone off their radar. As in Corinth, Christianity at best is one among many equally good religious options on the menu.

Leighton Ford indicates that North America now holds the distinguished honor of being the third largest mission field in the English-speaking world.[5] And the United States has more secular, unchurched people than most nations of the world,[6] yet many churches don't seem to operate in light of this fact.

Paul was a visionary church-starting entrepreneur, who sacrificed dearly to dive into the mess of a culture foreign to him. Those of us currently leading in churches need to prayerfully consider this: Are we raising up a generation of leaders ready to lay down their comfortable lives to dive into the muck of cultural America? Or are we just playing church—developing spiritual dependents who consume the goods off whichever church shelf will "feed me," or "puff me up with more knowledge," or even "feel postmodern"?

No longer can we afford to stand on the cliffs high above the cultural mudslide, chastising people for not climbing out of the mess to come up to higher ground. No longer can we feel content throwing our heroic lifelines of propositions intended to save. No longer can we idly sit by, bemoaning change and wishing to turn the clock back to nostalgic days gone by.

No, it is time for Christian leaders, tethered to the lifeline of God's Spirit and a community of faith, to gather up courage and plunge into the swirling mess of the cultural flow. Just as Paul said he did in Corinth, we too must "try to find common ground with everyone so that [we] might bring them to

Christ."[7] We must emulate the God who dove right into the sewer of life himself in the body of Jesus. And we must reawaken his dream—God's dream of swimming this rescue mission on earth through a new Body—the Body of his Church—Christ's Body re-presented.[8]

This great mystery of God, re-presenting himself in the world through those who truly trust in him, must come alive through us. This must be the first priority for leadership of the church in a post-Christian world: making the invisible Body visible.

Seeing Jesus

Brad showed up late that night. He confessed to the group what we already knew. I was amazed that he would be willing to admit using crack again, but even though he was not yet a Christian, he knew we cared about him. He sensed the mysterious hand of God's Spirit reaching out to him through this Body of new believers, and he knew he needed help.

Lana had opened up her heart to Christ during the past year. Now it was Brad's turn. That night this unlikely small group, now morphing into Christ's Body in the world, wrapped his arms around Brad with love and truth—at times confronting, as only those who have been through addiction can—at times encouraging, as wounded healers who have seen God's overcoming power. Brad prayed and asked for God's forgiveness. With his group surrounding him, touching him, praying for him . . . Brad told God, "I want what Jesus did to count for me. I need your power to do your will. Help me overcome so I can be the husband and father you intended." That intervention began the long journey for Brad and Lana we have seen many take, off the path of the addict and onto the way of Christ.

As I drove home that night, thinking about the miraculous life-change God had accomplished in that entire group, tears of gratitude filled my eyes. How many times I would drive away from a night with my small group, thanking God that I get to see Jesus alive—seeking and saving those who are lost, proclaiming the time of God's favor among the poor, the oppressed, the broken, the spiritual misfits of his day and ours. And I must say, God has used those people in my life as much as he has used me in theirs—for I too am a spiritual misfit. Through my friends, God reminded me that no one is more or less worthy of his grace, we all need it. And we must all grow up together into the community of people he intended us to be.

My small group is not an aberration, not even an extreme example. When we launched Gateway Community Church in 1998, we used to joke about our "Corinthian core." From ten people, the church grew to a couple thousand in the first five years, and I would say the lives of the people you just met are pretty typical. We keep seeing God draw hundreds and hundreds to faith in Christ every year out of similarly messy, broken, spiritually eclectic backgrounds. My small group lives in your city all around you, and if you have not gotten to know them yet, maybe it's because you're not looking up at the fields before you. This state of the union calls for a new kind of Christian leader. Are you ready? Look up! The harvest is great but the workers are few![9]

But God Causes the Growth

If the thought of reaching our post-Christian culture scares you, take heart! God can use anyone, because it's not ultimately up to us—it's up to him. But we do have a responsibility. Paul reminds church leaders in his letter to the Corinthians:

> I planted the seed, Apollos watered it, but God has been making it grow. So neither the one who plants nor the one who waters is anything, but only God, who makes things grow. The one who plants and the one who waters have one purpose, and they will each be rewarded according to their own labor. For we are God's co-workers; you are God's field. (1 Corinthians 3:6–9 TNIV)

As Christians in a post-Christian society, our job is to become cultural farmers. Church leaders, ministry leaders, and small group leaders must come to trust the God who is already at work all around us, making things grow. Our responsibility is not to make people grow or change. Our task is to create the right soil, a rich healthy environment, in which people can grow up in faith until the invisible God is made visible through his Body, the church.[10]

But how do we create soil in which the invisible is made visible? This is the art of culture creation and the focus of this book. As we labor in the field with him, creating a healthy come-as-you-are culture, God will cause the growth. As wise cultural farmers, we must realize God has given us responsibilities as his fellow laborers to create healthy cultural soil.

Jesus often used agricultural metaphors to describe the kingdom of God. I believe he did this not just because they related well in an agrarian society but also because there are general principles of growth to which they refer.

All life requires the right soil for healthy growth. Clearly this is true of plant life. Though the farmer never causes the growth, if he neglects the soil and it becomes hardened, or lacks nutrients or water, no growth will occur. If he does not protect the seed from the birds, before the plant ever has a chance, his adversaries will destroy his work. Conversely, if the farmer does his part to create the right soil, growth happens!

Children, psychologists tell us, also need the right soil in which to grow. Research confirms that children in loving, secure, truth-speaking family environments tend to thrive. It is the family culture that most influences healthy growth toward maturity.

But have we considered the soil needed for a healthy Christian community in a hard-packed, post-Christian society? God is responsible for the growth, for changed hearts, but the soil is the responsibility of the leaders and Christ-followers who make up that church. Creating a come-as-you-are culture is the most important task leaders can undertake to engage a post-Christian society, and yet we often give culture creation little mental effort. In fact, because culture is largely unseen, we are mostly unaware of the cultural soil we have created in our churches, small groups, or ministries.

In discussing the effect of culture on organizations, business consultant James Alexander notes how "the culture becomes highly ingrained to the point of becoming invisible to the members of the organization. That is why it is so difficult for group members to talk about their culture, because it operates at a level below our normal consciousness."[11]

But this explains why several churches may be trying to reach the same group with the same methods, but one just "feels" completely different than the other. That intangible "feel" is the culture. The culture is what seekers pick up on immediately, though it may be imperceptible to regular members. But the culture makes all the difference in the world in a post-Christian society. This is why effective leadership must be synonymous with creating the right culture.

Yet all too often, leaders implement new "seeker" services or "postmodern" services with cool music, candles, art, aesthetics, or whatever the latest conference hypes up, but miss the most essential nutrients for healthy Body-growth.

When I was Executive Director of Ministries for Willow Creek Community Church, I would see leaders come to conferences and get excited about leading people to Christ. But they would tragically assume it was the music and drama or other visible elements they were lacking, and they would go home to start a drama team or "contemporary" service with a new band and less worship, assuming "if we build it, they will come." But many missed the all-important culture created specifically to effectively reach one particular culture of Suburban-Chicago Baby Boomers. Much of the criticism aimed at the "seeker church" for being entertainment-oriented derives from this common mistake.

One time a staff member at Willow walked into the auditorium during a conference to witness a team of visiting church leaders measuring |

the auditorium. Curious, he asked them what they were doing. They said, "We love what's happening here, so we're just going to copy every last detail of it." Unfortunately, I suspect we could make the same error with emerging generational trends. We may end up with cool-looking candlelit venues, hip sounding music, a mosaic of "postmodern" do-it-yourself art in the service, or some other fad, and yet not really engage or penetrate our postmodern, post-Christian society at all! It's not the visible but the invisible that needs attention. It's not candles but community, not art but attitude, not liturgy but love that makes the difference in our broken world.

Are you planting and watering, tilling and fertilizing the culture of your church, small group, or ministry? Do you see the fruit of God's Spirit as secular people find faith and grow in your particular region? What does a come-as-you-are culture need to look like in a post-Christian society? What does it need to look like in your unique region or city? These are the meta-questions we will seek to answer in the following chapters. And I believe pondering these questions of culture creation can be beneficial regardless of whom you are reaching.

Whether you are in an emerging church or a church for the Boomer or Builder generations, whether a point leader or small group leader, understanding how culture gets formed and reflecting on your current culture is an essential task of leadership. But let me give you an overview of the threads of culture creation that will weave throughout the chapters that follow.

Defining Culture

First, what exactly is culture? Culture could be defined as the glue that holds any organization together. In churches, it encompasses the normal practices and behaviors of people as they determine what, why, or how they act or interact. But it is also the sum of all behaviors, attitudes, and styles of the people, programs, and services.[12]

Culture creation forms the texture of relational life and community in a local church. The outcome of an effective come-as-you-are culture is an engaging community of faith that God uses to transform individuals, neighborhoods, cities, and societies. It happens when leaders effectively contextualize the message of Christ for the surrounding indigenous culture, and out of the surrounding culture the community of Christ grows.

But we must beware that community alone is not the answer. There are life-giving communities created, but there are also repressive, toxic communities that form in local churches, small groups, and ministries.

Leadership Mindset

Creating a come-as-you-are culture begins with the mind-set of the leadership of a church. The way leaders think about themselves and the church creates the core from which the culture grows. As the leaders interact with others, they model the culture much as parents model the creation of a family's culture.

What do you and the other leaders in your church currently model culturally?

This book will present a vision of the church in culture that may challenge how you've thought of yourself and the church. Or it could be you will discover the culture you thought you or others were creating is not the culture spiritual seekers actually experience. Maybe the greatest value of reading this book will turn out to be not a new strategy or methodology you can implement, but a mindset shift. Instead of new methodology, maybe your views and attitudes that most shape the culture will morph. In culture creation, what happens in the hearts and heads of leaders has the greatest impact. For that reason, this book is more experiential than pragmatic. You'll experience lives and stories intersecting God's story of his church, challenging you to examine your view of yourself and your leadership.

Public Vibe

The "vibe" of the public service or group meeting also serves to create culture. The look and feel, the quality factor, the style of music, the way people speak and dress and interact publicly are very important. These elements signal to others what you are like, what to expect, and how to act. This public aspect of culture must be contextualized more than any other aspect to the tastes of the unchurched around you if you want to reach them.

> I went through a divorce two years ago and have just recently started to attend mass again, but I feel so much guilt and always feel like I just don't belong. So it was a very big step to walk into your church this past Sunday. I have to say I was very welcomed by everyone, and I loved the service and teaching. I just wanted to thank you and the staff for creating such a warm and loving environment for people to open up to even hear the message, knowing that whatever level they're coming in at is okay—they'll be loved for who they are! I know with any organization that attitude comes from the top and is duplicated by the whole organization, which can be good or bad, but yours is GREAT!
>
> —Gabrielle

In the following chapters, you will get a taste of the worship services at Gateway, and you will catch a vision for the vibe that affects the mood of small group communities. But remember, the visible aspects of a church are only a small part of the overall culture.

Vision-Casting

One of the most overlooked aspects of culture is how the average person, seeker, or believer, captures a vision of how to live and function in the church community. This aspect of vision-casting for culture creation is the most neglected and yet most powerful influence on cultural formation.

What gets communicated over and over and over again? What stories get told? What real-life spiritual journeys are highlighted to reinforce what the church is about? What does the average person think about when they think about your church, what it stands for, and their role in it? As I tell our leaders, we can have the coolest music, the most compelling communication, the most edgy technology, but if seekers don't like the people, they won't keep coming back. Our people are our secret weapon.

But how do you lead people to create the right culture? We will explore this question of vision-casting and storytelling to create the right culture throughout this book.

Organization

And culture creation cannot be divorced from organization. If the church is an organism, the Body of Christ, it must function in a coordinated way.

How do we organize in a way that enhances and supports culture much like a skeleton supports a body? Organization that is too rigid does not allow the flexibility and agility the Body needs to fully express itself. On the other hand, no organizational backbone hinders the Body from forming and expressing itself in a growing diversity of unified parts.

Hopefully you will catch a picture of some of the organizational structures that can be used to support and sustain the Body of the church to live out its cultural mandate and mission.

Understanding Context

Though principles of culture creation translate across cultures, they must be contextualized to the surrounding society in which people live.* So let me tell you a little about the uniqueness of Austin and our church to help you better translate these principles into your context.

Gateway is unique to the context of Austin. At the time of writing this, 50% of the people at Gateway are single, while Austin itself is nearly 60%

---

* For an in-depth treatment of contextualization to the surrounding culture, I highly recommend "The Cultural Perspective" section in *Perspectives on the World Christian Movement*, edited by Ralph Winter and Steven Hawthorne.

single. The majority of people at Gateway were formerly unchurched, but past estimates indicate that Austin's population is over 85% unchurched. On our yearly survey, 60% indicated they were not active Christ-followers when they first came to Gateway, though most say they are now active Christ-followers. The racial diversity of Austin is approximately 30% non-white, while Gateway is around 20% diverse in this respect. Approximately 75% of those attending are under age forty, yet we are watching God's Spirit draw hundreds and hundreds to faith every year of all backgrounds—especially out of this most cynical, jaded cohort of emerging America.

Through the real-life stories of people who have come to faith through Gateway Community Church, you will experience how a come-as-you-are culture can loosen up the hard-packed hearts of emerging generations. But understanding the uniqueness of *your context* is essential for effective culture creation. We will discuss principles of contextualization that can help you determine the way to culturally farm your unique soil—whether in your church, ministry, or small group. And my intent is to inspire Christ-followers and church leaders to overcome fears of diving in and engaging our post-Christian culture whatever the context, and to believe again that God can and will work through his followers in his local church to bring hope and healing to the world around us.

I want to clarify up front, I am not claiming what has happened at Gateway is the only way to reach our postmodern world or that we have the church everyone should imitate. In our diverse world, many diverse methods and strategies must be employed to create the right soil for the right context.

Gateway's not a perfect church—far from it!

Just as there are no perfect people, there are no perfect churches. We definitely do not claim to have all the answers or even know all the questions, but we see God at work, powerfully forming his church out of this broken, lost generation.

So this is simply the story of God's amazing work in our generation, seeking and saving those who were lost, and using his church to do his work. And my prayer in writing this book is that God would use it to help many more find faith through the ministry of local churches, parachurch ministries, and small group communities.

But before we talk specifics of culture creation to form fertile soil, we must first understand the struggles that created the hard-packed soil of the current generation. People hear God's Word, but often the seed lands on hard ground.

So the job of the Christian leader is to first take into account the context creating hardheartedness toward God's Word and Christ's church. What are the sociological struggles arising from the past forty years that keep people from finding faith through the local church? How do we live out and lead out Christian faith so that the soil of the local church becomes a place where people can grow despite these challenges? In the next chapter, we will explore these questions as we trace back to the source of the five greatest struggles our generation has with Christian faith and the church—struggles with Trust, Tolerance, Truth, Brokenness, and Aloneness.

STUDY GUIDE

Culture Check

1. How would people define the "feel" of your church after several experiences? Consider asking an unchurched neighbor to come two or three Sundays and give you raw, honest feedback about what he or she perceives people at your church value and what the experience was like for him or her.
2. Write down what you think your church values in reality. What do you desire it to value?
3. Write down *Leader Mindset*, *Public Vibe*, *Vision-Casting*, and *Organization*. As you read the remaining chapters, beside each word, make note of ideas to help create the kind of culture you desire.

Small Group Questions

1. How would we define the "feel" and "experience" of our group? (Is it safe? Like family? Educational? Reverent? Challenging?) Ask your group to write down anonymously on note cards the words that define how the group currently "feels." Have one person collect and read all the cards out loud, then discuss why this culture exists.
2. Now write down on another note card the words that describe the perfect "environment" you all hope to create for one another. Have someone read the words, then discuss why you want that environment and ways to help create that environment.
3. Read 1 Corinthians 9:20–23. What do you think Paul meant by "becoming all things"? How is the culture around us similar to or different than the culture of Corinth? What are some ways we can "be all things" to the surrounding culture without compromising following Christ?

Willow Creek Association
Vision, Training, Resources for Prevailing Churches

This resource was created to serve you and to help you build a local church that prevails. It is just one of many ministry tools that are part of the Willow Creek Resources® line, published by the Willow Creek Association together with Zondervan.

The Willow Creek Association (WCA) was created in 1992 to serve a rapidly growing number of churches from across the denominational spectrum that are committed to helping unchurched people become fully devoted followers of Christ. Membership in the WCA now numbers over 12,000 Member Churches worldwide from more than ninety denominations.

The Willow Creek Association links like-minded Christian leaders with each other and with strategic vision, training, and resources in order to help them build prevailing churches designed to reach their redemptive potential. Here are some of the ways the WCA does that.

- **The Leadership Summit**—a once a year, two-and-a-half-day conference to envision and equip Christians with leadership gifts and responsibilities. Presented live at Willow Creek as well as via satellite broadcast to over 130 locations across North America, this event is designed to increase the leadership effectiveness of pastors, ministry staff, volunteer church leaders, and Christians in the marketplace.

- **Ministry-Specific Conferences**—throughout each year the WCA hosts a variety of conferences and training events—both at Willow Creek's main campus and offsite, across the U.S., and around the world—targeting church leaders and volunteers in ministry-specific areas such as: small groups, preaching and teaching, the arts, children, students, volunteers, stewardship, etc.

- **Willow Creek Resources®**—provides churches with trusted and field-tested ministry resources in such areas as leadership, evangelism, spiritual formation, spiritual gifts, small groups, stewardship, student ministry, children's ministry, the use of the arts—drama, media, contemporary music—and more.

- **WCA Member Benefits**—includes substantial discounts to WCA training events, a 20 percent discount on all Willow Creek Resources®, *Defining Moments* monthly audio journal for leaders, quarterly *Willow* magazine, access to a Members-Only section on WillowNet, monthly communications, and more. Member Churches also receive special discounts and premier services through WCA's growing number of ministry partners—Select Service Providers—and save an average of $500 annually depending on the level of engagement.

For specific information about WCA conferences, resources, membership, and other ministry services contact:

Willow Creek Association
P.O. Box 3188
Barrington, IL 60011-3188
Phone: 847-570-9812
Fax: 847-765-5046
www.willowcreek.com

Share Your Thoughts

With the Author: Your comments will be forwarded to the author when you send them to *zauthor@zondervan.com*.

With Zondervan: Submit your review of this book by writing to *zreview@zondervan.com*.

Free Online Resources at
www.zondervan.com/hello

 Zondervan AuthorTracker: Be notified whenever your favorite authors publish new books, go on tour, or post an update about what's happening in their lives.

 Daily Bible Verses and Devotions: Enrich your life with daily Bible verses or devotions that help you start every morning focused on God.

 Free Email Publications: Sign up for newsletters on fiction, Christian living, church ministry, parenting, and more.

 Zondervan Bible Search: Find and compare Bible passages in a variety of translations at www.zondervanbiblesearch.com.

 Other Benefits: Register yourself to receive online benefits like coupons and special offers, or to participate in research.